AF843218

*Routledge Revivals*

# The Wealth Report

Until this book was first published in 1979, poverty studies had been exclusively concerned with studying the poor. This controversial book changed the whole debate about poverty in Britain by shifting the emphasis to a detailed examination of the rich. It looks at the distribution of income and wealth in the second half of the twentieth century and critically examines the claim that Britain was becoming a more equal society. It also discusses the massive shift of resources to the corporate sector since 1974. There are chapters on the mechanics for reviewing top salaries and the increasing problem of tax avoidance.

# The Wealth Report

Volume 1

Edited by Frank Field

Routledge
Taylor & Francis Group
Routledge Revivals

First published in 1979 by Routledge & Kegan Paul Ltd

This edition first published in 2026 by Routledge
4 Park Square, Milton Park, Abingdon, Oxon, OX14 4RN
and by Routledge
605 Third Avenue, New York, NY 10158.

*Routledge is an imprint of the Taylor & Francis Group, an informa business*

© 1979 Frank Field, Louie Burghes, Anthony Christopher, Alan Harrison, David Jordan, Chris Pond, Cedric Sandford, Ceri Thomas

All rights reserved. No part of this book may be reprinted or reproduced or utilised in any form or by any electronic, mechanical, or other means, now known or hereafter invented, including photocopying and recording, or in any information storage or retrieval system, without permission in writing from the publishers.

ISBN 13: 978-1-041-11912-8 (hbk)
ISBN 13: 978-1-003-66222-8 (ebk)
ISBN 13: 978-1-041-11913-5 (pbk)
Book DOI 10.4324/9781003662228

# The Wealth Report

Edited by
**Frank Field**

**Routledge & Kegan Paul**
London, Boston and Henley

*First published in 1979*
*by Routledge & Kegan Paul Ltd*
*39 Store Street, London WC1E 7DD*
*Broadway House, Newtown Road,*
*Henley-on-Thames, Oxon RG9 1EN and*
*9 Park Street, Boston, Mass. 02108, USA*
*Set in 10/12pt Press Roman by*
*Hope Services, Abingdon*
*and printed in Great Britain by*
*Lowe & Brydone Ltd., Thetford, Norfolk*
*© Frank Field, Louie Burghes,*
*Anthony Christopher, Alan Harrison, David Jordan*
*Chris Pond, Cedric Sandford, Ceri Thomas, 1979*
*No part of this book may be reproduced in*
*any form without permission from the*
*publisher, except for the quotation of brief*
*passages in criticism*

*British Library Cataloguing in Publication Data*

*The wealth report. – (Inequality in society).*

*1. Wealth – Great Britain*
*I. Field, Frank, b. 1942 II. Series*
*339.4'1'0941 HC260.W4 78-41078*
*ISBN 0 7100 0164 9*

To Barbara Wootton

# Contents

# Contributors

Louie Burghes studied sociology at London University and worked for over two years in the Urban Deprivation Unit of the Home Office as a Research Officer before joining Frank Field as his Personal Assistant. She contributed to *The Conscript Army*.

Anthony Christopher has been General Secretary of the Inland Revenue Staff Federation since 1977, and is a member of the TUC's General Council and its Economic Committee. He has been chairman of NACRO (The National Association for the Care and Resettlement of Offenders) since 1973. He is joint author of *Policy for Poverty*.

Frank Field taught in the London Colleges of Further Education in Southwark and Hammersmith before joining the Child Poverty Action Group in 1969. In 1966 he contested the Buckinghamshire South constituency seat for the Labour Party and was a councillor in Hounslow for four years. He has edited *Twentieth Century State Education*, *Black Britons*, *Low Pay*, *Education and the Urban Crisis*, *Are Low Wages Inevitable?* and *The Conscript Army*. He is the author of *Unequal Britain* and co-author of *To Him Who Hath*. Since 1974 he has also been Director of the Low Pay Unit.

Alan Harrison is Assistant Professor in the Department of Economics at McMaster University, Hamilton, Ontario and is joint author with A. B. Atkinson of *The Distribution of Personal Wealth in Britain.*

David Jordan studied economics and politics at the University of Bristol. He worked for a year as Information Officer with special responsibility for income maintenance with Age Concern before joining the Low Pay Unit as a Research Officer in January 1977. He has contributed to *An Ageing Population.*

Chris Pond studied economics at the University of Sussex and worked in the Department of Economics, Birkbeck College, before becoming a Research Officer at the Low Pay Unit. He has contributed to *Inflation and Low Incomes*, *Are Low Wages Inevitable?*, *The Conscript Army*, and *Why the Poor Pay More*, and is joint author of *Trade Unions and Taxation* and *To Him Who Hath.*

Cedric Sandford has been Director of the Bath University Centre for Fiscal Studies since 1974 and Professor of Political Economy within the university since 1975. He was a member of the Meade Committee and his publications include *Economics of Public Income*, *Taxing Personal Wealth*, *Hidden Costs of Taxation*, *Social Economics.* He is also the joint author of *An Accessions Tax* and *An Annual Wealth Tax.*

Ceri Thomas read geography at the University College of Wales, Aberystwyth, where he also undertook research into relative deprivation in rural Wales. In January 1977 he joined the Low Pay Unit as a Research Officer and has contributed to *Rural Deprivation: Essays on Rural Problems and Social Planning.*

# Acknowledgments

A number of people have helped in the production of this book. Sue Whiting, Jill Sullivan, Joan Hammell and Angela Wilson have been responsible for typing the manuscript for publication. David Jordan and Ruth Lister kindly read through much of the typescript and in doing so suggested a number of changes to the two sections I have written.

# Introduction

Frank Field

Back in 1913 R. H. Tawney delivered his inaugural lecture as director of the Ratan Tata Foundation. The foundation, which later became merged with, or lost within – whichever way you look at it – the Social Administration Department at the London School of Economics, was a forerunner of the poverty research institutes which have been established in the USA and Australia. During the course of this address, Tawney issued a powerful warning to those people who then, and subsequently, have made what must appear to the poor a very reasonable standard of living out of researching poverty. Tawney warned that an understanding of poverty required much more than the study of the poor themselves; specifically, a researcher 'will be wise to start much higher up the stream than the point he wishes to reach' adding, in case his message had not been fully grasped, 'what thoughtful rich people call the problem of poverty, thoughtful poor people call with equal justice the problem of riches' (Tawney, 1913).

It is easy enough to show what little heed has been paid to these remarks and, indeed, the present writer works for groups called the Child Poverty Action Group and the Low Pay Unit rather than a watchdog body on the rich. But, for reasons outlined by Ceri Thomas in Chapter 7, it is much easier to study the poor than those at the top end of the income wealth pyramid. There could be no better illustration of the difficulty of working to Tawney's guide-lines than to look at the work of the Ratan Tata Foundation directed by Tawney himself. Despite the warning about fixing one's gaze on the poor in isolation to the society in which they struggle to exist, a folly which Tawney expressed in the analogist terms of expecting to become a medical officer of health by merely strutting around hospital wards, the work of the foundation was largely concerned with studies of poverty. The energy of the researchers was spent (albeit most profitably) in studying the implementation of the first minimum wage set by the 1909 Trades Boards Act, the changes in health following the introduction of school meals, the effect of the school doctor service and so on, rather than starting work higher upstream.

The aim of this volume, which it is hoped will be the first of a regular series of reports on the rich, is to begin redressing the balance. For those contributors who work in what has become known as the 'poverty lobby', it is the first conscious attempt to extend the framework in which they campaign. And, because this move will be misunderstood, it is important to spell out the reasons for the change.

An insistence on making distributional questions the stuff of politics is met by a number of ploys. One is to emphasise the negativeness of such an approach. Why, one is asked, isn't more emphasis put on ways of expanding wealth rather than debating ways of dividing the existing cake? To argue otherwise is not tantamount to supporting a no growth policy. Whatever once were the attractions of this philosophy they are now distinctly less, and particularly so for those towards the bottom of the income pile, after experiencing a couple of years when national income fell. Irrespective of the size of the nation's wealth, the question of who gets what is still crucially important and never more so than at a time of low or negative growth. Again, as Tawney remarked, when the liner is sinking and the passengers leave for the life boats, there is no place for distinguishing between first- and second-class passengers.

Another argument deployed by those who occupy the commanding heights of privilege is that critics of the status quo are motivated only by envy. Of course, envy could be at work in the hearts of some critics, but man is not always driven by base motives. In 1913, L. H. Hobhouse wrote of the two functions of property as 'the control of things, which gives freedom and security, and the control of persons through things, which gives power to the owner' (Gore, 1913, p. 10). The demand that property for power should make a continual appearance on the political agenda does not spring from envy. Rather, it arises from a belief that issues affecting the community's welfare should be exposed to the public gaze and judged accordingly. This used to be so. Throughout the Middle Ages, for example, each part of a person's conduct, whether private or public, was viewed as but one of the numerous steps in the ladder stretching from hell to eternity. Tawney, commenting on the so called advance of civilisation since then, wrote:

> The most fundamental difference between medieval and modern economic thought consists . . . in the fact that, whereas the latter normally refers to economic expediency, however it may be interpreted, for the justification of any particular action, policy, or system of organisation, the former starts from the position that there is a moral authority to which considerations of economic expediency must be subordinated (Tawney, 1961, p. 52).

The initial step in the long haul back to a society where our economic appetites are once more subordinate to moral principles is to ensure a much wider and more informed debate about the nature of the society in which we live, and it is hoped the reports on the rich will contribute to this development. This first report has limited itself almost exclusively to questions concerning the distribution of income and wealth. The discussion begins here because of their importance in cementing together the whole network of unjustifiable and unjustified privileges which disfigure the face of British society. Other reports will look at the differences in health, education, jobs and mobility, as well as the distribution of privileges by sex.

What then are the main lessons which emerge from this first report? The assertion that wealth is now much more evenly spread throughout the community (as opposed to a more limited redistribution between the top 5 or 10 per cent) is not borne out by the research cited by Louie Burghes and Alan Harrison. The most recent work by A. B. Atkinson and Alan Harrison shows serious discrepancies in the series of data on the distribution of personal wealth beginning in 1911 and on which so many sweeping conclusions about redistribution are based (Atkinson and Harrison, 1978). They put together a new series covering the period from 1923 to 1972 on as a consistent a basis as possible recording carefully the two breaks in the data's continuity. Even so, the authors' work illustrates a slower downward trend in the redistribution of personal wealth from the top 1 per cent of wealth holders than does the Royal Commission; the Atkinson/Harrison series shows a fall at the rate of 4 percentage points a decade compared with a 7 percentage point per decade reduction recorded by the Commission. But the series also illustrates that while the top 1 per cent have been losing, the share of personal wealth going to the next 4 per cent in our hierarchy has been increasing.

What forces bring about changes in the distribution of personal wealth? Surprisingly, those changes which have occurred are not so much due to direct government action; rather, it is fluctuations in share prices which help to explain short-term changes in wealth holdings. Atkinson and Harrison found that their estimates showed a significant relationship over the past half century between changes in share prices and changes in the proportional wealth owned by the top 1 per cent (Atkinson, 1978). While Alan Day 'guestimated' that the collapse of the stock market between 1973 and 1974 resulted in the top 1 per cent of wealth holders losing between a quarter and a third of their wealth (1974), Atkinson records a much smaller reduction of four percentage points from 28 per cent to 24 per cent. But, to turn an old phrase on its head, it is important to remember that what comes down can also go up, and a stock market boom might well reverse this trend.

The second message which emerges strongly from this report indicates the powerfulness of the engine generating inequality in our society. There is room here to illustrate this in only two ways. The Royal Commission have presented data on wealth holdings for the period 1972-6 and this is reproduced in Table I.1.

TABLE I.1 *Distribution of wealth holdings 1972-6*

| Income group % | | Year 1972 £bn | Year 1976 £bn | Increase £bn | Increase % |
|---|---|---|---|---|---|
| Top | 1 | 51.9 | 70.0 | 18.1 | 17.5 |
| | 5 | 99.5 | 132.9 | 33.4 | 32.2 |
| | 10 | 124.2 | 172.9 | 48.7 | 47.0 |
| | 20 | 152.1 | 219.6 | 67.5 | 65.2 |
| Bottom | 80 | 32.5 | 68.6 | 36.1 | 34.8 |
| Total | | 184.6 | 215.0 | 103.6 | 100 |

(*Source*: Royal Commission, 1977, Table 39; *Economic Trends*, 1978)

This was the period of the stock market collapse which, as we have seen, led some people to believe that the very richest saw a sizeable chunk of their wealth vanish within a very short space of time. Although these scares were unfounded, the stock market collapse did have an adverse effect on top wealth holders because they hold a disproportionately large share of stock market assets. As we can see from the table, total personal wealth increased during the period 1972-6 by almost £104bn. The table also lists the percentage gains of different groups of wealth holders. This shows that even during a period which was unfavourable to the very richest – the top 1 per cent of personal wealth holders – they still managed to claim 17.5 per cent (or £18.1bn) of the increase in personal wealth during the five years under review. The top 10 per cent claimed 47 per cent of the increase over the same period (worth £48.7bn) while the increase to the bottom 80 per cent (£36.1bn) was only fractionally more than that which went to the top 5 per cent wealth holders (£33.4bn).

The second illustration of how powerfully entrenched inequality is in our society is to look at the distribution of unearned income. Table I.2 looks at the distribution of unearned income between different groups.

TABLE I.2 *Investment income 1973–4*

| Quantile groups % | % of investment income | Amount of investment income of gross £m |
|---|---|---|
| Top 1 | 34.4 | 1,006.8 |
| 2–5 | 21.0 | 614.6 |
| 6–10 | 7.5 | 219.5 |
| Top 10 | 62.9 | 1,841.0 |
| 11–20 | 8.4 | 245.8 |
| 21–30 | 5.5 | 161.0 |
| 31–40 | 4.6 | 134.6 |
| 41–50 | 4.8 | 140.5 |
| 51–60 | 5.2 | 152.2 |
| 61–70 | 3.9 | 114.1 |
| 71–80 | 2.4 | 70.2 |
| 81–90 | 1.5 | 43.9 |
| 91–100 | 0.8 | 23.4 |
| Total | | 2,926.8 |

(*Source*: Royal Commission, 1976a, pp. 43 and 130)

The unequalness in the distribution of earned income pales into insignificance compared with who gets what in the unearned income stakes. The table highlights, for example, the fact that the super rich, the top 1 per cent in the earnings distribution, picked up 5.3 per cent of all earned income together with 34.4 per cent of investment income. In money terms, this amounted to the top 1 per cent gaining a little over £1bn of the £2.9bn unearned income which was up for grabs during 1973–4. The top 10 per cent, while gaining 26.7 per cent of all earned income, cornered very nearly 63 per cent of unearned income – the princely sum of £1.8bn. In stark contrast, the bottom 30 per cent of the incomes pile were credited with only 9.5 per cent of earned income and a mere 4.7 per cent of unearned income.

That privilege and its reverse side, poverty, are firmly rooted in our society makes it even more important that reformers should match a clear understanding of the society in which we live with a vision of the commonwealth they wish to create. In the inaugural lecture cited at the beginning of this introduction Tawney remarked that the continuance of social evil 'is not due to the fact that we do not know what is right, but to the fact that we prefer to continue to do what is wrong.' He went on to add, 'Those who have the power to remove them have not the will, and those who have the will have not, as yet, the power.'

In the light of Cedric Sandford's contribution, this comment needs revision. Acting almost as though it was on Tawney's instructions, the Labour Movement has placed much more emphasis on putting people into office than concerning themselves with what the same persons should be doing once their hands are thrust on to what might euphemistically be called the levers of power. A clear programme of objectives is crucial for the Left in government. One commentator on Labour's 1973 programme invited us to look at the then Labour opposition front bench and commented: 'there they all are, older, fatter, balder, richer, but just as silly.' Cedric Sandford makes a much more serious charge against senior Labour politicians than that they are 'just as silly' as they ever were. The debate on the wealth tax in the Labour Movement throws into relief the stark ignorance of many of the leading protagonists about the kind of society Labour is in business to create.

The sad reflection is that many of those in the top echelons of the Labour Movement have yet to grasp the importance that wealth has in underpinning so many of the unjustifiable privileges in our society, let alone begin to devise the most effective combination of policies to bring about its much more even spread throughout the community. If the Labour Party is to be taken seriously by the electorate when it echoes Bacon's belief that 'wealth is like muck. It is not good but if it is spread', not only will it require a different set of policies from those at present pursued, but will, for a start, require a much less acquisitive attitude by Labour ministers to the rewards and perks of office; revolutions need to be lived as well as preached.

Another illustration of the Labour Movement's paralysis in thinking about, let alone acting against, the epicentres of privilege, is illustrated by the operation of bodies like the Top Salaries Review Body. David Jordan's essay records not only the history of this body, but the moral treadmill created by the establishment of such bodies. The determination of top salaries cannot be taken in a moral vacuum. To shunt off decisions about top rewards (or, come to that, any other rewards) to extra-parliamentary bodies, illustrates a fundamental misunderstanding of how moral decisions are taken. No matter how talented and distinguished the review chairman is, or how long the review staff labour in producing data, at the end of the day decisions about differences in rewards between one group and another are basically moral decisions. Leaving these key questions to outside bodies (who, not surprisingly, refuse to take them for politicians and instead couch their findings in terms of relativities) is yet another indication of the collapse of Labour's war against inequality.

A further lesson from this report centres on the question of taxation. Recently, the poverty debate has been characterised by the insistence of the need to take taxation into account when measuring cuts in the living standards of the poor. Such a lesson must now be learnt when examining the income gains for the rich. It is true that a number of writers have drawn attention to how the tax system has been remoulded to the advantage of the rich (see Field, Meacher and Pond, 1977). But there is a more immediate concern which goes beyond this argument.

In his successful attempts to sell the latter stages of incomes policy, the Chancellor was quick to make some of his tax cuts conditional on agreeing a ceiling to wage and salary increases. Weekly wage packets and monthly salary cheques were to be swelled by tax cuts but only if workers kept their side of the bargain on incomes restraint. Mr Healey knew that most taxpayers quickly reworked his figures to see how big a wage claim they would have to win (and the likelihood of winning) to give them the same *net* increase in pay which, for most, was theirs for the taking under an incomes policy backed up with tax cuts.

In the celebrations which followed fast on the heels of the patient swallowing the Chancellor's new medicine, one important consideration was overlooked. How did these tax changes affect the rich, not just simply in terms of the extent to which their tax bill was lowered, but on the much more important question of what size salary increase would they need to have won to have given them the same net increase in net take home pay resulting from tax changes? Table I.3 gives the tax

TABLE I.3 *Pay increases and tax cuts for different income groups, 1977 Budget*

| Annual earnings £ | Tax gains for a married couple plus two children under 11 years £ | Pay increase required to have same effect as tax cuts for a married couple with two children under 11 years | |
|---|---|---|---|
| | | Annual £ | As % of gross earnings |
| 2,000 | 94.88 | 247.90 | 12.4 |
| 4,000 | 114.88 | 281.65 | 7.0 |
| 6,000 | 134.88 | 287.51 | 4.8 |
| 7,000 | 167.13 | 393.42 | 5.6 |
| 8,800 | 340.89 | 844.76 | 9.6 |
| 10,900 | 445.54 | 1,532.26 | 14.1 |
| 13,200 | 567.34 | 2,243.63 | 17.0 |
| 16,000 | 705.19 | 3,203.76 | 20.0 |
| 19,675 | 761.99 | 4,301.12 | 21.9 |
| 21,175 | 761.99 | 5,007.00 | 23.6 |

(*Source*: Rooker, 1978)

gains for a family man with two children on different levels of earnings – from £2,000 to a little over £21,000. It also includes a calculation on what pay increase would be required to have the same effect as the tax cuts.

In one part of his contribution, Chris Pond reports on the difficulty very high income earners experience during periods of rapid inflation in winning salary increases which maintain the real value of their pay. But, as Table I.3 shows, if there's one lesson to be learnt about the rich it is never to underestimate their resourcefulness in keeping their place in the pecking order. One new way which is open to the rich to counter the worst ravages of inflation is to 'do a Healey'; to win important tax reduction which results in increases in living standards for which, if they'd been won by salary increases, would have brought down the final curtain on incomes policy. Table I.3 showed that a family man earning a little over £21,000 would have needed a pay increase of over £5,000 to give him the same increase in take-home pay that resulted in the tax changes embodied in the 1977 Budget. In other words, a £1 reduction in taxation for the very rich is equivalent to the net increase in income which would result from a seven- or eightfold increase in salary. Or expressing the value of the change yet another way, frozen salary increases by bodies like the Top Salary Review Body were implemented unnoticed by way of tax cuts.

This introduction need concern itself with only one further point. This book is dedicated to Barbara Wootton with affection and gratitude for a lifetime's service to the cause of greater equality. Recently, Barbara Wootton was invited to give the Blanche Colebrook Memorial Lecture. During her preparation for this, one waggish friend suggested to her that, given the resistance to bringing about major changes on the income and wealth front, her best course would be to present the audience with copies of *End Social Inequality* which was published under her name in 1941. While admitting that she had 'been pursuing an ideal of equality all my life but had been singularly unsuccessful in catching my prey', Barbara Wootton gave the following rallying cry:

> I was born into a Britain in which there were no old age pensions or family allowances, no National Health Service, no unemployment, sickness, maternity or funeral benefits, no attendance allowances for the disabled, no home-helps. If all these have been established within a single life-span, the younger members of this audience may hope to see what are now utopian visions actually translated into reality (Wootton, 1976, p. 11).

It is with this thought in mind that we should begin matching these social changes with a revolution in income distribution. Justice for today's poor is as linked to 'the problem of riches' as it was when Tawney delivered that inaugural lecture sixty-five years ago.

1

# The old order

Louie Burghes

Ask about wealth and the common view is how poor the once wealthy now are and how their loss has gone to make us all equal. But what is much more important is that the majority of the population in this country own but a fraction of its wealth, and if they have made any gains this century, or over the centuries, it emphasises not their relative affluence but from what a meagre position they started.

The lack of change is often easily glossed over by comparing different types of income and wealth for different groups. Polanyi and Wood, for example, wrote:

> The enjoyment of holidays abroad in summer and central heating at home in winter, the massive increase in the consumption per head of electricity, gas, wine and restaurant meals, are all visible signs of a widespread improvement in the standard of living. The decay of great houses, the prosperity of the supermarkets, are only two further pointers to what has been taking place (Polanyi and Wood, 1974, p. 12).

That the standard of living, and of incomes in general, has risen does not tell us about the distribution of either wealth or income in this country. In fact, looking back over the centuries, the landmarks of wealth and poverty remain strikingly familiar even if the relativities have changed. At the beginning of 1978, in contrast to Polanyi and Wood, A. H. Halsey wrote:

> The assumption of growing affluence is not beyond question. The old poverties of lack of property, low pay, poor health, inadequate

> education and bad housing still disfigure, and many would say disgrace, the powerful engine of production which we call industrial society (Halsey, 1978, p. 79).

Nor, despite the protestations of some commentators, is the question of the inequality of wealth beyond question. Wealth is important because of the many benefits that it confers. At one level there are, as Lydall and Tipping (1961) note, the benefits of freedom of manoeuvre, security against the unforeseen and power. In the second of the 1978 Reith Lectures it was 'property for power' that Professor Halsey saw as the distinguishing division in society:

> property for power by which I mean property which carries control over the lives of other people, and property for use – possessions that free a man from other people's control (Halsey, 1978, p. 80).

On the basis of this distinction he concluded,

> We can reasonbly say that, throughout the period we can collectively remember, three-quarters of us have been virtually propertyless in that area which covers the central part of our lives and our occupations – how we earn a living and how we relate to our fellow men. A tiny minority has monopolised wealth, and an even tinier minority has monopolised property for power (ibid.).

When those who argue about ever-increasing equality are listing the benefits to the average man, it is important to remember that there is all the difference in the world between a rise in real living standards and a change in the distribution of power-conferring wealth.

In this chapter we look at the extent of personal wealth in this country and the way that its distribution has changed over this century. But in interpreting the trends over the period we face two contradictory problems. A simplistic analysis of the statistical measures of wealth shows dramatic changes in the distribution; a careful analysis does not. But once we explore the technicalities of the measures we can get lost in a labyrinth in which we know that the end result is 'true' but are unclear as to its 'significance'. At the simplest the question is 'Do we have an equal distribution of wealth in this country?' Naive though it may appear, as a guide it proves indispensable and one of which many commentators have lost sight.

It is a truism to say that there are always problems with using statistics. There is never quite what one wants or needs; they are also remarkably out of date; their meaning and hence interpretation is always infinitely complex and highly ambiguous. For many people glazed eyes and boredom set in all too soon. All these usual problems are present in looking at statistics that measure the distribution of wealth; to some extent the problems seem even greater than with other social issues. But what is striking and what holds the attention is the alarming realisation that despite fine adjustments, definitional arguments, changes in series and increasing amounts of material to work with, the distribution of wealth is still very unequal.

We look first at the distribution of wealth before 1960, using 'unofficial' estimates mostly based on estate duty returns. We then look at the data since 1960, the year the Inland Revenue, again using estate duty returns, started producing their own estimates of the size and distribution of wealth. We go on to examine the criticisms of an adjustments to these figures pioneered by Jack Revell and extended by the Royal Commission on the Distribution of Income and Wealth. (The detailed critique and adjustments made by A. B. Atkinson and A. J. Harrison are analysed by Alan Harrison in the following chapter.)

## 1900–60

In the first edition of *A Survey of the Social Structure of England and Wales*, Carr-Saunders and Caradog Jones considered the still contentious issue of what constitutes wealth. They argued that wealth should be defined as 'the sum total of the exchangeable and transferable possessions of the inhabitants of this country' and that since human skills, now commonly referred to as human capital, are not exchangeable but are 'internal' skills, they cannot be included in a definition that corresponds to an ordinary conception of wealth (Carr-Saunders and Caradog Jones, 1927, p. 105). They do not deny the value of these assets, merely whether they should be included in calculating wealth. The same issues are under discussion today. In general, however, our inability to measure such wealth as human capital or social property has meant that their inclusion in calculations of wealth is patchy and therefore distorting. This chapter has not included estimates for them. The effect on the distribution of wealth from the inclusion of some components of human capital (occupational and state pension rights) has been looked at by the Royal Commission and is summarised here.

The estimates of wealth produced before 1960 differ from one another in a number of ways. First, they have not all been concerned with measuring the distribution of wealth as well as total wealth.

Second, they vary both in their base source and their methods of estimation. The most used technique has been the estate duty method. Using data from the collection of estate duty, estimates of the wealth of those who die are used as a sample and grossed up using a 'mortality multiplier' to produce estimates of the wealth of the living. (There is a detailed explanation of this method in the appendix.) The disadvantages of the method were the same then as they are now. Among the problems that the earlier writers tackled were: estimating the wealth of those who owned insufficient wealth for estate duty to be levied; estate duty avoidance resulting in estimates that are too low; and finding the correct mortality multipliers which need to allow for the interrelationships between death and age, health and wealth. This is still the most commonly used method, even today, although now more refined.

Sir Joshua Stamp produced some of the first estimates of the level of national income and wealth at the turn of the century. He defined the wealth of a country as '*either* the value of the objects found within its boundaries, *or* the wealth of the inhabitants, including their foreign possessions, and excluding wealth within the country held by people abroad' (Stamp, 1922, pp. 7 and 8). Such a definition was common to the pre-1960 commentators. Stamp, unlike many of the writers who have since produced estimates of personal wealth, used mainly income tax data as the basis of his estimates. He estimated that total national wealth in 1914 was just over £14,000m. Of this, £11,000m was estimated to be individual wealth. By 1922 he put an upper limit of £19,000–20,000m on total national wealth; £15,000m belonging to individuals.

He also looked at the distribution of wealth in 1919 adapting figures given by the Board of Inland Revenue in their memoranda on the *Taxation of War Wealth.* Figures for the United Kingdom showed that about two thirds of wealth was held by less than 400,000 people (less than 1 per cent of the population) and a third of wealth by 36,000 people (less than 1 in 1,000 of the population). Carr-Saunders and Caradog Jones reworked this data to give shares to the working population over 20 years of age. This gives estimates showing two thirds of wealth held by 2.5 per cent of this population and a third of all wealth by 2.5 persons in 1,000 (Carr-Saunders and Caradog Jones, 1927, p. 114).

Figures for the early part of the century for England and Wales were also produced by Professor Henry Clay; his estimates were for 1912–13 and 1920–1. Unlike Stamp, Clay used the estate duty method with different mortality multipliers for estates above and below £500 and estimates for small holdings of wealth – personal possessions and savings – for those estates that were below the tax exemption limit (£100 in 1911). He defined the population as those over 15 years who were classified as occupied in 1911. Total personal wealth was estimated at just under £7,000m in 1912-13 and just over £12,000m in 1920-1. In 1912-13, just under 68 per cent of it was held by just over 1 per cent of the population; in 1920-1, 64 per cent by 1.7 per cent of the population. (For further details, see Clay, 1924-6.)

Estimates produced by Sir Harry Campion overlapped those of Stamp and Clay. Campion's estimates were for 1911-13, 1926-8 and 1936. (Previously figures for 1911-13 and 1924-30 were produced by Daniels and Campion, 1935-6.) Campion warns that the estimates for total personal wealth exclude propety of persons under 25 years of age, settled property and allowances for evasion of taxation and undervaluation. The estimates cover England and Wales and use both general mortality multipliers and ones disaggregated to reflect social class. Campion estimated personal wealth for these years to be: £6,000-£7,000m in 1911-13; just under £14,000 to just under £15,500m in 1926-8 and just under £16,000 to £17,500m in 1936. He suggested that there had been some change in the distribution of wealth before and after the war, the top 1 per cent of wealth holders owning 70 per cent, 60 per cent and 55 per cent of total wealth respectively in 1911-13, 1926-8 and 1936. But the share of the top 5 per cent does not seem to have changed to such an extent. It fell from an estimated 85 per cent in 1911-13 to 80 per cent in 1928-8 and to between 75 per cent and 80 per cent in 1936. (For further details see Campion, 1939.)

Kathleen Langley added to this series, producing comparable figures for 1936-8 and 1946-7. She followed Campion on both mortality multipliers and on the treatment of small holdings of wealth; he in turn had followed Clay on the latter. Her analysis concentrates on changes over time in the numbers of wealth holders within different ranges of wealth. Looking at the changing share of the top 1 per cent for the entire period covered by herself and Daniels and Campion, she concluded that the distribution of capital was becoming more equal. The share of the top 1 per cent had been 70 per cent in 1911-13; 60 per cent in 1924-30; 55 per cent in 1936-8 and 50 per cent in 1946-7. But between the earliest and the latest dates, the amount of wealth that was held by the top 10 per cent or so of wealth holders only declined by about 10 percentage points indicating less redistribution than would appear from the changing share of the top 1 per cent. (For further details see Langley, 1950 and 1951.)

In contrast to earlier estimates, those for the 1950s were not produced from estate duty statistics (although they were used) but from the results of social surveys. The surveys were carried out by the Institute of Statistics at Oxford, one each for the three years 1952–4. Income units in private dwellings in Great Britain were used as the sample base and they carried out, for example, just under 2,500 interviews for the 1954 survey. As a method of collecting information, sample surveys suffer from a number of disadvantages – and collecting information on personal wealth in this way is no exception. People tend to be reluctant to discuss their personal finances and this increases both the number of people who refuse to take part in the survey and the unreliability of any information given. In the second of the Oxford surveys, in 1953, the overall response rate was just over 66 per cent but varied by income group from just under 69 per cent for the lower groups to just over 46 per cent in the upper groups. In the 1954 survey, the overall response rate was slightly higher and the difference between the two groups slightly narrower. But surveys have their advantages; for instance they will pick up ownership of some types of personal wealth usually left out of estate duty returns.

Looking at the results of the Oxford surveys, differences between the individual years are not thought to be significant. Taken together, however, the last two years in particular give an indication of the distribution of wealth in the period. The following were among the main points to arise from the results. In 1953 average individual net worth was estimated at £800 per income unit; £1,000 in 1954 (when one third of the income units were found to have no wealth at all). In 1953, the top 3 per cent of income units held 50 per cent of the total net wealth, and the top 10 per cent, 75 per cent of wealth. More than 50 per cent of the income units shared less than 1 per cent of net wealth between them. In 1954 the top 5 per cent held 60 per cent of net wealth and the top 20 per cent, 90 per cent of wealth. The distribution of the different types of assets was also found to be very uneven. Only 5-7 per cent of the income units, for example, owned stocks and shares and other securities. (For further details see, for example, Hill, 1955.)

The drawbacks associated with both the estate duty and survey methods led Lydall and Tipping to make use of both sources of information to produce what they thought would be more accurate estimates of total wealth and its distribution. Although they produced estimates for total personal wealth from 1951 to 1958 (total wealth for each year respectively was £30,000m and £38.000m) they did not feel that the data were reliable enough to produce estimates of the distribution for each year. Instead they used their estimates from the estate duty returns for 1951-6 to produce an estimate for the beginning of 1954. They supplemented these data with information from the 1954 survey to estimate wealth below the estate exemption limit (before 1954, £2,000; after 1954, £3,000).

This suggested that total personal wealth in 1954 was about £40,000m. Of this, £31,000m was owned by 3m people and £9,000m by 32m people. The top 1 per cent of wealth holders in 1954 were therefore estimated to own 43 per cent of total personal wealth; the top 10 per cent, nearly 80 per cent. If these figures are more accurate than those from the surveys alone, they suggest that wealth might have been more concentrated in 1954, than the survey figures suggested for 1953. (For further details of the methods they used, see Lydall and Tipping, 1961.)

### *Long-run trend*

What conclusions can we draw from these figures? The individual commentators certainly thought that the distribution of wealth was becoming more equal. But how has the picture been changing over the whole period? Unfortunately that is not something that these figures can tell us. They do not provide a consistent series but snapshots of the distribution of wealth at different points in time based on different assumptions and different estimating methods. But the figures have been used by some commentators to present series from the beginning of the century to 1960 and beyond as if they were a consistent series.

There are two well-known long-run series. First, that given by Polanyi and Wood (Table 1.1) and, second, that reproduced by the Royal Commission in their first report and credited to Revell (Table 1.2). Taking the Polanyi and Wood figures, Atkinson and Harrison have pointed out that the series is not as consistent as the authors suggest nor is it from only two sources – Lydall and Tipping and the Inland Revenue – to whom it is attributed. In fact the early figures are from Daniels and Campion (1911-13 and 1924-30) and Campion (1936). The 1951-6 figures are from Lydall and Tipping and the figures from 1960 are from the Inland Revenue.

The coverage of the figures from 1960 is quite different from that for the earlier periods. The figures from 1960 are for Great Britain and for those aged 15 years and over and do not make allowance for the

TABLE 1.1 *Long-run trend: from Polanyi and Wood, 1974, pp. 17 and 19*

Wealth ownership, 1911–13 to 1970
per cent of total personal wealth
(based on mortality rates corrected for social class)

| Proportion of adults | England & Wales<br>Adults aged 25 and over<br>1911–13 | 1924–30 | 1936 | 1951–6 | Great Britain<br>Adults aged 15 and over<br>1960 | 1965 | 1970 |
|---|---|---|---|---|---|---|---|
| | as presented by Lydall and Tipping | | | | our estimates from Inland Revenue | | |
| % | % | % | % | % | % | % | % |
| Top 1 | 66 | 60 | 56 | 42 | 39 | 34 | 31 |
| 5 | 86 | 83 | 81 | 68 | 64 | 62 | 56 |
| 10 | 90 | 90 | 88 | 79 | 76 | 75 | 70 |
| Bottom 90 | 10 | 10 | 12 | 21 | 24 | 25 | 30 |

(*Source*: 1911–13 to 1951–6: Lydall and Tipping, 1961, p. 92. 1960 to 1970: estimates from *Inland Revenue Statistics*)

Wealth ownership in inter-percentile groups: 1924–30 to 1970
per cent of total personal wealth
(based on mortality rates corrected for social class)

| Proportion of adults | England & Wales<br>Adults aged 25 and over<br>1924–30 | 1936 | 1951–6 | Great Britain<br>Adults aged 15 and over<br>1960 | 1965 | 1970 |
|---|---|---|---|---|---|---|
| | as presented by Lydall and Tipping | | | our estimates from Inland Revenue | | |
| % | % | % | % | % | % | % |
| Top 1 | 60 | 56 | 42 | 39 | 34 | 31 |
| 2–5 | 23 | 25 | 26 | 25 | 28 | 25 |
| 6–10 | 7 | 7 | 11 | 12 | 13 | 14 |
| 11–20 | 6 | 6 | 10 | 15 | 14 | 17 |
| Bottom 80 | 4 | 6 | 11 | 9 | 11 | 13 |

(*Source*: as above)

wealth of the excluded population. The figures before 1960 are for England and Wales only, and for the population aged 25 years and over.

The second series was reproduced by the Royal Commission from Revell. Again the series is not consistent. For the earliest two periods Revell used estimates produced by Daniels and Campion and the 1936–1936–8 estimate is Langley's. (For a detailed summary of the distinction between these series, see Chapter 6 in Atkinson and Harrison, 1978.)

It is these misleading series that underlie the conclusion that there

TABLE 1.2 *Long-run trend: from Royal Commission 1975, Table 41*

Trends in the distribution of personal wealth up to 1960
Percentage shares of personal wealth owned by given quantile groups of the population aged 25 and over, assuming that persons not covered by the estate duty returns have no wealth; at specified dates between 1911-13 and 1960
England and Wales (Series B)

| Quantile group % | Percentage share of personal wealth 1911-13 | 1924-30 | 1936-8 | 1954 | 1960 |
|---|---|---|---|---|---|
| | % | % | % | % | % |
| Top 1 | 69 | 62 | 56 | 43 | 42 |
| 2- 5 | 18 | 22 | 23 | 28 | 33 |
| 6- 10 | 5 | 7 | 9 | 8 | 8 |
| 11-100 | 8 | 9 | 12 | 21 | 17 |
| (Cumulative basis) | | | | | |
| Top 1 | 69 | 62 | 56 | 43 | 42 |
| Top 5 | 87 | 84 | 79 | 71 | 75 |
| Top 10 | 92 | 91 | 88 | 79 | 83 |

(*Source:* J. Revell, 'Changes in the social distribution of property in Brtain during the twentieth century', Third international conference of economic history, Munich, 1965)

has been a dramatic redistribution of wealth this century. Even if we put aside the major reservation of using data which are not part of a consistent series, the figures themselves would not support the view that a major redistribution has taken place. Looking at the top half of Tables 1.1 and 1.2 it is clear that equality in the distribution of wealth is not just around the corner. What these figures show is that although the share of the top 1 per cent has declined, it was all but accounted for by increased shares to both the top 2-5 per cent and 6-10 per cent of wealth holders. The top 1 per cent may have lost some of its share, but those groups just below have gained considerably. Atkinson (1972) concluded that 'It seems therefore that what redistribution there has been has not been between the rich and the poor, but between the rich and the very rich' (p. 22) and that this 'reflects in part the rearrangements of wealth *within* families rather than redistribution *between* rich and poor families' (p. 24). It is only now that we have a consistent long-run trend (calculated by Atkinson and

Harrison). The next chapter looks at what this tells us about changes in the distribution of wealth over time.

### *Inland Revenue data – from 1960*

The Inland Revenue statistics constructed from the estate duty returns provide wide-ranging information about the amount of wealth in the country, the numbers of wealth holders, estate duty paid, asset composition and the distribution of wealth among the population. The series since 1960 is not, however, geographically consistent. Before 1974, the Inland Revenue estimates were for Great Britain only; in that year they produced estimates for both Great Britain and the United Kingdom. Since then figures have only been produced for the United Kingdom, but the distribution for Great Britain and the United Kingdom are remarkably similar for that year (see Table 1.3).

The Inland Revenue's statistics show that between 1964-5 and 1974-5 there was a small decline in the number of estates assessed for estate duty (from about 296,000 to about 285,000) but that there was a considerable increase, for the same period, in the number of estates valued at over £15,000 (from just over 21,500 to just under 44,500) (Inland Revenue, 1975, Table 92). In 1975-6 there were over 310,000 estates assessed and just under 57,000 estates valued at over £15,000 (Inland Revenue, 1977a, Table 97). The net capital value of estates rose from just under £2,000m in 1970-1 to just under £3,000m in 1974-5. Estate duty paid in both years was about £350m. While the net capital value of estates rose it seems that estate duty did not. Figure for the United Kingdom for 1975-6 were respectively just under £3,500m and just under £330m (an even more surprising drop) (Inland Revenue, 1977a, Table 99).

Using the estate duty method the Inland Revenue calculate total personal wealth in this country and estimate its distribution. From the Inland Revenue statistics we can see that the estimated net wealth of individuals in this country has increased from £51,000m in 1960 to £157,000m in 1974 (Inland Revenue, 1970, Table 122 and Inland Revenue, 1977a, Table 111). In 1975 total net wealth in the United Kingdom was estimated at just under £160,000m (Inland Revenue, 1977a, Table 111).

Table 1.3 shows the Inland Revenue's estimates of the distribution of wealth in this country since 1960. The top half of the table shows that the bottom 80 per cent of the population of wealth owners have only increased their share of wealth by 11.3 per cent percentage points

TABLE 1.3 *Trends in the distribution of personal wealth since 1960, from Royal Commission, 1977, Table 33*

Percentage shares of estimated personal wealth of given quantile groups both of the population covered by the Inland Revenue estimates and of the total population aged 18 and over, with Gini coefficients; at specified dates between 1960 and 1975
Great Britain 1960–74
United Kingdom 1974 and 1975 (Series A and B)

| Quantile group % | 1960 | 1962 | 1964 | 1966 | 1968 | 1970 | 1972 | 1973 | (GB) 1974 | (UK) 1974 | (UK) 1975 |
|---|---|---|---|---|---|---|---|---|---|---|---|
| | % | % | % | % | % | % | % | % | % | % | % |
| Population covered by Inland Revenue estimates (Series A) | | | | | | | | | | | |
| Top 1 | 28.4 | 27.2 | 25.9 | 23.6 | 24.2 | 20.7 | 22.1 | 21.8 | 18.4 | 18.3 | 17.2 |
| 5 | 50.9 | 48.8 | 48.5 | 43.7 | 45.2 | 40.9 | 41.8 | 38.8 | 36.7 | 36.7 | 35.0 |
| 10 | 63.1 | 60.7 | 60.5 | 56.0 | 57.1 | 51.9 | 53.9 | 50.9 | 49.0 | 49.1 | 47.3 |
| 20 | 76.2 | 73.9 | 74.1 | 70.8 | 71.2 | 66.4 | 68.5 | 66.6 | 64.9 | 65.0 | 63.3 |
| Bottom 80 | 23.8 | 26.1 | 25.9 | 29.2 | 28.8 | 33.6 | 31.5 | 33.4 | 35.1 | 35.0 | 36.7 |
| Gini coefficient | 73 | 72 | 72 | 67 | 68 | 65 | 66 | 65 | 63 | 63 | 62 |
| Total population aged 18 and over (Series B)* | | | | | | | | | | | |
| Top 1 | 38.2 | 36.0 | 34.4 | 31.8 | 32.7 | 29.0 | 29.9 | 27.6 | 25.3 | 25.2 | 23.2 |
| 5 | 64.3 | 60.7 | 59.3 | 56.7 | 59.0 | 56.3 | 56.3 | 51.3 | 49.9 | 49.9 | 46.5 |
| 10 | 76.7 | 74.0 | 73.5 | 71.8 | 73.8 | 70.1 | 71.9 | 67.2 | 66.0 | 66.1 | 62.4 |
| 20 | 89.8 | 88.4 | 88.4 | 87.8 | 89.4 | 89.0 | 89.2 | 86.4 | 85.5 | 85.6 | 81.8 |
| Bottom 80 | 10.2 | 11.6 | 11.6 | 12.2 | 10.6 | 11.0 | 10.8 | 13.6 | 14.5 | 14.4 | 18.2 |
| Gini coefficient | 89 | 87 | 87 | 86 | 87 | 86 | 86 | 84 | 83 | 83 | 81 |

(*Source*: Inland Revenue.)
*Assuming that persons not covered by the Inland Revenue estimates have no wealth.

between 1960 and 1974. But this trend seems slight in comparison to the disproportionate amount of wealth owned by only a small section of the population. In 1974 the top 1 per cent of wealth owners still owned over 18 per cent of personal wealth; 5 per cent just under 37 per cent and the top 10 per cent all but 50 per cent. The bottom 90 per cent share the remaining 50 per cent of the country's wealth.

But these figures show the distribution of wealth only among wealth holders identified from the estate duty statistics. It therefore omits those who are likely to have little or no wealth and on whose wealth there is no data – almost half the population; this is the Inland Revenue's A Series. An alternative method – to include those who have no wealth – is the basis of the Inland Revenue's B Series. Although neither of these extreme methods is generally considered adequate, the Inland Revenue say of the B Series that the figures 'provide a useful upper limit to the actual degree of inequality in the ownership of wealth' (Inland Revenue, 1976a, p. 162).

The Inland Revenue's B Series not unexpectedly shows far more inequality in the distribution of wealth. But less obviously it also shows that there has been less of a change in the direction of equality than the A Series would suggest. The figures show the share of wealth of the top 1 per cent as just over 25 per cent (rather than just over 18 per cent); the share of the top 5 per cent as all but 50 per cent (rather than just under 37 per cent); and the share of the top 10 per cent as 66 per cent (rather than nearly 50 per cent). The share of the bottom 90 per cent is a mere 34 per cent (compared with 50 per cent) and the bottom 80 per cent is 14.5 per cent (compared with 35 per cent).

Figures produced by the Royal Commission in their most recent report help to put this into perspective. They have calculated the minimum wealth that an individual would have to own to be included among the various percentile groups. The figures for the A Series are: £11,700 to be in the top 20 per cent of wealth holders; £17,900 for the top 10 per cent; £26,800 for the top 5 per cent and £66,000 for the top 1 per cent. For the B Series, the figures are: £6,500 for the top 20 per cent; £12,000 for the top 10 per cent; £18,400 for the top 5 per cent; and £46,100 for the top 1 per cent (Royal Commission, 1977, Table 28).

Another way of measuring the distribution of wealth and the difference produced by the diferent series is to use the Gini coefficient (see Table 1.3 and the appendix for an explanation of it). While the coefficient for the A Series shows a decline of 10 points for the period from 73 to 63, that for the B Series shows a smaller move and from a higher base (89 to 83) suggesting both greater inequality and only a slight diminution of it.

*Distribution by wealth owned*

Whatever the degree of change in the distribution since 1960 there can be little doubt that the distribution of wealth among the population is still remarkably uneven. Another way of demonstrating this unevenness is to look at the proportion of the population that own different amounts of wealth.

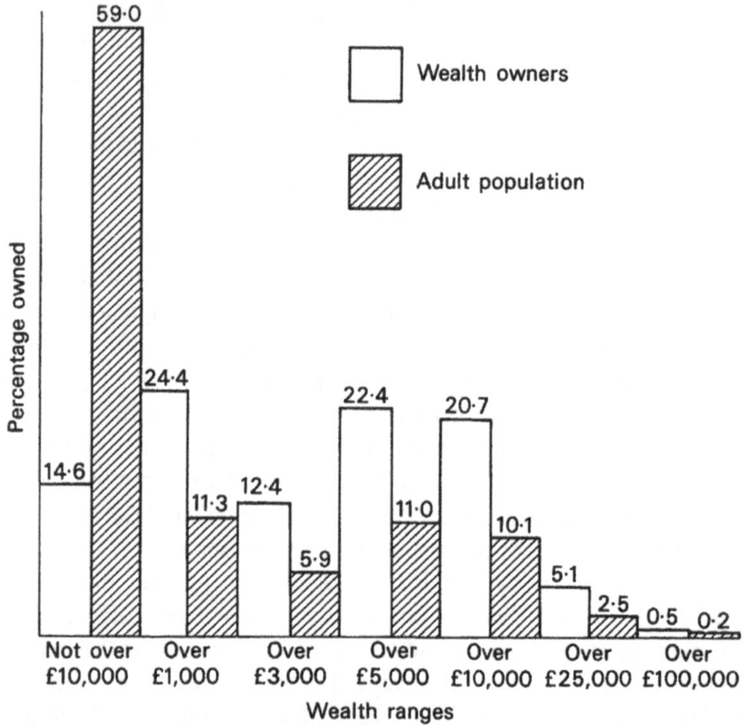


FIGURE 1.1 *Inland Revenue estimates of total personal wealth in the United Kingdom, 1975: distribution among wealth owners and adult population.* (Source: *Inland Revenue, 1977, Tables 114 and 115*)

Looking at the figures in Figure 1.1, we can see that the majority of those who do own wealth only hold amounts in the lower ranges; and when we look at wealth ownership among the total adult population this tendency is much more marked. In 1975, in the United Kingdom, nearly 15 per cent of wealth holders were estimated to own less than £1,000; but, taking the entire adult population, those estimated to have less than £1,000 increases to almost 60 per cent. At the other extreme, less than 5 per cent of the population owned more than £25,000 and only 0.5 per cent over £100,000 (A Series). Looking at the B Series, an even smaller proportion of the population are estimated to own these amounts: 2.5 per cent and 0.2 per cent respectively (Inland Revenue, 1977, Tables 114 and 115). Again in 1975, and also for the United Kingdom, there were estimated to be 69,000 individuals with over £100,000 and 29,000 with over £200,000 (Inland Revenue, 1977a, Table 111). What we do not know is exactly how wealthy these 29,000 individuals are.

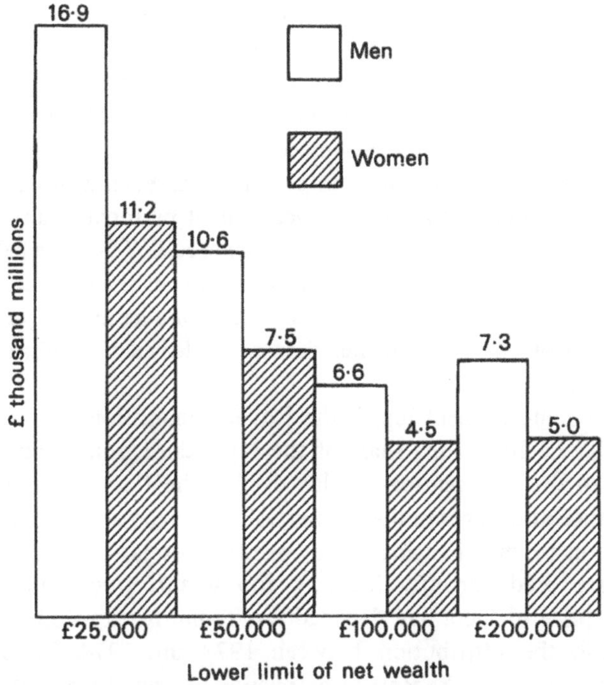


FIGURE 1.2 *Personal wealth in the United Kingdom, 1975, by sex* (Source: *Inland Revenue, 1977, Table 111*)

Taking the same estimates for total personal wealth from the Inland Revenue for the United Kingdom in 1975, we can look at the distribution of the wealth holding between men and women (Figure 1.2). Despite differential life expectancy, men hold more than twice the amount of wealth owned by women and there are more male wealth holders than there are female. Although women hold more wealth than men in the wealth range below £1,000, in all other ranges there are both more men, and they hold more wealth. In 1975, of £190,300m of total net personal wealth, men owned £115,900m; women £74,300m. There were over 12m men identified as holding wealth; but only 8.75m women. Although there were only 50 per cent more men than women wealth holders, they owned nearly twice as much between them. Figure 1.2 shows the difference in wealth holding between men and women.

### *The importance of assets and valuation*

A particular problem with measuring wealth is valuation. It is particularly important because wealth groups vary greatly in their asset holdings. Not only are the most 'valuable' assets owned by those in the highest wealth groups, but the way in which they are valued affects the distribution, an issue which is examined in the next chapter.

Among the top wealth groups (over £200,000) physical assets (of which dwellings are the most important), shares and other company securities accounted for over 70 per cent of personal wealth in 1975. In contrast, those whose wealth did not exceed £5,000 have below average holdings of all the physical assets and higher than average holdings of cash and bank deposits, national savings, life assurance policies and other cash assets. (For further details see Royal Commission, 1977, Table 29).

In their most recent report the Royal Commission pointed out the noticeable decline in the share of the top wealth groups between 1973 and 1974. In commenting on this decline the Commission noted the importance of changes in the market/values of land and company shares in relation to the changing values of other assets. The fact that these assets are predominantly held by top wealth groups and that the current price of them had declined was found to explain much of the change in the distribution between 1973 and 1974. To bring this analysis up to date, the Royal Commission projected from 1975 figures to produce estimates for the United Kingdom (on both the A and B Series) of the distribution of wealth in 1976. The increase in the inequality of the distribution that was projected could be accounted for, they suggested, by the rise in the price of company shares in 1976 compared with other assets. Looking at the top 1 per cent, 5 per cent and 10 per cent groups, all three increased their shares on both the A and B distribution. On the B Series, the top 1 per cent from just over 23 per cent to 24.5 per cent; the top 5 per cent from 46.5 per cent to just under 48 per cent and the top by 1 per cent from 62.4 per cent to 63.4 per cent (Royal Commission, 1977, Table 38).

### *Official and unofficial estimates compared*

The Inland Revneue estate duty data do not, however, include all the wealth of everyone who dies. The deficiencies in the data have been summarised as resulting from 'missing people' and 'missing wealth' (see the appendix for details); as a result, personal wealth is under-estimated. In this section we look at the results when corrections are made for these deficiencies.

The balance sheet method has generally been used to produce alternative estimates of wealth (and its distribution); this method was pioneered by Revell. Revell was interested in producing an estimate for a national balance sheet of which the personal sector was a part and he used alternative estimates of wealth (to the estate duty figures) to do so. Not surprisingly, given the element of missing wealth from the estate duty figures, one of the main findings of the work using a balance sheet method is how far the estate duty estimates of personal wealth fall short of the balance sheet figures. Despite the criticisms Revell made of both the estate duty figures and the method, he considered the latter useful and made adjustments to produce his own estimates of total personal wealth. He compared these results for 1957–61 with personal sector wealth from the national balance sheet. Despite his adjustments the estimates still fell short of the balance sheet figures although they were, as expected, greater than the Inland Revenue's estimates for 1960 and 1961. For example, in 1961 the net worth of the personal sector was estimated at £54.2bn by the Inland Revenue, £65.3bn by Revell (using the estate duty method) and £77.6bn from the balance sheet. But the comparison between Revell's estimates and those from the balance sheet showed enough consistency for Revell to conclude that the principle of adjustment was correct, that the mortality multipliers that he had devised were an improvement on the Inland Revenue's and that he could account for the difference between the two sets of figures because of the limitations of the estate duty estimates in terms of valuation or coverage.

This pioneering work by Revell was extended with Alan Roe producing sector balance sheets from 1957 to 1966 (see Roe, 1971, and a summary of the work in Revell and Roe, 1971). Balance sheet estimates have been used since by both the Royal Commission and by Atkinson and Harrison. The former followed the method developed by Revell very closely whereas, as we see in the next chapter, Atkinson and Harrison have developed more sophisticated techniques. The Royal Commission have used the balance sheet estimates to produce an estimate of the distribution of wealth including an estimate of the wealth holding of the population assumed not to own wealth in the Inland Revenue's A and B Series. They have called this the C Series. (The difference between the Inland Revenue's estimate of total wealth at just over £190 billion and the Royal Commssion's balance sheet total of just £240 billion for 1975 (both United Kingdom) is nearly £49 billion; the Inland Revenue's estimate being just under 80 per cent of the Royal Commission's balance sheet total.) Since the purpose of the Royal Commission's C Series is, among other things, to allocate wealth to this excluded population, we would expect the C Series to indicate a more equal distribution of wealth.

The figures in Table 1.4 show that while there may be a move in that direction, it is not particularly marked and although, on the basis of this series, the top 1 per cent, and the 4 per cent below them may have experienced a decline in their share of wealth over the period, the two

TABLE 1.4 *Trends in the distribution of wealth on an adjusted basis, Series C, from Royal Commission, 1977a, Table 39*

Percentage shares of personal wealth owned by given quantile groups of the total population aged 18 and over, on an adjusted basis, 1972-5
1972-4 Great Britain
1975 United Kingdom

| Quantile group % | % share of estimated personal wealth | | | |
|---|---|---|---|---|
| | Series C | | | |
| | 1972 | 1973 | 1974 | 1975 |
| Top 1 | 28.1 | 28.0 | 25.0 | 24.3 |
| 2-5 | 25.8 | 22.5 | 22.4 | 21.8 |
| 6-10 | 13.4 | 14.2 | 14.1 | 13.9 |
| 11- 20 | 15.1 | 16.5 | 16.6 | 16.2 |
| 21-100 | 17.6 | 18.8 | 21.9 | 23.8 |
| Cumulative basis | | | | |
| Top 1 | 28.1 | 28.0 | 25.0 | 24.3 |
| 5 | 53.9 | 50.5 | 47.4 | 46.1 |
| 10 | 67.3 | 64.7 | 61.5 | 60.0 |
| 20 | 82.4 | 81.2 | 78.1 | 76.2 |

(*Source*: 1972 figures from Table 34, Report no. 1; 1973 and 1974 figures from Table 35, Report no. 4; 1975 figures from Table 38, Report No. 5)

quantile groups below them shared some of the increase. To put the change in perspective, it is worth noting that the top 20 per cent still owned more than 75 per cent of total personal wealth; the bottom 80 per cent less than 25 per cent. The Royal Commission have also pointed out that the trend towards equality is far less marked in the C Series (than in the other series). They point out that the share of the top 1 per cent is shown to have declined by about 2 percentage points a year according to the B Series, whereas the C Series suggests that there was a sharp decline between 1973 and 1974 (as a result of the change in the relative value of different assets – see above) but much smaller falls in other years.

It was as a further refinement of the C Series that the Royal Commission looked at the effect of including the value of pensions in the distribution of wealth. They looked separately at the effects of occupational and state pensions on the distribution, both pensions taken at their actuarial value representing the capitalised value of future income flows. But this similarity (of valuation) masks an essential difference between them. While the state pension is nothing but a 'future income flow', occupational pensions may give other benefits. Some occupational pensions, for example, can be cashed in or borrowed against. Neither are true of the state pension. It is a significant difference which distribution figures do not distinguish.

It was argued earlier that one reason for excluding pension rights was because they represent such a small part of what might be called 'social wealth'. There are also technical problems. For example, the effect of including occupational rights is to reduce the share of the top 10 per cent (and of all the groups within the top 10 per cent) but to increase the share of the bottom 90 per cent. But the Royal Commission point out that this is rather misleading since only about a third of the population have rights to occupational schemes and the above figures hide the fact that the share of the bottom two thirds will actually have fallen. The effect on the distribution (the D Series) of the inclusion of occupational pension rights is to reduce the share of the top 10 per cent by 4.9 percentage points from 59.9 per cent to 55.0 per cent which is the gain made by the bottom 90 per cent (though we know that the bottom two thirds will not have gained) increasing their share from 40.1 per cent to 45.0 per cent. Most of the reduction in the share of the top 10 per cent is concentrated in the top 1 per cent of wealth holders whose share is reduced by 3.4 percentage points from 24.4 per cent to 21 per cent.

Since the Royal Commission have assumed in their analysis that every adult has a right to a state pension, the effect on the distribution is much more marked and ownership shifts in favour of men and the old and away from women and the young. The effect of the inclusion (producing the E Series) is measured against the distribution which includes occupational pension rights (the D Series). In this case the share of the top 10 per cent falls by 15.5 percentage points from 55 per cent to 39.5 per cent and the bottom 90 per cent increase their share from 45 per cent to 60.5 per cent. The share of the top 1 per cent is reduced by 7.1 percentage points – just over half the total loss of the top 10 per cent. But the Royal Commission are wrong to assume that every individual has state pension rights. Until 1975, when the contribution condition for retirement pensions was changed, those who were least likely to have complete contribution records were people who had been unemployed, and given what is known about the characteristics of the unemployed this would suggest that they are most likely to be found at the bottom of the wealth distribution. Not only then are pensions merely one part of 'social wealth' which cannot all be allocated in the distribution but there are limitations with the assumptions about pensions themselves which may mean that the distribution is more misleading than illuminating when they are included.

An alternative balance sheet estimate produced by the Central Statistical Office puts total personal wealth for 1975 (United Kingdom) at £290bn. This is about £40bn higher than the Royal Commission's and £94bn higher than the Inland Revenue estimate; indeed it is almost a half of the Inland Revenue's total estimate. (The difference between the Royal Commission and the Central Statistical Office figures reflects their construction of different balance sheet methods; the Royal Commission closely following Revell, the Central Statistical Office not doing so.) Of the £94bn difference, the Central Statistical Office estimate that £32bn was due to wealth missing from the estate duty statistics because of estates falling below the tax exemption limits and assets not being liable to taxation. The total can be divided between £20bn for excluded joint property and small estates and £11bn for excluded trusts (*Economic Trends*, 1978, p. 102). The Central Statistical Office also produced an estimate for 1976 of £325bn – evenly distributed this would be about £8,000 a head. In fact, of course, since the distribution is so unequal, the top 7 per cent, with a quarter of all personal wealth, would own about £150,000 if they divided it equally among themselves.

*Conclusion*

Looking at the distribution of wealth this century and the methodology behind it and the analyses of the distribution reveals striking aspects in both. Viewed from additional and different perspectives the analyses widen, the conclusions change. One of the striking methodological issues is the tendency for stuaies to start by looking at the top of the wealth distribution and how the wealth holders' position has changed. As a result, the major conclusion of many studies has been couched in terms of how much the top wealth holders have lost. But if we start from the bottom of the distribution our conclusions might be different. We might ask, for example, 'Why is the distribution not more equal?' and 'Why have the majority gained so little?'

The perspective of just looking from the top down has also led to some strange statistical comparisons. For example, when talking of the losses from the top percentiles (say top 10 per cent) these are often taken implicitly as gains to the majority (say the bottom 90 per cent) as if the two groups were of equal size. The impression can be given that, individual for individual, we are becoming more equal in our wealth holdings. In fact if we look at the effect that the increase in home ownership may have had, it suggests that, not only will the loss of the top 10 per cent not go so far among 90 per cent of the population, but that within the bottom 80 per cent the divisions could have increased.

Taking these facts into account and looking again at the distribution of wealth (Table 1.4) we see that the bottom 80 per cent owned less than a quarter of total personal wealth in 1975; this was less than the top 1 per cent of the population in the same year. The next 4 per cent of the population owned almost as great a share of total personal wealth – just under 22 per cent. The top 5 per cent, then, owned some 46 per cent of total personal wealth, just less than twice that of the bottom 80 per cent of the population. However fast the distribution has been changing, the top wealth holding groups still undoubtedly have a disproportionate share of the total.

2

# Recent changes in the distribution of personal wealth in Britain

Alan Harrison

As Louie Burghes has reminded us, over the last few years a great deal of attention has been focused on the related questions of whether the distribution of wealth is becoming less concentrated, and, if so, whether the trend is gaining pace or slowing down. In this chapter we examine these questions using new estimates of the distribution of wealth. These estimates have been constructed, as far as possible, on a consistent basis, in order to avoid the problems which occur when the questions mentioned above are addressed using either a variety of differing sources or one source which is nevertheless not adequate for the purpose.

The chapter* is arranged as follows. First, we briefly describe the method by which the estimates have been derived and contrast our approach with those used by the Inland Revenue (when deriving the official estimates) and by the Royal Commission on the Distribution of Income and Wealth (when adjusting the official estimates). Second, we present the actual estimates and use these to answer the questions posed in the previous paragraph. Finally we turn to a consideration of some of the factors which influence the distribution of wealth, and examine their quantitative impact.

## Estimating the distribution of wealth

Since the advent of the Royal Commission, and the regular reports on its standing reference, the need to begin a chapter such as this with a lengthy discussion of the basis of the estate multiplier method (the most widely-used method in Britain for estimating the distribution) has diminished somewhat. The *Initial Report* of the Commission (Royal Commission, 1975) contains a full account of the method, together with an explanation of why adjustments to the basic estimates are necessary and details are given in the appendix to this book. Suffice to say here, therefore, that the method makes use of data on estates which come to the notice of the Estate Duty Office, on the assumption that those who die in any one year are a representative sample of the living. Grossing-up is carried out by reference to information on differential mortality among age/sex groups, and the result may be seen most simply as an estimate of the wealth of all living persons whose wealth in that year would be dutiable, if they were to die, plus the wealth of some proportion of the persons who would not be liable to pay duty. (Estate duty has of course actually been succeeded by capital transfer tax, but it is not thought likely that this will cause any serious problems for estimates of the distribution of wealth. The change is anyway not relevant to the period under consideration in this chapter.)

The adjustments which can be made to the estimates relate to such matters as the representativeness of the estate data sample, the suitability of estate duty wealth as an indication of wealth in the hands of the living and the like. They can be grouped conveniently into four categories:

- **A** mortality multipliers;
- **B** people missing from the estate data;
- **C** wealth missing from the estate data on account of valuation differences;
- **D** wealth missing from the estate data for reasons other than valuation.

In the next few pages we explain the purpose of these adjustments and outline the precise nature of the adjustments actually made to our estimates in each case.

The term mortality multiplier refers to the factor which is applied to the basic estate statistics to gross them up to an estimate of the wealth of living persons. It is derived from the mortality rate: if, for example, one person in every 1,000 in a particular age/sex group were to die in a particular year, a multiplier of 1,000 would be applied to the number and values of all estates in that age and sex group. It is widely accepted that some consideration should be given to the observed correlation between longevity and social class, and the assumed correlation between social class and wealth. In consequence social class multipliers are usually applied, at least above some level of wealth, and this is the approach adopted by the Inland Revenue and followed by the Royal Commission. Both apply the mortality multiplier for social classes I and II to all estates above £5,000 (£3,000 before 1970), and use a lower multiplier for the smaller estates. However, this involves a sharp jump in the multiplier at the cut-off point, and an argument can be made for an approach which more smoothly graduates the multipliers with estate size.

Such an approach is the one favoured by Atkinson and Harrison (1978, pp. 67-9) and adopted here. To achieve this they fit a straight line from the general multiplier at the population midpoint to the social class multiplier at the midpoint of the combined social classes I and II. The relevant multiplier for each of six estate ranges is then read off at the population midpoint for the range. Thus, if the social class and general multipliers are respectively 135 and 100, and the midpoint of the top two social classes is at 8.35 per cent of the population, the gradient is (135-100) ÷ (50.0-8.35) or 0.84 per 1 per cent of the population. An estate range midpoint of 15 per cent, for example, would therefore yield a graduated multiplier of 129. The effect of such an adjustment turns out to be fairly minor and, if anything, testifies to the robustness of the estimates under different assumptions about mortality multipliers; but, when combined with alterations to some more technical aspects of the application of the multipliers by the Inland Revenue and the Royal Commission, the differences in the estimates are more pronounced (the more technical aspects mentioned here are discussed at length by Atkinson and Harrison, 1978, Chapter 2, especially pp. 30-1) as we shall see later in the chapter.

Category B refers to the group of people referred to by Atkinson and Harrison as the 'excluded population': those who, if they were to die, would not trouble the Estate Duty Office. The size of this group naturally varies with such factors as the estate duty exemption level, and is also larger, the smaller are the multipliers used. Making allowance for the existence of this group is relatively straightforward, but problems occur when attempts are made to allow for the likely extent of its wealth. The most extreme approach is to assume it equal to zero, and this is the basis of one set of estimates prepared by the Royal Commission, which it describes as Series B (Royal Commission, 1975, Table 45). The Royal Commission goes on to adjust its estimates for the wealth of the excluded population, but the resulting figures do not distinguish this adjustment from that for category D.

Atkinson and Harrison make a variety of allocations to adjust for this missing wealth. Groups of assets are considered individually and in each case three adjustments are made. An attempt is made to provide a lower band on concentration (where wealth is allocated as far as is reasonable to the excluded population), a central estimate and an upper bound on concentration. The figures presented in this chapter are the central estimates, but Atkinson and Harrison do give an indication of the impact of adopting either of the alternative assumptions (1978, p. 101).

Once the wealth of persons missing from the statistics is allowed for, there remain the problems associated with the fact that even the wealth of the included population is, in a number of respects, not adequately captured. Category C refers to one important aspect of this question, that of valuation. The sorts of assets affected by the method of valuation include household goods, life insurance policies and occupational pension rights – all assets which are valued for estate duty purposes differently from the appropriate valuation for living persons' wealth. To adjust for this, Atkinson and Harrison introduce two bases, realisation and going concern valuations (p. 5). The former refers to a value determined by a sale in an open market, the latter to a value on the assumption that the asset is retained.

This distinction relates closely to the concept of marketability used by the Royal Commission since the non-marketable assets, for example, are those with zero realisation value (notably state and occupational pension rights). This relationship can be seen from the following schema:

| | Method of valuation | |
|---|---|---|
| Type of market | Realisation | Going concern |
| perfect market | X | X |
| imperfect market (gap between buying and selling price, but latter non-zero) | Y | Y′ |
| no market | zero | Z |

The Commission presents estimates of (X+Y′), marketable assets only, and of (X+Y′+Z); the estimates used here are of (X+Y) and of (X+Y′+Z), although in the latter case this excludes social property. (The Commission's coverage of social property is limited to state pensions.) The choice of (X+Y) rather than (X+Y′) is based on the fact that there seems little case for attaching a special significance to a zero realisation value. Instead it seems preferable to treat marketability as varying continuously, and indeed the Royal Commission seems elsewhere to acknowledge this when it suggests that 'different approaches to personal wealth hinge essentially on varying degrees of marketability of assets' (1975, pp. 9-10).

The other aspect of missing wealth, category D, arises because of the provisions in estate duty law which allow wealth to be transferred without duty being paid or at a reduced rate of duty. This does not always lead to wealth not appearing in the estate statistics, but it is nevertheless true that substantial amounts are missing; as the Inland Revenue puts it, 'certain elements are omitted because no duty is payable on them either because of special exemptions or because they fall outside the scope of estate duty law' (Inland Revenue, 1974, p. 175).

As we mentioned earlier, the Royal Commission adjusts for this aspect of missing wealth and category B simultaneously, so that, although an appendix in the Initial Report outlines the allocation for both categories, the published estimates do not allow the reader to assess the separate effect of the adjustments. Atkinson and Harrison, by contrast, present estimates for category B separately, and then for B, C and D together, and, in addition, show the effect on one year's estimates of each adjustment separately. A further difference between the Commission and Atkinson and Harrison exists in the approach taken to the question of what amount should be allocated. Here the Royal Commission computes, for each group of assets, the amount of each already accounted for by the estate data. This is subtracted from the personal sector balance sheet total for each asset, and the residual is taken to be the amount to be allocated in adjustment categories B and D. Additionally, to an unspecified extent, the allocation also incorporates an adjustment for category C since the Commission notes that the residual 'may be attributed to the errors introduced by the various deficiencies in coverage and valuation of estate multiplier approach' (1975, p. 85).

This statement, of course, implies the uncritical acceptance of balance sheet totals, whereas, in fact, the personal sector totals are nothing more than residuals from estimates for other sectors; the divergence between the balance sheet and estate totals may, therefore, partly reflect errors in these other estimates. The adjustments made by Atkinson and Harrison attempt to take this into account by following certain general principles:

(i) They are only made where there is good reason to expect that the divergence corresponds to a source of wealth which is missing from the estate data or which is incorrectly valued.

(ii) As far as possible, they are only made when the balance sheet totals can be rated as fairly reliable. (Estimation of national balance sheet totals was pioneered by Revell (1967) who assigns different ratings to the totals, ranging from A (very reliable) to D (very unreliable).)

(iii) They are not made when there are likely to be offsetting adjustments elsewhere.

A further feature of the adjustments made by Atkinson and Harrison is that the precise nature of category D adjustments depends on category B adjustments. This is simply because the amount which can be allocated to the included population will be lower (higher) the higher (lower) is the amount allocated to the excluded population. Since the Royal Commission does not vary the allocation in category B, however, this does not arise in the case of its category D adjustments.

Before proceeding to a discussion of the actual estimates, one final point should be mentioned. For one group of assets, land and buildings, the difference between the balance sheet and estate totals is very substantial. Moreover it can be attributed to any number of different factors, so that Atkinson and Harrison choose not to incorporate the adjustment for this group into categories B-D, preferring instead to make a separate set of adjustments described as category E. (For further details, see Atkinson and Harrison, 1978, pp. 99-100 and appendix III.) The assumption made in the estimation of the figures used in this chapter is that half of the discrepancy between the two totals in the case of dwellings is allocated to the excluded population, and the remainder of the value of dwellings plus the whole of the difference in the case of 'other land and buildings' is allocated to the included population, proportionately to estate holdings. The Royal Commission, however, makes the adjustment for land and buildings within categories B-D.

## The distribution of wealth, 1966-72

In the previous section we have explained the detailed adjustments which Atkinson and Harrison have made to the data to meet common criticisms made of it. To summarise very briefly, allowances are made for the wealth of the excluded population and wealth missing from the estate data, and the mortality multipliers used are graduated with estate

TABLE 2.1 *Effects on shares of top 1 per cent and 5 per cent of different adjustments (1968)*

| Assumptions | | | | | | Top 1% | 5% |
|---|---|---|---|---|---|---|---|
| A | B | C1 | C2 | D | E | | |
| ✓ | × | × | × | × | × | 34.7 | 60.5 |
| ✓ | ✓ | × | × | × | × | 33.6 | 58.6 |
| ✓ | ✓ | ✓ | × | × | × | 36.8 | 60.9 |
| ✓ | ✓ | ✓ | × | ✓ | × | 39.0 | 62.6 |
| ✓ | ✓ | × | ✓ | ✓ | × | 34.0 | 58.1 |
| ✓ | ✓ | × | ✓ | ✓ | ✓ | 32.9 | 57.0 |
| Unadjusted Royal Commission estimates | | | | | | 32.7 | 59.0 |

Note: The table is adapted from Atkinson and Harrison, 1978, Table 5.1. The Royal Commsssion figures are from the 1975 report, Table 45. C1 and C2 refer respectively to realisation and going concern valuations. Where neither is applied, the estate valuation is used, which for most assets is based on realisation.

size. The effect of sequentially making these allowances can be seen in Table 2.1 where estimates of the shares of the top 1 per cent and 5 per cent in 1968 are given for various assumptions and contrasted with unadjusted Royal Commission figures. The effects can be summarised as follows:

| | Change in share of top 5 per cent (percentage points) |
|---|---|
| B | –2.00 |
| C1 (realisation) | +2.25 |
| D | +1.75 |
| C2 (going concern) | –4.50 |
| E | –1.00 |

It should be noted that the adjustments are interdependent and that their marginal contribution depends on the other assumptions made, but the interesting fact to emerge is that the effects are generally relatively small and tend to cancel each other out, so that the final estimates are very close to the preliminary Royal Commission estimates. This is not to say that this is true for all years, however, and indeed there are good reasons to believe that 1968 was atypical. In consequence the examination of the results for a more extended period is necessary.

TABLE 2.2 *Shares of top wealth groups 1966–72*

| | 1966 | 1967 | 1968 | 1969 | 1970 | 1971 | 1972 |
|---|---|---|---|---|---|---|---|
| Top 1% | | | | | | | |
| Royal Commission | 31.8 | 32.1 | 32.7 | 29.0 | 29.0 | 27.6 | 29.9 |
| A/B/C1/D/E | 34.8 | 35.1 | 36.9 | 34.2 | 33.3 | 31.6 | 34.7 |
| A/B/C2/D/E | 31.1 | 31.3 | 32.9 | 30.2 | 29.4 | 28.1 | 31.4 |
| Top 5% | | | | | | | |
| Royal Commission | 56.7 | 57.2 | 59.0 | 54.0 | 56.3 | 52.1 | 56.3 |
| A/B/C1/D/E | 58.7 | 58.6 | 60.6 | 58.0 | 55.6 | 54.5 | 58.2 |
| A/B/C2/D/E | 55.4 | 55.2 | 57.0 | 54.2 | 51.9 | 50.5 | 54.7 |
| Top 10% | | | | | | | |
| Royal Commission | 71.8 | 72.3 | 73.8 | 69.4 | 70.1 | 67.4 | 71.9 |
| A/B/C1/D/E | 71.3 | 71.5 | 72.8 | 69.0 | 69.2 | 68.3 | 71.2 |
| A/B/C2/D/E | 68.5 | 68.6 | 69.8 | 65.7 | 66.1 | 64.8 | 68.2 |

(*Source*: Atkinson and Harrison, 1978, Table 5.4; Royal Commission, 1975, Table 45)

In Table 2.2 we present figures comparable with three of the lines in Table 2.1 for the shares of the top 1 per cent, 5 per cent and 10 per cent for the years 1966–72. The unadjusted Royal Commission estimates are compared with estimates under assumptions A/B/C1/D/E and A/B/C2/D/E. The restriction to the years 1966–72 is a consequence mainly of data constraints which were in operation at the time the estimates were constructed. These constraints would not, even now, allow years before 1966 to be studied, although estimates for more recent years than 1972 are, of course, possible. However, even the figures in Table 2.2 allow us to draw a number of conclusions of considerable interest.

First, if we take the estimates for 1969–72 and average these to yield a figure for the distribution of wealth at the beginning of the 1970s, we have:

| % | C1<br>% | C2<br>% |
|---|---|---|
| Top 1 | 33 | 30 |
| Top 5 | 57 | 53 |
| Top 10 | 69 | 66 |

In other words, on this basis, it seems that the conventional wisdom of the top 1 per cent owning around a third of total personal wealth, and the top 5 per cent more than a half, is broadly true. Second, turning to the changes over the period, the figures suggest a decline in the shares of top groups until 1971 and then a reversal of this trend in 1972. This is evident regardless of which series we consider, including the unadjusted Royal Commission figures (with the exception of the top 1 per cent where the 1972 estimate is 2 percentage points below that for 1966). The 1972 figures generally appear rather different from those for earlier years, and the Inland Revenue has suggested that this probably reflects 'the very big upsurge in the price of Stock Exchange securities' (Inland Revenue, 1974, p. 176), a factor which was undoubtedly important, and which we examine in more detail below. Finally, if we break the period at 1970, and attempt to evaluate the effects of Labour and Conservative administrations separately, there is no clear indication that the policies of either had any significant influence on the distribution of wealth. This is not, however, surprising since the distribution of any stock is likely to change only very slowly as a result of government action, particularly if, as is the case in Britain, the stock remains untaxed in the absence of it being transferred between holders.

## Recent data

Do more recent events look as though they have radically changed the conclusions of the Atkinson and Harrison series of data? To judge whether this is so we turn our attention to the estimates published by the Royal Commission in its two reports on the standing reference (Royal Commission, 1975, 1976a). As we have mentioned, these estimates are, for a number of reasons, not directly comparable with those of Atkinson and Harrison used earlier, but they at least give some indication of more recent trends.

Of the Royal Commission's various estimates, probably the closest we can get to either of the Atkinson and Harrison estimates is to compare those listed as A/B/C2/D/E in Table 2.2 with those which the Royal Commission describes as C Series. Conveniently, the latter are calculated for 1972 as well as 1973 and 1974, so that the overlapping years' estimates give some indication of the magnitude of the discrepancy introduced by the differing assumptions. Both sets of figures for 1972 plus the Royal Commission's figures for 1973 and 1974 are given in Table 2.3. These show the share of at least the top

TABLE 2.3 *Shares of top wealth groups, 1972–74*

| | | Top | | |
|---|---|---|---|---|
| | | 1% | 5% | 10% |
| 1972 | A/B/C2/D/E | 31.4 | 54.7 | 68.2 |
| 1972 | Royal Commission | 28.1 | 53.9 | 67.3 |
| 1973 | Royal Commission | 28.0 | 50.5 | 64.7 |
| 1974 | Royal Commission | 25.0 | 47.4 | 61.5 |

(*Source*: Royal Commission, 1975, Table 34 for 1972 estimates; 1976, Table 35 for 1973 and 1974)

1 per cent to be relatively constant for 1972 and 1973 (putting aside for a moment the differences between the two estimates for 1972), but in 1974 there appears to have been an appreciable fall in this figure, which the Royal Commission attributes to the 'exceptional fall in stock market prices' (1976a, p. 64).

The discrepancy between the estimates of the share of the top 1 per cent in 1972 arises in part as a consequence of the different allocations adopted by Atkinson and Harrison and the Royal Commission, although a more significant portion of it results from the different multipliers used by Atkinson and Harrison. These have the effect of increasing the share of the top 1 per cent and reducing the shares of the groups below the top 1 per cent by a roughly corresponding amount, as can be seen by comparing the first and last lines of Table 2.1. It is not, however, the graduation with estate size *per se* which is the dominant influence here, but rather the more technical aspects of the different multipliers alluded to earlier (Atkinson and Harrison, 1978, chapter 2). The outcome can be seen in Table 2.3 by comparing the first two lines: the share of the top 1 per cent in 1972 was, according to the Royal Commission, 3 percentage points below the figure estimated by Atkinson and Harrison, whereas the Royal Commission calculates that the share of the next 9 per cent was 2 points higher than the equivalent estimate of Atkinson and Harrison. (It must be borne in mind, when considering the evidence in Table 2.3, that there is no reason why the difference between the two estimates for 1972 would necessarily apply in 1973 and 1974 also, although it seems likely that the underlying trend in the Royal Commission's estimates would be apparent.)

Taking the period as a whole, the evidence from Tables 2.2 and 2.3 suggests a number of conclusions. First, the share of the top 10 per cent appears to have stayed remarkably stable, so that, to the extent that the top 1 per cent has lost ground, the effect has only filtered down to the 9 per cent immediately below the top 1 per cent. Second, there does appear to have been some limited reduction in the share of the top 1 per cent, particularly between 1973 and 1974. However, this change must be viewed with some caution. The fall in the final year is based on a rather crude comparison of two different sets of estimates; and furthermore Atkinson and Harrison report a statistical test of the time trend in their estimates between 1966 and 1972 (those used in Table 2.2) which suggests that the downward trend is not significantly different from zero in either case (p. 132). Put another way, the errors introduced as a consequence of estimating the distribution of wealth from a sample could alone explain all the variation observed in the share of the top 1 per cent over the period. Overall, the safest conclusion is that the distribution of wealth in the early 1970s was little different from that observed in the early 1960s.

## Factors influencing the distribution of wealth

We have so far concentrated our attention solely on establishing what changes occurred in the distribution of wealth between 1966 and 1974, but now we turn to the more difficult question of what factors affect the shares of top groups in the distribution. Having done this, we conclude the chapter with a brief review of various measures which a government could use if it wished to bring about some redistribution of wealth.

Atkinson and Harrison conducted a lengthy investigation of the variables which can be expected to influence the distribution, using a series of estimates spanning the fifty years 1923-72. (These estimates are less comprehensive than those used in Table 2.2. In particular the multipliers are not graduated with estate size, and only adjustments in category B are made.) Possible candidates include the extent of saving out of earned income which is likely to be important for the share of the bottom 90 per cent (£7,000 and below in 1970). Within this general category, increasing owner-occupation, the spread of pension schemes, and the acquisition of consumer durables are all likely to play a part. However only the first and third of these are relevant, given the estimates used by Atkinson and Harrison, and they attempt to measure the effect of these via the growth in 'popular' wealth – the value of owner-occupied housing plus the value of consumer durables.

In the upper part of the distribution, an important influence is likely to be the tendency of assets held by the wealthy to increase in value. One particular asset which features prominently in the portfolio of the top 1 per cent is shares, and the index of share prices and the dividend yield (after tax and inflation) can be expected therefore to have some effect on the proportion of total wealth owned by the top 1 per cent.

A further potential influence on the distribution is that of taxation, and in particular taxes on investment income and estates. In the case of the former, it is the combination of the rate of income tax rate on unearned income and the capital gains tax rate which is relevant. Income tax can be implicitly measured if the dividend yield (mentioned above) is computed net of tax, and, for the purposes of their investigation, this is what Atkinson and Harrison do. (This does not, however, make any allowance for capital gains tax.) To establish the importance of estate duty, Atkinson and Harrison construct a variable measuring the cumulative impact of the tax since 1923.

The outcome of the statistical assessment of the influence of these various factors is interesting, if a little confusing. In particular, an unambiguous conclusion is not forthcoming. On the one hand, the decline in the share of the top 1 per cent between 1923 and 1972 (from 61 per cent to 32 per cent) is explained by the spread of 'popular' wealth, with the upward movement in the share prices working in the opposite directions. On the other hand, an alternative, and arguably less plausible, result suggests a dominant role for estate duty in the reduction of concentration, offset by higher share prices again.

Since the effect of the share price index is the only one to be unambiguous, it is of interest to use this result to predict the effect of the fall in share prices in 1974 in an attempt to establish whether the fall in the Royal Commission's estimates of the share of the top 1 per cent between 1973 and 1974, seen in Table 2.3, can indeed be attributed to this factor. Between mid-1973 and mid-1974 share prices fell by about 40 per cent, equivalent to a fall of about 85 points in the index used by Atkinson and Harrison. This in turn suggests a fall in the share of the top 1 per cent of approximately one eighth, so that 28.0 per cent would become 24.5 per cent whereas the actual estimate for 1974 is 25.0 per cent. The Royal Commission's stated opinion that the share price fall led to the 3 percentage point reduction in the share of the top 1 per cent seems therefore to be supported by the analysis carried out by Atkinson and Harrison. Furthermore, although the share is indeed sensitive to the behaviour of the stock market, wilder estimates of its influence, for example by Alan Day, appear to be ruled out of court. Day asserted that 'the squeeze on wealthy individuals . . . is already taking place with a vengeance because of the stock market collapse' (1974).

In the light of the foregoing discussion the relative constancy in the shares of the top groups in the distribution of wealth between 1964 and 1974 can most likely be explained by certain equalising influences being offset by higher share prices. When the stock market has suffered a reverse, as in 1974, there has been a reduction in the concentration of wealth, although the effect should not be exaggerated. Estate duty, if it has had any influence, has conducted a 'holding operation', preventing an increase in concentration; it may even be that, as many observers have suggested, it has had no impact whatsoever. The question we must then ask, and the one to which we will attempt some tentative answer, is 'What other methods are at a government's disposal if it wishes to achieve any substantial amount of redistribution?'

There has, of course, already been one development in this context which we should mention: the introduction of the capital transfer tax. This tax, which replaced estate duty, applies to all transfers of wealth. It is the liability of the person making the transfer and is levied cumulatively, although the scale of rates on lifetime transfers is lower than that on those made at death. In turn, the latter rates are below the old estate duty rates. The most important feature of the tax, from the point of view of redistribution, is the inclusion of lifetime transfers, previously regarded as a significant avenue of avoidance under estate duty. However, it must be said that it was not the only avenue, and other means still exist for those concerned to pass on their wealth largely intact. In particular, agricultural land and woodland are still favourably treated, so that the death-bed acquisition of growing timber, for example, is not a thing of the past.

A further feature of the tax, which is likely to lessen its redistributive force, is that it is levied on the total transferred by the donor, rather than on the total of all transfers received by a particular donee. This means, of course, that there exists less of an incentive to wealth holders to divide up their wealth and to favour those not previously in receipt of a gift. Also, the effect of the new tax on the distribution is likely to manifest itself only slowly, particularly if it causes wealthy people to postpone making gifts which they might otherwise have made while still alive.

A measure which could be expected to have a more immediate influence on the distribution, were it to be introduced, is an annual wealth tax. Such a tax can take a number of forms and, in particular, can be a substitute for an existing tax or a net addition to the tax system. If the former approach is adopted, the most likely taxes to be replaced are the investment income surcharge or the highest rates of income tax, and the original green paper on an annual wealth tax suggested that it might 'give relief on total liabilities so as to benefit most those who receive a high taxable return on their assets' (*Wealth Tax*, 1975, p. 10). However, if the tax is to be redistributive, it should involve an increase in the tax burden, at least on those holding capital. Indeed, an important aspect of a redistributive wealth tax is the opportunity it affords of imposing an implicit average rate of tax greater than 100 per cent on very high investment incomes, but not a marginal rate over 100 per cent on the income from a given capital. The structure of such a tax is also dependent on the purpose it is designed to achieve. The threshold of the tax, for example, should be much higher, if it is to be redistributive, than if it is to be a substitute for some other tax, and the desirable rates of tax, also, will be determined by the objectives of the tax. But, as Cedric Sandford points out in Chapter 6, the Labour Party has still to think through the long-term goals for such a tax.

Another fiscal measure which offers possibilities for redistribution of wealth is the tax on capital gains. At present, these are treated much more favourably than other forms of income which are subject to income tax, since gains are only taxed on realisation and then at a reduced rate, and there seems little doubt that capital gains have been a major element in the creation of new fortunes, relatively untroubled by taxation. However, the reform of the capital gains tax is typically advocated as an alternative to an annual wealth tax, and it is important, therefore, that, if both are being considered, they should be designed to act in a co-ordinated way.

The measures discussed so far are aimed at restricting the growth of large wealth holdings. It is also possible, however, to attempt to reduce concentration by encouraging growth in smaller wealth holdings through a variety of non-fiscal means. For many years various governments have been concerned to encourage small savings. The most important recent innovation in this direction has been the introduction of index-linked bonds, with the novel guarantee of a positive real rate of return. The bonds have been of two forms: one for those of retirement age, with a maximum holding, and a contractual savings scheme over five years with a maximum monthly payment. Both provide full indexation, and neither is subject to tax. This latter provision means, however, that the bonds are particularly attractive to higher rate taxpayers, and a sensible alteration to the scheme would be to limit this concession, perhaps by substituting a fixed tax credit.

Government interest in capital-sharing has, on the other hand, been much less. The aim of such a scheme is to provide workers with a share in retained profits. This would be paid into a workers' investment fund, and could be withdrawn after a specified period. A number of European countries have operated or proposed such schemes, and the government might consider at least an inspection of the European experience, to assess whether anything along similar lines might be introduced in Britain.

## Note

*This chapter draws heavily on Atkinson and Harrison (1978), and I am grateful to Tony Atkinson for permission to use material from the monograph.

3

# The high paid and the crisis of living standards

Chris Pond

The deterioration of the British economy since 1974 has caused a 'crisis of living standards' from which few groups have been exempt. But it is now widely believed that the harshest effects of that crisis have been borne by higher paid professional and managerial groups, whose previous position in the structure of relative rewards has collapsed. As the British Institute of Management has put the case: 'The impact of flat rate pay policies, inflation and an increasing burden of direct taxation at the higher managerial levels, has been proportionately much greater on managers, and skilled and professional workers than on other sectors of the community. . . . Differentials must be brought back' (BIM, 1977, pp. 5–6).

Such protestations have not fallen on deaf ears. Announcing tax concessions designed to provide disproportionate benefit to 'middle management', the Chancellor of the Exchequer lamented in his April 1976 Budget Statement: 'middle managers in industry . . . have seen their net pay severely reduced in real terms over recent years by inflation and incomes policies of successive governments' (*Hansard*, 1976, col. 276). In chapter 6 Professor Sandford describes how the commitment to a wealth tax has evaporated since Labour come to office in 1974, and here we demonstrate that the same government's approach to income tax has also changed fundamentally since that date.

Much of this change in the direction of public policy is the result of the concerted campaign on management differentials. In this chapter, we therefore examine the evidence of a decline in the relative rewards of this group, paying particular attention to the three factors specifically identified as causes of this deterioration: inflation, taxation and incomes policy. We also examine in detail the approach of the Labour government to personal taxation in the twelve budgets implemented in its first four years in office. To provide a backdrop to this discussion, we begin by considering briefly changes in the distribution of incomes since the late 1950s.

## The distribution of incomes

The first two chapters show that the redistribution of wealth since the 1960s has been largely confined to the highest income groups. What about the changes in that other component of economic inequality, the distribution of incomes? Data on the distribution of incomes, as with that on the distribution of wealth, are subject to a number of pitfalls of which we should be aware before considering the published evidence.

The most comprehensive source of data on income distribution is that compiled by the Central Statistical Office (CSO) and known as the Blue Book series. This combines data from the Inland Revenue's *Survey of Personal Incomes* (SPI) and the Department of Employment's *Family Expenditure Survey* (FES). The amalgamation of these two sources is necessary since neither offers a satisfactory picture of the distribution of incomes on its own.

Being primarily a by-product of the administrative process of tax collection, the SPI adopts a definition of income which is inappropriate when trying to assess the distribution of incomes. Income is defined as 'total net income' which is gross income minus 'allowable deductions' such as work expenses, mortgage interest payments and superannuation contributions. Since higher income groups benefit most from such allowable deductions, this definition of income tends to understate the share of income going to the top half of the distribution. Then again, income which is not assessable for tax, such as national insurance unemployment and sickness benefits (but not pensions), supplementary benefits and non-taxable fringe benefits is excluded altogether from the data. It also excludes income which is below the effective exemption limit (equivalent to the single person's tax allowance). While this once caused serious problems, one of the consequences of 'fiscal drag' has been to push increasing numbers of the low paid into tax (see below) and therefore into the Inland Revenue's statistics. In addition to these problems, income data are collected on the basis of 'tax units' (rather than individuals or households). If a wife's or child's income is aggregated with a husband's for tax purposes, this appears as one income in the Inland Revenue figures. Finally, income is measured on an annual basis, so that low recorded annual incomes may represent high weekly incomes received for a relatively short period of time. These are just some of the questions which the SPI fails to ask about the distribution of incomes. But there are still more questions for which the answers given are known to be inadequate, largely due to the Survey's association with the process of tax collection. The Inland Revenue data inevitably fail to include that income which circumvents the normal channels leading to the Exchequer, either through avoidance or evasion. Titmuss argued as long ago as 1962 that this alone was sufficient to offset, or even reverse, the modest post-war redistribution of incomes apparent in the statistics (Titmuss, 1962) and we know that the problem has, if anything, worsened in recent years. Since both the opportunity and the incentive to avoid declaring income increases the further one moves up the income scale (and beyond the normal channels of the PAYE system), the distortion created by this under-recording is likely to minimise the degree of economic inequality. Investment income, in particular, is thought to be inadequately recorded.

The Family Expenditure Survey suffers from its own problems. The sample size is small (representing approximately 1 in every 2,800 households) and the response rate, at about 70 per cent, is not good for a survey of this kind. Non-response is thought to be even higher amongst higher income groups and the self-employed, older and smaller families. Income is known to be understated, especially investment income, part-time earnings and fringe benefits. Indeed the Survey records the value of concessionary coal and coke or potatoes from an employer, but neglects the more important fringe benefits such as a company car enjoyed mainly by higher occupational groups. Finally, those who have been away from work for less than three months are treated as if they received their normal earnings prior to this demise.

The Blue Book distribution represents the marriage between these two somewhat inadequate sources, with data on certain incomes below the exemption limit and non-taxable benefits from the FES being grafted on to the SPI data. But the dominant partner remains the Inland Revenue's SPI, many of whose less fortunate characteristics are reflected in the offspring. The Blue Book series is still calculated on the basis of annual income (retaining the problem of part-year incomes); income is still recorded net of allowable deductions (including mortgage interest payments and superannuation); non-taxable income and income in kind (including fringe benefits) remains under-recorded as is much investment income; and those who manage to manoeuvre their income intact through the tax system (legally or illegally) remain outside the statistics (see Royal Commission, 1975, appendix F). In short, the statistics on the distribution of incomes reflect the adequacy with which the tax system itself encompasses the whole range of incomes, and this we know is far from perfect. Bearing these qualifications in mind, Table 3.1 shows how the distribution of incomes has (apparently) changed since the late 1950s. The figures are given both before and after tax.

Two facts emerge clearly from the data presented in this table. In the first place, it reveals the persistence of extreme inequality even in the distribution of income. Although not as marked as inequalities in wealth, it remains true that the top 10 per cent of income recipients command more than a quarter of all incomes before tax, while the poorest 10 per cent hold only 2.6 per cent of the total. Indeed, the share of income going to the highest decile is proportionately ten times as large as that going to the bottom decile. This top tenth continue to enjoy a larger share of pre-tax income than that shared amongst the entire lower half of the income distribution. The inclusion of the effects of income tax barely affects these general conclusions, as an examination of the lower half of the table reveals. Second, it emerges that over that entire period there has been very little change in this unequal distribution. Certainly the share of the top 10 per cent has declined since the late 1950s, but by less than 3 percentage points before tax (from 29.4 per cent of income to 26.6 per cent). And this decline has been largely confined to the very highest income groups. The top 1 per cent have seen their share of total income fall by 2 percentage points (from 8.4 per cent to 6.2). The top 2–5 per cent have lost even less ground, releasing less than 1 percentage point in their share of income (from 11.5 to 10.6 per cent). And the top 6–10 per cent have actually *improved* their share of income over the period.

The small decline in pre-tax income experienced by the top 10 per cent is balanced by an equivalent increase in the share of the rest of the population. But that increase is rather unequally distributed amongst the lower 90 per cent: as the Royal Commission has noted, 60 per cent of this increase accrued to the top 40 per cent of income recipients within this group, whose share of income increased from 47.5 per cent to 49.2. Meanwhile the poorest 50 per cent of income recipients have enjoyed an increase in their share from 23.1 per cent to only 24.2 per cent over the entire period since 1959. The Commission therefore

TABLE 3.1 *Percentage shares of income, before and after income tax, received by given quantile groups; 1959, 1964, 1967 and 1968–9 to 1974–5*

| United Kingdom | | | | | | | | | | | Income Unit: tax unit |
|---|---|---|---|---|---|---|---|---|---|---|---|
| Quantile group % | 1959 | 1964 | 1967 | 1968–9 | 1969–70 | 1970–1 | 1971–2 | 1972–3 | 1973–4 | 1974–5 | Income range 1974–5 (lower limit) |
| *Before income tax* | % | % | % | % | % | % | % | % | % | % | £ p.a. |
| Top 1 | 8.4 | 8.2 | 7.4 | 7.1 | 7.0 | 6.6 | 6.5 | 6.4 | 6.5 | 6.2 | 8,585 |
| 2–5 | 11.5 | 11.3 | 11.0 | 10.7 | 10.8 | 11.1 | 11.0 | 10.8 | 10.6 | 10.6 | 4,983 |
| 6–10 | 9.5 | 9.6 | 9.6 | 9.3 | 9.4 | 9.8 | 9.8 | 9.7 | 9.7 | 9.8 | 4,097 |
| Top 10 | 29.4 | 29.1 | 28.0 | 27.1 | 27.2 | 27.5 | 27.3 | 26.9 | 26.8 | 26.6 | 4,097 |
| 11–20 | 15.1 | 15.5 | 15.2 | 15.4 | 15.5 | 15.9 | 15.9 | 15.8 | 15.6 | 15.8 | 3,238 |
| 21–30 | 12.6 | 12.6 | 12.6 | 12.9 | 13.0 | 13.2 | 13.2 | 13.1 | 12.9 | 13.1 | 2,732 |
| 31–40 | 10.7 | 10.9 | 11.1 | 11.0 | 11.0 | 10.9 | 11.0 | 11.0 | 11.2 | 11.0 | 2,296 |
| 41–50 | 9.1 | 9.2 | 9.1 | 9.4 | 9.4 | 9.0 | 9.2 | 9.2 | 9.3 | 9.3 | 1,913 |
| 51–60 | 7.5 | 7.4 | 7.7 | 7.6 | 7.6 | 7.4 | 7.4 | 7.5 | 7.5 | 7.6 | 1,509 |
| 61–70 | 5.9 | 5.8 | 6.0 | 6.2 | 6.1 | 5.9 | 5.9 | 5.9 | 5.8 | 5.8 | 1,168 |
| 71–80 | 4.4 | 4.3 | 4.8 | 4.7 | 4.7 | 4.6 | 4.5 | 4.8 | 4.7 | 4.6 | 909 |
| 81–90 | 5.3 | 5.2 | 3.4 | 3.4 | 3.3 | 3.1 | 5.6 | 5.8 | 3.5 | 3.6 | 680 |
| 91–100 | | | 2.2 | 2.3 | 2.2 | 2.5 | | | 2.7 | 2.6 | – |
| *After income tax* | % | % | % | % | % | % | % | % | % | % | £ p.a. |
| Top 1 | 5.3 | 5.3 | 4.9 | 4.6 | 4.7 | 4.5 | 4.6 | 4.4 | 4.5 | 4.0 | 5,856 |
| 2–5 | 10.5 | 10.7 | 9.9 | 9.8 | 9.7 | 10.0 | 10.0 | 9.8 | 9.8 | 9.7 | 3,846 |
| 6–10 | 9.4 | 9.9 | 9.5 | 9.2 | 9.2 | 9.4 | 9.5 | 9.4 | 9.3 | 9.5 | 3,260 |
| Top 10 | 25.2 | 25.9 | 24.3 | 23.6 | 23.6 | 23.9 | 24.1 | 23.6 | 23.6 | 23.2 | 3,260 |
| 11–20 | 15.7 | 16.1 | 15.2 | 15.5 | 15.6 | 15.9 | 15.9 | 15.8 | 15.5 | 15.8 | 2,670 |
| 21–30 | 12.9 | 12.9 | 13.0 | 13.1 | 13.3 | 13.3 | 13.4 | 13.2 | 13.2 | 13.2 | 2,250 |
| 31–40 | 11.2 | 11.1 | 11.0 | 11.5 | 11.4 | 11.2 | 11.3 | 11.2 | 11.2 | 11.4 | 1,926 |
| 41–50 | 9.9 | 8.8 | 9.7 | 9.7 | 9.7 | 9.5 | 9.4 | 9.5 | 9.5 | 9.4 | 1,604 |
| 51–60 | 7.2 | 8.0 | 7.7 | 8.1 | 8.1 | 7.8 | 7.8 | 8.0 | 7.8 | 7.8 | 1,315 |
| 61–70 | 6.6 | 5.6 | 7.1 | 6.6 | 6.7 | 6.5 | 6.4 | 6.5 | 6.4 | 6.4 | 1,080 |
| 71–80 | 5.2 | 5.1 | 4.9 | 5.3 | 5.2 | 5.2 | 5.1 | 5.5 | 5.4 | 5.3 | 870 |
| 81–90 | 6.0 | 6.5 | 7.1 | 6.6 | 6.4 | 6.7 | 6.6 | 6.8 | 4.2 | 4.4 | 676 |
| 91–100 | | | | | | | | | 3.2 | 3.1 | – |

(*Source*: Royal Commission, 1977, p. 21)

note that the distribution of income within the bottom 90 per cent became even more unequal over the longer period of 1949 to 1971-2. This, they suggest, is largely due to demographic changes over the period.

Given the widespread belief that the system of taxation in Britain is radically progressive, we would expect the shares of the top and bottom income groups to change fundamentally when income tax is taken into account. In fact, the share of income enjoyed by the top 10 per cent is changed very little by the deduction of tax, falling from 26.6 per cent to 23.2. And most of this decline is again concentrated in the top 1 per cent. The share of the next 9 per cent of income recipients falls from 20.4 to only 19.2 per cent. Correspondingly, the share of the bottom 10 per cent increases by only 0.5 of a percentage point (from 2.6 per cent to 3.1) by the inclusion of tax. We would also expect the effects of income tax to accelerate the decline in the share of the highest income groups if the commonly held view that taxation is becoming increasingly progressive were true. In fact, the Royal Commission found a rather different situation: 'For the top one and ten per cent the decline in the share of post-tax income is less marked than the decline in the pre-tax share. The pattern is reversed however at the bottom of the distribution' (Royal Commission, 1977, para. 65). It appears that for the group with which we are concerned in this chapter – the top 10 per cent of income recipients – taxation actually managed to mitigate the decline in their income share. We consider some of the reasons for this below.

## *Differentials and the high paid*

We have seen that the redistribution of incomes since the late 1950s has been largely confined to the very highest income groups. Here we focus on a relatively small section of these high income recipients – those who derive their income mainly from employment. The Royal Commission on the Distribution of Income and Wealth, considering their reference to examine higher incomes from employment, defined this group as those earning £10,000 a year or more in 1974-5 (and the equivalent in other years). Inland Revenue data provided them with an estimate (subject to the reservations outlined above) of 65,000 people who had incomes from employment at or above this level. This small group of people represented just 3 in 1,000 (0.3 per cent) of all recipients of employment incomes, but received 2.1 per cent of all such incomes before tax. They therefore absorbed proportionately seven times as much income from employment as their representation in the population would justify.

The Commission found a remarkable rigidity in the position of this group over a considerable period of time. First, they found that those with incomes at the equivalent of £10,000 and above (at 1974–5 prices) remained constant throughout the 1960s, both in total numbers and as a proportion of the employed population. During this period, the numbers remained at between 50,000 and 55,000, representing 2 or 3 out of every 1,000 income recipients. There does appear to have been some increase in the numbers in the early 1970s. Second, the proportion of all those with incomes above £10,000 whose incomes above this level came primarily from employment has remained at about 30 per cent since the late 1950s (the earliest date for which figures are available). Although for most of the population, incomes from work are the most important source, this is far from the case with the highest income groups. And of course there is a significant overlap in the highest income groups between income from employment and investment income. As the TUC pointed out in their evidence to the Royal Commission, over 80 per cent of those with incomes of £10,000 or more in 1971-2 had some investment income, compared with only 22 per cent of all income recipients. Investment income also represented more than a third of the average incomes of the over £10,000 group but only 6 per cent amongst the population of income recipients as a whole (Royal Commission, 1976b).

Again using Inland Revenue data, the Commission found that there had been some decline in the earnings of these highest income groups compared with the average (median) income recipient. The highest decimillile (top 0.01 per cent) of all income recipients – with an income of £23,000 or more in 1973–4 – received 24 times as much as the median in 1959–60, but only 16 times as much in 1973–4. Over that same period, the richest millile (top 0.1 per cent) fell from an income equivalent to 10 times the median to just over 8 times, and the highest percentile (top 1 per cent) from 4 times the median to 3.75 times. The highest decile (top 10 per cent) actually enjoyed a slight *increase* in their relative position. It appears therefore, that if any squeezing of differentials took place over that period, it was confined to the top 1 per cent of income earners, representing less than 250,000 people.

Of course, an immediate criticism of this finding is that it takes no account of the effects of income tax, thought to be one of the major causes of increased equality of incomes. The Royal Commission attempted to take account of this by adjusting the gross income data for tax, assuming that in each case the family received allowances as a married couple with two children under 11. No other allowances – for mortgage interest, life assurance and pension schemes, business expenses, etc. – were taken into account here. As we show later, this assumption is particularly unrealistic, since these additional allowances are one of the main reasons for the lack of effective progressivity in the tax system.

Considering the gross employment incomes of males alone, the Commission found that before tax the ratio of the highest decimillile, the millile and the highest percentile to the median were respectively 21, 10 and 4 in 1959-60, and 15, 8 and 3.5 in 1972-3. Adjusting the figures for tax, the ratios changed to 11, 7 and 3 times the median in 1959-60 and to 7, 5 and 3 times in 1972-3. Whereas, according to this set of data, even the top 1 per cent suffered some decline in its relative position before tax this effect was mitigated when taxation was taken into account. As the Commission noted: 'Over the whole period the effect of tax appears to have offset slightly the fall in the ratio of the highest percentile to the median but to have acted in the opposite way at the highest millile and decimillile levels' (Royal Commission, 1976c, para. 49). In other words the effects of taxation, rather than accelerating the decline in differentials, acted to reinforce the pressures which confined this decline to the very highest income groups, with no further distribution lower down the income scale. Indeed, these conclusions are based on the nominal tax liability of the high paid, ignoring the many reliefs which reduce that liability in practice. As we show in a later section, the reason for this lack of effective redistribution through the tax system is that taxation is becoming increasingly less progressive.

The Inland Revenue data, subject as it is to a number of deficiencies, appear to show that the belief in a fundamental collapse of the relative rewards of the highest paid is unfounded. The data available only take us to 1974-5. Is it possible that the situation has deteriorated significantly for this group since that date, perhaps under pressure of the policies pursued by the Labour government who took office in 1974? To try and answer this question, we now turn to an examination of the impact of incomes policy, inflation, and taxation on this group paying particular attention to the period since 1974. This leads us to modify further the findings presented above, based on Inland Revenue data. Unfortunately the three factors which we consider are inextricably intertwined so that divisions between the effects of each can only be artificial. However, to clarify the argument we will try and separate

TABLE 3.2 *Earnings of higher paid males in relation to the median, 1959–60 and 1972–3*

| | Highest decimillile | | Highest millile | | Highest percentile | |
|---|---|---|---|---|---|---|
| | Amount (£) | Ratio to median | Amount (£) | Ratio to median | Amount (£) | Ratio to median |
| | | | Before tax | | | |
| 1959–60 | 13,134 | 21 | 5,854 | 10 | 2,345 | 4 |
| 1972–3 | 24,072 | 15 | 12,590 | 8 | 5,665 | 3.5 |
| | | | After tax | | | |
| 1959–60 | 6,952 | 11 | 4,190 | 7 | 1,864 | 3 |
| 1972–3 | 10,748 | 7 | 7,443 | 5 | 4,247 | 3 |

(*Source*: Royal Commision 1976, p. 41)

Note: Tax liability is calculated assuming that at each level income recipients are married with two children aged under 11. No other allowances or reliefs are taken into account. The figures are therefore likely to understate the true dispersion between higher earnings and the median.

the effects of each as far as possible, bringing all three together at the end. We begin by considering the effects of inflation.

### *Inflation*

The acceleration of inflation is perhaps the most important single influence on the distribution of incomes which we have experienced in recent years. Certainly it has had more impact on the degree of economic inequality than government measures intended to achieve that effect. Partly this is due to the effects of rising prices and money incomes pushing people into continually higher marginal rates of tax – an issue to which we return below. But the main reason is simply that, at high levels of inflation percentage increases in pay to keep pace with rising prices require such large cash increases at the highest income levels that these would be both socially and (from the employer's point of view) financially unacceptable. Taking the highest earnings group considered by the Royal Commission – those earning £23,000 and above in 1973-4 – this group would have needed increases of over £5,000 in 1976-7 just to keep pace with the percentage increase in prices. To maintain their position in the *percentage* income distribution, this group would have had to obtain a cash increase over the period of almost £16,000. Analysis of company accounts reveals that some of the highest paid actually received increases of that size and above (*Labour Research*, 1977a). Our own examination of salary surveys described later also reveals surprisingly large increases for some management groups. For many others however such large increases in cash pay were not granted, and the percentage differential of the highest income groups inevitably fell.

It would be wrong to assume that this has been a process of long run decline, as is often suggested. The effect of inflation acting in this way is a relatively recent phenomenon. The Royal Commission's calculations showed that gross incomes of even the highest income groups increased well ahead of inflation until 1973-4 – the year in which the annual rate of price rises moved into double figures. And there is evidence that those with higher incomes from employment are better insulated from the effects of inflation than are those whose high incomes derive from other sources.

In the first National Management Survey, the British Institute of Management explained that gross salaries need not rise by the same percentage as the Retail Price Index 'to enable executives to maintain the same standard of living. A standard of living is dependent on much more than the gross salary of the individual. In fact the use of gross salary as a measure may be misleading, since it ignores pension provisions and the availability of mortgage or other loans. The total compensation package on which living standards are based is made up of net income plus fringe benefits, which may include stock options and loans at advantageous rates, as well as other benefits which are more difficult to measure.' And the report went on to explain: 'It seems unlikely that salaries will keep pace with (the currently high) rate of inflation. Executives and management do not, of course, remain static within any particular salary structure, and the expectation of most managers is that they will be promoted within a company, or promote themselves by changing jobs' (BIM, 1974, p. 15). In this way, management and professional workers are better able to insulate their living standards from inflation than is the case with their manual counterparts, for whom the earnings profile is both lower and flatter.

Statistics on gross salaries are therefore somewhat misleading as an indication of changing relativities for management groups. There are, in addition, other ways in which inflation has tended to redistribute income, not always against the better off and rarely reflected in the official data. It redistributes income from those who lend money to those who borrow it, for instance, although the effect of this on vertical inequality is difficult to disentangle. It also redistributes income towards those whose assets increase faster in price than the general rate of inflation. Although we are concerned in this chapter with earned incomes, it is worth while to note that many of those with high employment incomes also own a disproportionate amount of assets, and in this context, housing may be of particular importance. As Louie Burghes' chapter has shown, the very large increases in house prices in recent years have had considerable effect on the distribution of wealth and, since ownership remains concentrated in the upper half of the income distribution, inflation has an inegalitarian impact through this mechanism.

Perhaps the most important aspect of the recent inflation as far as income distribution is concerned has, however, been its differential effect through changes in the living costs of different groups. The effects which inflation has on particular households are determined by their expenditure patterns and by the extent to which relative price changes are biased against the type of goods which are most important in their budgets. In recent years, the costs of necessities have risen fastest in price, while those of 'luxuries', services and consumer goods have risen relatively modestly. As a result, the 'cost of living' of the poorest households has risen significantly faster than that of the rich. The Low Pay Unit has estimated, for instance, that in the three years to March 1977, prices rose by 5 percentage points more at the lowest decile than at the highest (Low Pay Unit, 1977).

The highest income groups considered in this chapter are excluded from the expenditure weightings used to construct the Retail Price Index. The Index is, nevertheless, used to calculate the changes in the living standards of this group. The Royal Commission itself warned 'although we have no alternative to using the RPI in looking at higher level employment incomes in the light of changes in the value of money', such an approach is likely to yield results which are less than accurate. The Commission estimated that the cost of living of those excluded from the RPI (receiving over £145 a week in the first half of 1977) had increased by only 1 or 2 percentage points less than the official index over the period 1962-75. Taking a higher definition of income, our own calculations (using unadjusted fixed weight indices) suggest that the cost of living of households with incomes of over £10,000 (in 1976) increased by about 2 percentage points less than the General Index over the much shorter period January 1974 to December 1977. Although a crude estimate, this does give some indication of the importance of differential inflation at the higher levels.

Of course neither of these estimates can show the full differential impact, since they are based on the average price quotations used in the RPI itself, and the prices paid by different groups are known to vary widely. Those able to buy in bulk or to 'shop around', to avoid expensive hire purchase arrangements and so on, are likely to be able to offset at least some of the effects of rising prices. Since it is impossible to assess the importance of this, the general conclusion must be that differential inflation at least modifies the decline in differentials reflected in the official data. Indeed, at the level of the highest percentile where the recorded decline in relative earnings is only marginal, the differential effect of inflation may be to reverse the trend when measured in real terms (for a further discussion see Pond, 1977a). An additional caveat must be that much expenditure at the highest levels is not undertaken by individuals or households at all, but is paid for directly by companies as fringe benefits. We return to this in a later section.

*Taxation*

Britain's system of personal taxation is generally believed to be highly progressive. Indeed, it is often argued that incentives to take additional responsibility through promotion are rapidly disappearing. This belief is largely mythical. In a recent British Institute of Management Survey, 96 per cent replied that they intended actively to seek promotion, or would accept it if offered. As we have already noted, the effects of taxation on the distribution of earned income are very moderate indeed, and have in fact helped to confine the decline in relative rewards to the very highest income groups. Table 2.3 shows in detail how this has come about.

For at least a quarter of a century, the burden of direct taxation has been moving steadily away from the highest income groups. Between 1959 and 1974-5 the proportion of total income tax paid by the top 1 per cent of tax units more than halved – from 34.5 per cent to 15.8 per cent, and by 1976-7 it has fallen again to 13 per cent. The top 10 per cent paid almost 65 per cent of all tax in 1959, but only 42.2 per cent in 1974-5 and only 36 per cent in 1976-7. As a result, the remaining 90 per cent of taxpayers contributed 57.8 per cent of tax in 1974-5 and 64 per cent in 1976-7 compared with just over 35 per cent in 1959 (Royal Commission, 1977. The 1976-7 figures from *Hansard*, 1977b, cols 455-6). Only a small part of this decline in the share of tax paid by the highest groups can be attributed to the decline in the share of income which they held. For a more satisfactory explanation, we need to look more closely at changes in the tax system itself.

Over the period, 1959 to 1974-5, the average rate of tax paid by the bulk of the population, the lowest 90 per cent, more than doubled. Meanwhile, the richest 10 per cent of taxpayers faced an increased burden of only 25 per cent and the richest 1 per cent an increased burden of only 10 per cent. That average rates of tax in the UK at the end of this process are less penal than most people believe is reflected in the fact that in 1974-5 the top 10 per cent paid less than 30 per cent of their income in direct tax, while even the richest 1 per cent contributed less than half of their income in tax (47.1 per cent, compared with 43.2 per cent in 1959). In fact, these figures overstate the average tax rate of high income groups since tax is shown as a proportion of income net of allowable deductions such as mortgage interest or superannuation. As a proportion of gross income, tax rates would be even lower than those recorded in the table.

For the most important explanation of why the increase in tax

TABLE 3.3 *Percentage shares of income before tax, average tax paid as percentage of income before tax, and percentage shares of tax paid; by quantile groups of income before tax; 1959, 1967, 1972–3, 1973–4 and 1974–5, from Royal Commission, 1977, p. 26*

United Kingdom — Income unit: tax unit

| Quantile group of income before tax % | Percentage share of income before tax | | | | | Average tax paid as percentage of income before tax | | | | | Percentage share of tax paid | | | | |
|---|---|---|---|---|---|---|---|---|---|---|---|---|---|---|---|
| | 1959 | 1967 | 1972–3 | 1973–4 | 1974–5 | 1959 | 1967 | 1972–3 | 1973–4 | 1974–5 | 1959 | 1967 | 1972–3 | 1973–4 | 1974–5 |
| | % | % | % | % | % | % | % | % | % | % | % | % | % | % | % |
| Top 1 | 8.4 | 7.4 | 6.3 | 6.5 | 6.2 | 43.2 | 43.3 | 41.6 | 42.0 | 47.1 | 34.5 | 23.3 | 18.4 | 17.7 | 15.8 |
| 2–5 | 11.5 | 11.0 | 10.8 | 10.6 | 10.6 | 19.1 | 20.6 | 22.6 | 21.9 | 25.4 | 20.2 | 16.1 | 16.7 | 15.1 | 14.8 |
| 6–10 | 9.5 | 9.6 | 9.7 | 9.7 | 9.8 | 11.3 | 14.6 | 16.9 | 18.6 | 21.8 | 10.2 | 10.6 | 11.6 | 11.4 | 11.6 |
| Top 10 | 29.4 | 28.0 | 26.8 | 26.8 | 26.6 | 23.5 | 24.5 | 25.1 | 25.6 | 29.1 | 64.9 | 50.0 | 46.7 | 44.2 | 42.2 |
| 11–20 | 15.1 | 15.2 | 15.8 | 15.6 | 15.8 | 7.8 | 13.3 | 15.1 | 15.8 | 19.3 | 11.6 | 15.0 | 16.5 | 16.2 | 16.6 |
| 21–40 | 23.3 | 23.7 | 24.2 | 24.1 | 24.1 | 5.7 | 11.1 | 12.9 | 14.5 | 17.2 | 13.1 | 19.5 | 21.8 | 22.7 | 22.8 |
| 41–60 | 16.6 | 16.8 | 16.7 | 16.7 | 16.9 | 4.9 | 9.1 | 10.4 | 12.1 | 15.2 | 7.8 | 11.4 | 12.1 | 13.1 | 14.1 |
| 61–80 | 10.3 | 10.7 | 10.7 | 10.5 | 10.4 | 2.6 | 4.7 | 3.8 | 5.3 | 7.2 | 2.6 | 3.7 | 2.9 | 3.6 | 4.0 |
| 81–100 | 5.3 | 5.6 | 5.8 | 6.3 | 6.2 | 0.1 | 0.8 | – | 0.4 | 1.0 | – | 0.4 | – | 0.2 | 0.3 |
| All groups | 100.0 | 100.0 | 100.0 | 100.0 | 100.0 | 10.5 | 13.6 | 14.4 | 15.4 | 18.3 | 100.0 | 100.0 | 100.0 | 100.0 | 100.0 |

Note: – indicates less than 0.1.

(*Source*: pre-1974–5 figures derived from Blue Book: 1974–5 figures derived from CSO table in *Economic Trends*, April 1977)

burdens has been biased in favour of the higher income groups, we have to return to the issue of inflation. Inflation has the effect of increasing the amount of tax paid by all income groups, unless allowances are increased in line with rising prices. This is because the allowances – representing the proportion of income that is free of tax – become an increasingly smaller proportion of total income. At the same time, an increase in money incomes to keep pace with inflation may push the wage-earner into a higher rate of tax. This has resulted in a higher tax burden amongst all income groups but it has been accompanied by pressures which direct a larger share of that increased burden towards the lower paid. This is first because tax-free personal allowances represent a larger proportion of the incomes of this group (being flat rate) so that their erosion by inflation has a harsher impact than at higher income levels. Second, an increase in money incomes at the lower levels which takes a family into the tax system for the first time involves a jump in marginal tax rates from 0 to 34 per cent in 1977–8, whereas at higher levels, the increase in marginal tax rates is rarely more than 5 per cent. This last effect has been compounded by modifications to the tax system which have reduced the progressiveness of the tax structure itself. Throughout the 1950s three reduced rates of tax applied before the standard rate (which stood at 30 per cent in 1959) came into force at about average earnings. The reduced rates were withdrawn in stages throughout the 1960s until they were finally abolished by the Labour government in 1970. This converted the income tax structure into the basically proportional form in which it exists today, and this has been exacerbated by the repeated lengthening of the 'basic rate band' of tax before higher rates apply. It also meant that in the past quarter of a century the marginal rate of tax faced by the average wage-earner has trebled, while that experienced by the higher paid (on twice the average wage) has remained the same, or even fallen (Pond, 1977a).

So while increasing money incomes can involve moving into higher rate bands of tax, this is only the case at the very bottom and the very top of the income scale – those crossing the threshold for the first time and those subject to the higher rates of tax – a group representing only 4 per cent of taxpayers. As Professor F. W. Paish found in his analysis of tax changes since the war, 'The effect of inflation on the percentage paid in tax in constant real incomes is substantial at the lowest levels of income subject to tax, decreases as the average rate rises towards the standard rate, and leaves greater gain as soon as the surtax threshold is reached (Paish, 1975).

Professor Paish attempted to isolate the effects of inflation on tax burdens by calculating the amount of tax paid on 'real income equivalents' over the period since the war, for a married couple with two children aged under 11. While the average rate of tax of a family earning the equivalent of £1,000 at 1950-51 prices (i.e. £2,630 in 1973-4) remained virtually constant between then and 1973-4, that faced by a similar family on the 1950-1 equivalent of £10,000 (£26,300 in 1973-4) *fell* from 63.2 per cent to 55.1 over the same period. The importance of deliberate changes in the tax structure was also revealed by Paish's calculation that while the marginal rate of tax (the rate of tax paid on each additional pound of income) faced by a family on the lowest level of income (equivalent to £500 in 1950-1 and to £1,315 in 1973-4) had increased from 18p to 30p in the £, that faced by the highest group (equivalent to £10,000 in 1950-1) fell from nearly 86p in the £ to less than 74p. We return later to consider the effects of tax changes since 1974.

Changes in tax rates in recent years have therefore tended to benefit the higher paid, offsetting to some extent the effects of inflation pushing 'surtax' payers into increasingly higher rates. However, it is impossible to know just how much tax is actually paid by specific groups of individuals. The calculations presented above on the shares of total taxation contributed by various groups of income recipients are the best we have. This is because the true tax liability of individuals may vary greatly from the notional liability as calculated by the Royal Commission (and used in the calculations by Paish presented above). In addition to their basic personal allowances, taxpayers can claim for a large number of other forms of expenditure such as mortgage interest relief, life assurance, superannuation, bank loan interest (for house purchase or improvement), fees to professional bodies and work expenses. In some of its calculations the Royal Commission added 5 per cent of salary as additional allowance against tax, which affected the conclusions very little. At higher levels of income, however, such allowances are known to be significantly more important than this.

More than twenty years ago, the Royal Commission on the Taxation of Profits and Incomes warned that the 'erosion of the tax base' brought about by these allowances and reliefs meant that 'the tax system, behind a facade of formal equality, metes out unequal treatment to the different classes of the taxpaying community (Royal Commission, 1955, Memorandum of Dissent). The unequal treatment derives from the fact that such allowances and reliefs are not distributed equally between taxpayers, and because the larger the allowances granted to one group, the higher the rate of tax which must be paid by others. The unequal distribution of the value of tax allowances is due to the fact that it tends to be mainly higher income groups who undertake the expenditure relieved from tax (mortgage interest is exempt, rent payments are not; fees to professional bodies are exempt, but trade union subscriptions are not; life assurance and superannuation contributions are free of tax, national insurance contributions are not). But it is also due to the fact that the value of the allowances increases, the higher the marginal rate of tax faced by the recipient (Field, Meacher and Pond, 1977).

All this helps to explain why post-tax differentials at any point in time are considerably larger than theoretical calculations suggest and why the tax system is less progressive than is generally accepted. But why has the change in management differentials been less dramatic than their spokesmen would have us believe? There are two reasons for this. The first is simply that the number of allowances which can be claimed against tax, and the amount of income which is thereby exempted, has proliferated in recent years. Since it is the higher paid who benefit most from such allowances, this has helped shift the burden of taxation further away from this group. Second, unlike the personal allowances claimed by all taxpayers which are expressed as flat-rate sums (and therefore tend to decline in value with inflation), the expenditure reliefs tend to be expressed in percentage terms, so that their value increases with incomes and inflation. For example, a salary earner who contributes a percentage of his gross pay to a tax allowable pension scheme will find that as his income rises, so does the amount which can be offset against tax. So the allowance acts as a brake against fiscal drag and, at the margin, the increase in the value of the allowance may be sufficient to prevent the taxpayer moving into the next higher band of tax. Or consider the effect of mortgage interest relief – now generally acknowledged to be the most significant fiscal benefit paid through the tax system. On reasonable assumptions, a salary earner on £20,000 could derive double the net benefit from a 10 per cent pay rise if he had a maximum (£25,000) mortgage than if he had no mortgage at all.

These factors ensure that the increasing tax burden of the high paid is considerably less dramatic than many management pressure groups would have the public and policy-makers believe. But the campaigns to convince the British public that the situtION was otherwise had their desired effect on government approaches to incomes policy and taxation. Below we illustrate this with an analysis of budget changes in the period 1974-7. In the next section we consider how the development of incomes policy has reflected a similar concern about management differentials.

### The government response: taxation

An analysis of Budget Statements in the four years from March 1974, when the Labour government came to power, is a revealing exercise. It shows clearly how the priorities of the government shifted from a desire to ensure a fairer distribution of income and wealth to a preoccupation with the exigencies of conventional economic management. The development of the government policy on the wealth tax which Professor Sandford describes in Chapter 6 represents one example of this. Here we examine the changing attitude of the Labour government to personal taxation.

Mr Healey's first Budget took place just three weeks after Labour took office. On 26 March 1974 the Chancellor told the Commons that 'The Labour Party has pledged itself to achieve a major redistribution of both wealth and income. It has always been our aim to use the taxation system to promote greater social and economic equality.' The Chancellor, therefore, announced changes in direct taxation intended to 'ensure that the rich bear a higher share of the tax burden than they have under the last Government' and that 'everyone who enjoys an income somewhat above the average must expect to have to make some contribution through taxation to the cost of the essential measures intended to protect the living standards of those who earn less than the average.' This he tried to achieve by raising the tax threshold, increasing the basic and higher rates of tax and lowering the level of income at which the higher rates became payable. Other measures intended to shift the burden towards higher income groups included the introduction of a surcharge on surtax (which was to be implemented anyway by the previous government), a reduction in the level of unearned income at which the investment income surcharge applied, and the restriction of tax relief on mortgages to a maximum of £25,000 allowable only on the principal place of residence. At the same time share option and incentive schemes, then popular as a fringe benefit to many managerial staff, were to be taxed 'as part of the pay for the job' (*Hansard*, 1974a, col. 317).

The same attitude to the use of taxation as an instrument of redistribution was reflected in Mr Healey's November 1974 Budget (the third of that year). 'There must be room for those at the bottom to see their living standards rise', he told the House. 'This means sacrifices for those at the upper end of the scale. The main instrument for achieving this necessary redistribution of wealth and income is our system of personal taxation' (*Hansard*, 1974b, col. 274). Such a redistribution could not begin, he explained, until the main Budget of the following spring. But when that Budget came, the Chancellor's measures were framed in a different environment. Whereas his statement of a year earlier had stressed the importance of co-operation between government and workpeople through the social contract, he now warned against the continuation of the 'excessive' wage increases which had characterised the first stage of that contract: 'The immediate effect of excessive wage settlements is to increase private consumption, with damaging effects on the balance of resources in the economy, which the Government must seek to remove by increasing taxation' (*Hansard*, 1975b, col. 281). The basic rate of tax was increased by 2p in the £. The Chancellor did stress the need, however, 'to ensure that the burden of taxation which I regard as necessary at the present time is shared fairly between those best able to bear it . . . this theme of fairness runs through all my proposals in the personal tax field.' However, personal allowances were again increased by less than the amount necessary to offset inflation so that almost three quarters of a million exempted low paid workers were dragged back into tax. The burden of taxation on the lowest paid was thereby substantially increased, despite Mr Healey's assertion that 'poor families will be affected least by my strategy of moving resources away from private consumption' (*Hansard*, 1975b, col. 320).

By the time Mr Healey came to present his April 1976 Budget, he was looking for further reductions in living standards to effect a further shift of resources to the corporate sector (see Chapter 6). His adjustments to personal taxation consisted of a small increase in children's and personal tax allowances, the latter being conditional on agreement to a further stage of pay policy. The 'conditional' reliefs included an increase in the threshold for higher rate tax by £500 a year.

The TUC agreed to a low wage limit and the conditional tax reliefs were granted. The cost of this second part of the package was nearly three times the value of the unconditional benefits given to children and the elderly. One tenth of this cost was devoted to raising the threshold at which higher rates of tax apply. Mr Healey explained the reasons for this scale of priorities in the following way: 'The threshold for higher rate tax has been eroded by inflation so that it now lies between one and a half times and twice average earnings. Unless I adjust it this year, the numbers subject to higher rate tax will rise from

1.3 million in 1975-76 to 1.9 million in 1976-77.' So whereas two years earlier the Chancellor had taken action to increase the number of higher rate taxpayers, he now sought to reduce marginal tax rates on the better off. His rationale for this was that 'I believe that it is desirable in any case to reduce the extent to which fringe benefits are used as a substitute for pay increases at the higher levels' and to this end the Chancellor had introduced measures to increase the taxation of company cars and low interest or interest free loans. These measures were, as a result of a concerted campaign, seriously modified before being implemented. But already he felt a need to compensate those who would thereby lose part of the benefits of such perquisites: 'The counterpart of action on fringe benefits must be some reduction in the income tax burden, particularly on middle managers in industry who have seen their net pay severely reduced in real terms over recent years by inflation and incomes policy of successive governments.' This budget therefore marks the turning point in the Labour government's approach to personal taxation.

In his March 1977 Budget Statement, announcing the adjustments he proposed to make to the structure of income tax, the Chancellor pointed out that the benefit would fall disproportionately on middle management. 'I should have liked to have been able to do more for senior managers as I should have liked to do more for those at the bottom of the earnings scale. But I have felt it necessary this year to concentrate relief where it is most needed' (*Hansard*, 1977a, col. 282).

The basic personal allowances were raised by significantly less than the rate of inflation, allowing the tax threshold to fall yet again. Child tax allowances were not raised at all (as the first stage of the Child Benefit Scheme) so the number of low paid taxpayers once again increased. The Chancellor pursued his strategy of reducing the burden of taxation on middle management by once again increasing the higher rate tax thresholds. And in this case the increases were significantly more than the rate of inflation would have justified. The number of people liable to higher rate tax was thereby almost halved. And the costs of the concessions to higher rate taxpayers were approximately one third of the amount of revenue given to all taxpayers as an increase in allowances.

The Chancellor therefore amended the income tax structure to the benefit of the better off at the expense of the progressiveness of the entire system. But such changes could do little to restore differentials and relativities between the great majority of people who pay tax at the standard rate. For this purpose another mechanism was employed: a reduction in the tax rate from 35 to 33 per cent. Increases in allowances and reductions in tax rates both serve to reduce the overall tax burden. However, they do have different effects on the distribution of that burden. A reduction in the tax rate benefits a taxpayer in proportion to his level of taxable income (after deducting tax free allowances). The higher one's income the greater the value of a reduction in marginal tax rates. The overall impact of the March 1977 Budget was therefore to shift the burden of taxation significantly further down the income scale. The Trade Union Research Unit, analysing the Budget effects, noted that a family on £25,000 a year would obtain a benefit approximately nine and a half times as large as that conferred on the average wage-earning family (on about £4,000). 'In terms of after-tax pay, this Budget, like the one a year earlier, has given the largest increases to those families at the top end of the income scale' (TURU, 1977).

This view of the Budget was not restricted to trade union circles. *The Economist* anticipated that 'The pips shouldn't even murmur this time', while the *Sunday Times* felt that the budget changes were cause for 'the sound of laughter from the executive washroom'. The CBI's official reaction to the Budget announcement confirmed the overall effect: 'Nearly all the CBI's budget representations were to a greater or lesser degree accepted. The overall shape of the budget was bang in line with what we campaigned for.' But this enthusiasm from the representatives of management groups was dampened somewhat when the Finance Committee refused to accept the full Budget proposals in their original form. Two Labour backbench members, Jeff Rooker and Audrey Wise, pointed out the inegalitarian nature of the original proposals – that no less than two thirds of the revenue devoted to tax concessions would go to those earning more than the average wage. They therefore forced through two fundamental amendments: the first was that the main personal allowances should be automatically linked to the Retail Prices Index to prevent a further decline in the real value of the tax threshold dragging even larger numbers of low paid families into the tax net; the second was that the £1,000 millions set aside to reduce the basic rate of tax by 2p in the £ (and benefiting most the higher paid) should be used to raise still further the allowances to lift 365,000 low paid out of tax altogether. In the event, the government were forced to accept a further increase in personal allowances, a reduction in the basic rate of tax of only 1p in the £ (instead of the proposed 2p) and the commitment to index the main personal allowances unless given Paliamentary approval to the contrary (see *Hansard*, 1977d, cols. 57–144).

In October of the same year, the Chancellor once again rose to announce his Budget changes. This time the main change in personal taxation was to increase the personal allowances. The tax cuts were worth eight times as much for a married couple on six times the average wage as for those on the average. Nevertheless, this unequal distribution of concessions was inevitable given the current structure of British taxation. The Chancellor noted that there was a strong case for raising the tax threshold to the level of the Supplementary Benefit level, thereby returning to the age-old principle that the poor should be exempt from tax, and for introducing a reduced rate band of tax. This, he said, would have to wait until the spring 1978 Budget.

Over the period since 1974, we have therefore witnessed a quite fundamental shift in the Labour government's attitude to personal taxation. From viewing the income tax system as a means of achieving a fundamental redistribution of income and wealth we find that policy towards taxation developed into a means of increasing post tax differentials between different sections of the community. The reasons for such a change in approach are complex and lie outside the scope of this chapter, although it is perhaps safe to suppose that the campaign by management groups on the need to restore their previous position in the income hierarchy at least played a part. Suffice it to say that the same developments in government attitude are reflected in the wealth tax debate (see Chapter 6) and in incomes policies, which we consider in the following section.

## Incomes policy

The third force believed to be behind the collapse of management differentials is that of incomes policies. The obvious point should perhaps first be made that a policy on incomes can only affect those who are included and, except nominally, it cannot be said that the highest income earners were included in the four stages of wages policy (a more appropriate term than the more comprehensive incomes policy) which have occurred since 1974. The reasons are outlined below.

Stage one of the social contract stretched from September 1974 to July 1975. Wages were to rise by no more than the percentage increase in prices: a twelve month gap between wage rises was to be observed; and – as a means of improving the relative position of the low paid – a minimum wage target of £30 a week was established by the TUC. The second stage also stressed the importance of fairness for the low paid. Beginning in August 1975 a flat rate £6 limit on pay increases (intended to give larger percentage increases to the low paid) was to be implemented. A maximum income of £8,500 a year was specified beyond which no pay rise at all was payable. It was largely through arguments that the flat rate policy had eroded differentials that this approach was abandoned in the following stage of the policy which ran from August 1976. This time a 5 per cent maximum increase was specified but was subject to a minimum increase of £2.50 and a maximum of £4 – again as payment of lip service to the need to protect the living standards of the lowest paid. However, even this meagre protection was withdrawn in stage four of the policy which began one year later. All increases were now to be limited to 10 per cent, and the TUC formally abandoned its minimum wage target. No concessions were now made to the commitment to protect the low paid; the fear of reduced differetials had become the more immediate priority.

The development of pay policies in the years since 1974 (as with taxation policy) therefore exhibits a clear trend from a formal commitment to protect the low paid to a desire to re-establish differentials. This change in policy resulted from the belief that differentials, especially those of higher paid professional and management groups, had been severely eroded by flat-rate policies. How true is this now popular belief?

The most comprehensive source of data on earnings over relatively short periods is the Department of Employment's New Earnings Survey (NES). Unfortunately, the earnings of the high paid are poorly represented in the survey. Nevertheless, the survey probably gives us a fairly clear impression of how relative earnings change from one year to the next. The overall picture which emerges from the NES, as from the Inland Revenue data on incomes which we considered above, is one of considerable rigidity. Over the period since 1970 (the earliest date for which NES results are available on a comparable basis) the relative positions of the quantiles of the distribution compared to the median remain virtually unchanged. The lowest percentile has remained at about one half the median and the lowest decile two thirds the median since 1970 (and indeed, it has remained at about this level since 1886); the lower quartile has hardly deviated from 80 per cent of the median or the higher quartile from 125 per cent; the upper decile has maintained its position at about 160 per cent of the median. What is more remarkable is the fact that the shape of the distribution for women hardly differs from that of men, except that the dispersion is somewhat wider at the upper end.

The exception to this picture of rigidity is the group with which we are most concerned in this chapter – the top 1 per cent of earners. It appears that, since 1970, the relative earnings of this group have declined steadily from over 300 per cent of the median in 1970 to 265 per cent in 1976 and to 264 per cent in 1977. The most probable explanation for this is not the impact of pay policies but the effects of inflation. As we described above, given the sheer size of the cash increases necessary to maintain percentage differentials against inflation, it is unsurprising that the relative earnings of the very highest groups fell during this period, and the rate of decline in their relative position matches well the pattern of inflation.

Between 1970 and 1974, the earnings of the top 1 per cent fell by 5 percentage points a year. Between 1974 and 1975, however, when inflation approached 20 per cent, the fall in the relative position of the highest percentile accelerated to over 15 percentage points. If the arguments that flat-rate pay policies have had a significant effect on differentials were correct, we would expect a further dramatic fall in this group's relative position in 1975–6. In fact that period witnessed an actual improvement, albeit slight, in the relative position of the top 1 per cent. It should be emphasised that, throughout the whole period, these changes were isolated amongst the very highest groups of male wage-earners, the top 10 per cent's relative position remaining virtually unchanged.

The extent to which inflation can compress the percentage earnings distribution despite very large cash increases is also well illustrated by the NES data. The information given above related to the structure of earnings, but not to the changes in the earnings of particular individuals. Department of Employment analyses of individuals' earnings have shown that people can move about freely within the earnings distribution without the shape of the overall distribution changing. As some receive very large increases lifting them out of the lowest ranges somebody else takes their place, either by undergoing a cut in wages or entering the job market for the first time (DE, 1977). Looking at the period 1970–4 the Department found that cash increases for manual men ranged between £9.80 and £18.30, while non-manual men received cash increases of between £17.80 and £39.40 over that same period. For all non-manual men, percentage increases over that period represented an average of 65.2 per cent, compared with 61.8 per cent for manual men. So if we look at the earnings of individuals, rather than of 'jobs' reflected in the whole distribution, the picture of reduced differentials changes fundamentally. Although it is true that within each group, taking manual and non-manual separately, the lowest paid received the biggest percentage increases, it was also the case that within each income band non-manual workers received bigger percentage increases than their manual counterparts.

The Low Pay Unit undertook a special analysis of the New Earnings Survey data for the years 1975–6 (the period of the £6 pay policy) to see what had happened to differentials (or more precisely relativities) over this period. The analysis traced the changes in earnings of those individuals who appeared in both surveys (the 'matched sample'). This helped to overcome the effects of some people leaving and others joining on the average earnings for the group. For instance, the increase in average earnings will be depressed if better paid members of the group concerned leave (through promotion or retirement) and are replaced by others on lower earnings. Amongst professional and management groups on steeply sloping incremental scales, this must be important. For instance, it was found that the average earnings of accountants between the two years increased by 16.6 per cent if the complete sample was considered, but by 22.6 per cent once attention was focused on only those individuals who were in the group in both years.

The increase between April 1975 and April 1976 – a period most of which was covered by the £6 flat-rate pay policy – registered as 17 per cent for manual men, but 22 per cent for non-manual workers, a conclusion similar to that reached by the Royal Commission for the earlier period. The average increase for all men together was 19.3 per cent. The Unit then turned to consider which groups received bigger increases than this and which received smaller percentages. Table 3.4 summarises the findings.

Being a flat-rate pay limit, we would expect that the largest percentage increases would have gone to the lower paid manual groups. In fact, the top half of the table, showing those who received increases above the average, contained only one manual group and the only non-manual groups to fall below the average level of percentage increases were those engaged in selling, which includes poorly paid shop assistants and sales representatives. The average earnings of those who found themselves above the line in terms of increases was £82 a week, and their cash increase was £14.80. The average earnings of their less fortunate counterparts below the line was £63.20, and their cash increase was an average of only £9.10.

Examining the assertion that the differentials of middle management had suffered significantly, the Unit found that the best paid management group received 189 per cent of the earnings of the lowest paid

TABLE 3.4 *Increase in average weekly earnings April 1975 to April 1976 (including overtime pay) and based on the matched samples, all men*

| Occupational group | | Average earnings £ | Increase £ | % | |
|---|---|---|---|---|---|
| Professional and related in education, health and welfare | (N) | 95.9 | 19.90 | 26.2 | |
| Security and protective service | (N) | 77.0 | 14.30 | 22.8 | |
| Professional and related in science, technology and related fields | (N) | 89.7 | 16.60 | 22.7 | |
| Professional and related supporting management and administration | (N) | 97.6 | 17.60 | 22.0 | |
| Clerical and related | (N) | 63.8 | 11.50 | 22.0 | |
| Literary, artistic and sports | (N) | 85.1 | 14.30 | 20.2 | |
| Materials processing (excl. metals) | (M) | 65.4 | 10.90 | 20.0 | |
| Managerial (excl. general management) | (N) | 82.8 | 13.40 | 19.3 | |
| | | | | | Average increase |
| Miscellaneous manual workers | (M) | 62.6 | 10.00 | 19.0 | |
| Selling | (N/M) | 65.4 | 10.30 | 18.7 | |
| Farming, fishing and related | (M) | 50.0 | 7.70 | 18.2 | |
| Painting, repetitive assembling product inspecting, packaging and related | (M) | 65.5 | 9.90 | 17.8 | |
| Making and repairing (excl. metal and elec.) | (M) | 64.7 | 9.40 | 17.0 | |
| Catering, cleaning, hairdressing and other personal service | (M) | 55.90 | 8.0 | 16.7 | |
| Processing, making, repairing and related (metal and electrical) | (M) | 70.9 | 10.10 | 16.6 | |
| Transport operating, materials moving and storing and related | (M) | 66.0 | 9.20 | 16.2 | |
| Construction, mining and related not identified elsewhere | (M) | 68.1 | 7.30 | 12.0 | |

(*Source*: Pond, 1977b)

group (who were farmworkers) in 1975 and 195 per cent in 1976. Their differentials had actually increased. A wider analysis showed this pattern to be fairly consistent throughout the earnings distribution. Ranking occupational groups according to their average earnings in 1976. The analysis revealed that of the six groups who earned more than the average in 1976, five had increased their differential over the average wage-earner and one had maintained the same percentage differential. Of the ten occupational groups who earned below the average only two managed to improve their relative earnings, one remained the same, and seven fell behind.

The Unit then took the analysis one stage further, adjusting the figures for nominal tax liability (although not for the additional tax allowances discussed above). The pattern of changes in after-tax differentials was almost identical to that before tax, except that one of the non-manual groups who had enjoyed an actual increase in their relative position (Literary, artistic and sports) had to remain content with staying in the same position once tax was taken into account. Of the two groups with below average earnings who had managed to improve their pre-tax relative position, one had this advantage confiscated by tax, leaving its earnings unchanged.

How could this situation of widening relativities despite a flat-rate pay policy be explained? One reason was that the analysis considered the period April 1975 to April 1976, while the policy ran from August to August. But, as the report argued, 'at least eight months of the period over which this widening of relativities took place saw the existence of a flat rate pay policy. Either one must argue that the polarisation of rewards to different groups was extremely large in the first four months of the period, and that the £6 redressed part of the balance, or that a substantial part of the increase in earnings inequality took place during the period of the flat rate policy itself' (Pond, 1977b). More plausible reasons were that non-manual groups were in receipt of incremental pay increases on top of the pay policy supplement (as the policy allowed) and that individuals in these groups were also obtaining increases through job changes and promotion, either real or artificial. As Baroness Wootton has pointed out, 'every wage policy is at risk of circumvention by phoney promotions or job changes' (Wootton, 1977). Non-manual occupations offer greater opportunities for artificial regrading and promotions than is the case with manual jobs.

There were also forces at work to depress the earnings of lower paid manual workers: the fact that many groups of the lowest paid didn't receive the full £6 and that the pay policy supplement couldn't be used calculate overtime pay (which is obviously of more importance to manual grade workers). So, while the flat-rate policy may have involved some compression of differentials within bargaining groups, the belief in a collapse in the structure of rewards between groups in the labour market did not stand up to careful examination.

Although governments earnestly protest that pay policies are comprehensive in their coverage, distributing the burden of sacrifice fairly, management organisations have never suffered from such illusions. Reporting on their salary survey findings for the period July 1975 to July 1976 AIC/Inbucon stated that, 'Overall the executives covered by this year's survey obtained an increase of around 8.5 per cent during the last twelve months. The overall average is up by £494 and the median by £550. In view of the Government's pay policy, it may seem surprising that these figures are above £312 (£6 a week), the maximum increase permitted under the policy. It must however, be remembered that the policy came into force on 1st August 1975, while the Survey covers the period 1st July 1975-1st July 1976' (AIC/Inbucon, 1976). The survey's findings are additionally surprising given the fact that, under that stage of pay policy, those earning £8,500 or more should have received no increase at all.

The following year's AIC/Inbucon survey, broadly covering stage two of the pay policy in which increases were to be limited to 5 per cent, subject to a maximum increase of £4 a week (£208 a year), yielded equally embarrassing results: 'this year's sample of executives obtained increases of around 8.7 per cent between 1st July 1976 and 1st July 1977. The median has risen by £536 and the average by £605. Those figures are, of course, above the £208 maximum allowed in Stage 2 of the Government's pay policy.' Indeed, General Managers received increases of 13.3 per cent at the median (10.3 per cent at the average). But this was not the whole story. Total remuneration (salary plus bonus, commission, share of profits, directors' fees, etc.) increased by 10 per cent (£608 at the median and £729 at the average) while that for the median managing director (earning £10,000 in 1976) rose by 15 per cent over the year (AIC/Inbucon, 1977).

The British Institute of Management survey for 1977 (covering the period January 1976 to January 1977) confirmed that for many management groups increases during their period were well above pay limits. The average gross salary of chief executives rose by £811; other directors enjoyed an increase of £677 over the year, senior heads of functions received an additional £520 a year. In every case the change in salary over tax was significantly larger than the gross change (BIM, 1977).

These figures understate the true size of management increases. The salary levels reflected not the pay of individuals but the average pay of those who made up that group sample at any one time. As the BIM were careful to warn, 'a number of people may receive rises in pay yet the average for the management level in which they find themselves may be static or even decrease. This will particularly be so where promotions move individuals into higher responsibilities; their new salaries will probably be less than those of the people they replace, and so too will their successors not enjoy as high levels of pay as they did.' The Institute estimated that individuals could receive personal increments of up to 4 per cent without this registering any increase at all in the average salary of their group. Based on the matched sample of companies taking part in the 1976 and 1977 surveys, the BIM concluded that the evidence 'suggests that many managers, faced with a continuing reduction in their real standard of living over the past twelve months, have been changing jobs to obtain reasonable salary increases' (BIM, 1977).

### ------And with a fringe on the top

At the beginning of this chapter, we considered the evidence on the distribution of incomes given by the CSO Blue Book estimates. As long ago as 1962, Richard Titmuss warned that 'as a result of the growth of "fringe benefits" the Blue Book figures of salaries and wages are becoming increasingly inappropriate as a guide to income differentials' (Titmuss, 1962). What was true then is even more so today. The official data on incomes can only reflect fringe benefits to the extent that they are taxable and, perhaps more important, to the extent that they are declared for tax. This leaves a severe gap in our information on income distribution, and a gap which is getting wider every year.

Yet those arguing the case that management differentials have been eroded by inflation, incomes policy and taxation frequently ignore the importance of fringe benefits as a determinant of living standards for the higher paid. However, largely because of the effects of taxation and incomes policy, management groups have turned increasingly towards the use of such additions to income. Their importance has increased both in terms of their scope and number as well as in value and in the proportion of employees receiving them. The British Institute of Management found for instance that 65 per cent of companies interviewed had provided increased benefits between 1970 and 1973 and half had improved provision still further by 1978.

The value of such benefits can be quite considerable. AIC/Inbucon estimated that 'total remuneration', that is basic salary plus cash benefits, exceeded basic salary by 5 per cent for all management groups in their 1977 survey, and by 10 per cent in the case of managing directors. But, of course, not all fringe benefits are expressed as cash payments. The main forms of benefits which companies now provide their management are a company car (at higher levels sometimes with a chauffeur) or car allowance, subsidised lunches, subsidised housing or assistance with house purchase, free life assurance, free medical assurance, share option schemes (nowadays less popular because of tax changes) and bonus schemes.

The two fastest growing forms of additional benefit appear to be the company car and free medical insurance. 14.5 per cent of managers were entitled to medical insurance in 1969, but by 1977 this had more than doubled to 38.8 per cent. Similarly, under half (49.7 per cent) of managers had sole use of a company car in 1969, but this proportion had increased to almost two thirds (63.8 per cent) by 1977. At the higher executive levels, the importance of the company car has become an almost universal benefit: between 1971 and 1977, the proportion of managing directors with a company car had increased from 92.5 per cent to 95.2 per cent; general managers receiving this perk increased from 81 per cent in 1969 to 94.8 per cent in 1977, while company secretaries provided with a car increased from under 62 per cent to 75.4 per cent (AIC/Inbucon, 1977). In addition to these common benefits, a number of others have emerged since 1970, according to the BIM survey of company practice published in 1974: accident and travel insurance, general loan facilities, company canteens and restaurants, share incentive schemes, widows' and dependants' pensions, increased luncheon voucher entitlements, cash discount cards, service, attendance and recruitment bonuses, company financed holiday/conferences abroad, study leave, confidential personal advisory services. Most recently, company credit cards have been added to the list.

The reasons for such an increase in benefits is clear: first they are increasingly used as a means round taxation. As the BIM survey found, 'Most managers see benefits primarily as reducing tax liability on total remuneration' (Murlis, 1974). The second main reason for their growth in recent years, few would dispute, is their value as a means round incomes policies.

A profile of the proportion of managers receiving each type of benefits in 1977 is given in the BIM salary survey. 44 per cent of top managers and 41 per cent of supporting managers received holidays of five weeks or more: 14 per cent of managers (and 41.5 per cent of directors) had special 'fire-proof' service contracts; virtually all (99.7 per cent) firms gave travel/accident insurance to their management; 8 per cent of executives received free or assisted housing; 27 per cent of managers (42 per cent of directors) received free telephone or telephone allowance; 4 per cent received help with children's school fees; 22 per cent received medical insurance; 15.4 per cent received loans at advantageous rates; 14.2 per cent of directors had prime use of a chauffeur driven car (and almost 90 per cent of these *also* had sole use of a company car) together 91.4 per cent of directors and 51 per cent of supporting managers had sole use of a company car; 35.4 per cent of executives received bonus payments (BIM, 1977). Bearing this in mind, it is fruitful to reconsider our earlier discussion about the differential effects of inflation. Given the provision of assistance with a wide range of expenditure, the comparison of management gross salary increases with the General Index of Retail Prices appears to be particularly inappropriate.

## Managing on a shoe string?

In the preceding sections we have tried to build up a picture, using the statistics available to us, of the effects of the recent recession on the living standards of higher paid management and professional groups. Despite considerable evidence that these groups have succeeded in insulating themselves from the full effects of the 'crisis' in ways not open to other sections of the working population, we often hear that managers find it difficult to 'make ends meet'. The concept of 'relative deprivation' is clearly important for this group as it is for the poor. The difference is that this group's living standards are measured in relation to those of their counterparts abroad, to the prosperity they enjoyed in an earlier period, and perhaps to the aspirations which they have held for a certain life style.

In May 1974, the British Institute of Management reported that 'managers at all levels were suffering from a feeling of injustice, that differentials were being whittled away and the salary restrictions, combined with recent taxation, were bearing on them unfairly' (Royal Commission, 1976b, p. 28). This feeling apparently persisted despite the fact that the BIM survey of the same year showed that gross salary increases of job levels ranged between 21 per cent and 29 per cent (compared with an increase in the RPI of 20 per cent) and that actual increases for individual managers could be considerably above this level:

that over 40 per cent of managers earned bonus payments on top of this ranging between 12 and 25 per cent of basic salary; and that substantial fringe benefits were provided as an additional supplement. In 1976 a number of companies sponsored the Opinion Research Centre to undertake a survey of the attitudes of management. The researchers had already noted the chnage in the government approach to this group which we outlined earlier in this chapter: 'The Chancellor of the Exchequer has already made it clear that he has for some time been concerned about the rewards of management and, within his constraints, would like to do something to help. In order to help Mr Healey and his Treasury advisers evaluate the urgency of this problem in the light of other pressures, it was felt that the attitudinal and factual information should be made available for public discussion as soon as possible.'

The starting point used by the researchers was unequivocal. 'That the managerial class have fared particularly badly in the last few years is no longer a matter of dispute. The Prime Minister and the Chancellor of the Exchequer have both gone on record accepting the basic case'. The aim of the survey was to illustrate the effects of this apparently self-evident fact on the motivation of British managers. Summarising their findings, the ORC painted a dismal picture of the life styles of British managers: many were having to make economies or living off capital; many were maintaining their living standards only by their wives going out to work; others were indulging in 'moonlighting'. As a result, morale and motivation were said to be damaged by a feeling that managers were not considered important. Therefore many no longer cared about their job, cared little about promotion or would like to leave the country.

A detailed examination of the published tables in the survey report, however, revealed a rather different picture. For instance, less than half (45 per cent) of managers interviewed felt that they were worse off than three years ago – a remarkable achievement given the general decline in living standards associated with the recession of that period – and less than a fifth (19 per cent) thought they were much worse off. The report explained that this could be because managers had received promotion to better paid jobs or that their wives had taken up employment. When asked what economies they had been forced to make as a result of the recession, 42 per cent replied that they had found none necessary at all. The economies which the remainder were asked to list included doing their own repairs, gardening and painting and the wife dispensing with domestic help (which befell only 1 per cent of the sample). 1 per cent also had to remove their children from private education, although none was forced to dispense with private medicine. In no category of expenditure did more than a quarter of the sample have to make economies. One half (51 per cent) of the managers had been forced to lower the expectations for consumption which they had held three years ago, but 45 per cent had attained their aspirations. The biggest disappointment (experienced by 17 per cent) was that they could not, as they had hoped three years earlier, buy a bigger or better *second* car. Future expectations were only dampened for a minority: one third thought that their standard of living in three years' time would be lower than at present; 39 per cent expected it to be higher and a quarter thought it would be about the same. Asked whether they considered that a reduction in their own standard of living was a necessary consequence of pay policy, 36 per cent thought that it was not, but 57 thought that it was.

The survey then went on to ask whether the sample were having difficulty saving in various ways. 80 per cent reported no problem in maintaining a mortgage; 82 per cent had no problem giving children a private education; 83 per cent experienced no difficulty in paying for a life assurance policy and 86 per cent managed to finance their pension contributions. On none of these items did the report specify the reason for the lack of such difficulties – i.e. was it because they did not undertake such expenditure or because their employers undertook the expenditure for them? Were managers living off capital to maintain these commitments? 63 per cent answered that their capital reserves were either the same or better than they had been three years ago. Only 8 per cent of managers claimed that they were drawing on capital to supplement their income.

Of course attitude surveys are notoriously unreliable especially where, as in this case, the respondents have a vested interest in presenting a dismal picture. The way in which the questions were asked and the choices of issues to be included further weaken the reliability of the ORC survey. Nevertheless, such sources clearly have an impact on public and government opinion on the well-being of higher income groups. It is therefore interesting to note that the data published in the survey report contradicted, in many cases, the statements presented in the text. If any conclusions can be drawn from the survey, it is that the subjective views of many managers support our earlier conclusions about changes in management living standards.

A similar survey of management attitudes was carried out two years later by Political and Economic Planning (PEP) on behalf of the British

Institute of Management. A preliminary analysis of the first 500 replies presented a picture similar to that which emerged from the ORC survey. When asked how satisfied the respondents were with their earnings (which averaged £8,932), 10 per cent replied that they were 'very satisfied' while another 46 per cent reported that they were 'fairly satisfied'. PEP noted that 'there is no unanimous outrage amongst managers about their pay rates.' 78 per cent of the sample said that dissatisfaction with their jobs occurred 'hardly ever' or 'not very often'. And of those who expressed regular dissatisfaction with their jobs, taxation and pay came third in a list of six most frequent causes of the discontent. Criticisms of the organisation or of superiors were both more frequent causes of dissatisfaction. 56 per cent of respondents felt that taxation and incomes policies had a bad effect – but almost half did not see them as detrimental. The results also refuted the belief, commonly expressed, that taxation and the reduction of differentials have eroded the desire for betterment and promotion: 96 per cent said they would be prepared to accept promotion if offered and 60 per cent of these intended to actively seek it (Cowton, 1978).

## Conclusion

Contrary to widely held beliefs, the distribution of incomes over the past two decades has changed very little. Redistribution has been modest and has been confined to the very highest income groups. Nevertheless, the belief persists that inflation, incomes policies and taxation have together brought about a collapse in the structure of differentials and that these forces have been at their most vociferous since the Labour government came to office in 1974. The evidence presented in this chapter suggests that both these propositions are open to question. The higher paid have apparently managed to sidestep the constraints of incomes policy: inflation has affected high income groups less severely than the rest of the community; and recent trends in taxation have reduced significantly the contribution of the higher paid to public funds. These factors together cast considerable doubt on the premise that the relative living standards of the rich have been eroded. While this view still pervades public debate, management attitude surveys suggest that it is less widely believed amongst some high income earners themselves.

# 4

# Tax avoidance

Anthony Christopher

If a man is born with riches the evasion, or avoidance, of taxes probably represents the most important element in the compound of what is required in keeping them. If he is born poor, but aims to be wealthy, then contriving to contribute as little as possible to the Inland Revenue is certainly desirable and at modern tax rates probably essential.

The rich have been remarkably successful in keeping a hold on their wealth and almost certainly because of, rather than despite, the now replaced estate duty. It is not much of an oversimplification to say that only the greedy, or dead unlucky, needed to pay it. As we have seen in Chapter 2, at the present time only 15 per cent of the privately owned marketable wealth of Britain is shared by 80 per cent of the population. About twenty years ago they shared 10 per cent of the wealth. Most of the redistribution which has taken place has been amongst the wealthiest 20 per cent: from the very wealthy to the rather rich.

As the Royal Commission on the Distribution of Income and Wealth put it: 'on the evidence available, the role of inheritance in influencing the distribution of wealth at the top end of the scale is substantial and that there has been no marked changed in the pattern of inheritance, at least up to the mid 1960's' (Royal Commission, 1975, p. 120).

The distribution of gross income, i.e. income before tax, follows the same pattern: the top 2 per cent of incomes aggregating to the same total income as that shared by the poorest 30 per cent. Taxation and social security benefits alter the net result to some degree – for example the top 10 per cent of households have their share of total net income reduced from 27 per cent to 23 per cent. But, as Chris Pond suggests in Chapter 3, there has been a valuable easement for those on the highest earnings in the shape of fringe benefits. In its third report the Royal Commission looking at higher income from employment found, hardly surprisingly, that the higher grade management jobs attract increasingly large fringe benefits of which the most valuable overall is undoubtedly pension provision. But the list is long and certainly lengthening: cars, housing, education, holidays, loans, share options and expense accounts generally. Some of these things are arranged within the framework of the law, including the tax law; superannuation, for example. Others are taxed, but for a mixture of reasons, inadequately. To have the private use of a company Rover 3500 in return for a notional taxable income of £500 or a BMW 730 at a notional income of £800, cannot be bad. Why else would the provision of a company car be the most sought after perk in business today?

In this chapter we turn our attention away from the 'perks' industry and begin to examine the main forms of tax evasion and avoidance. We then consider the ways by which some taxpayers minimise (sometimes to the point of zero) their tax liability. Lastly we look at the tax advantages of being self-employed.

## Capital taxes

If an escape route from taxes on capital is not found a rich man is in real trouble.

The main capital taxes in Britain have been estate duty, now replaced by capital transfer tax, and capital gains tax. The old estate duty was remarkably successfully avoided by means of trusts and giving wealth away during one's lifetime. In 1974-5 £83m was returned as gifts *inter vivos* during the seven years before the deaths of about 7,000 people who left net estates valued at over £15,000. At its peak in 1971-2 estate duty amounted only to £450m. Capital gains tax that same year totalled £150m – today it is over twice that sum, but the capital transfer tax is estimated to bring in only £300m in the current year.

The development land tax has been in force for rather more than a year. 'The build up of work', say the Board of Inland Revenue, 'has been rather slower than had been expected' (Inland Revenue, 1977b, p. 9). Estimated yield this year is £5m. Part of the explanation was given by *The Economist* on 7 January 1978 under the heading 'Development untaxed'.

New taxes open up new markets for tax experts. The novel tax may be neutralised before it reaches the statute book. This happened to the development land tax, which came into force in August, 1976. From that date profits on property development were to be taxes at rates of up to 80%. In practice, the potential taxable profits have already been minimised in the books of those property companies that acted before the legislation came in; high base values were established for the development land via a little-publicised scheme which involved shunting assets around a group.

The principles involved were these. First, if an asset is sold by one group company to another, the group can elect for any corporation tax on capital gains to be paid for either of the two companies. Second, losses on past trading can, in certain circumstances, be offset against current or future profits for tax purposes.

Here is how the scheme is worked:

Step 1: The company owning the development site, which is in the books at an out-of-date value of £400,000, buys redeemable preference shares in a loss-making property and share-dealing company laid on by the tax expert. The preference shares are unusual: as well as conferring a right to the normal fixed-rate dividend, they give a right to a dividend dependent on profits. This appearance whereby preference shares masquerade as ordinary share capital means that the property and share-dealing company can be treated as a subsidiary in the main property group.

Step 2: The company owning the development land sells it to the newly acquired dealing company for its current market value of £1m. Using the group election, the £600,000 profit is not taxed in the development company. It will fall into the loss-making dealing company. There the losses will soak up the liability to corporation tax on the capital gains.

Step 3: The preference shares are then redeemed or sold so that the dealing company leaves the group.

Step 4: The dealing company then sells the development land at a commercial profit back to another subsidiary in the original property group. The consideration for this transaction establishes the base cost of the development land for development land tax purposes; the £600,000 profit on the sale of the land to the dealing company, meantime, escapes corporation tax.

Generally speaking, the success with which the rich have kept their wealth 'in the family' has been by avoiding the taxes on it. Already the tax base of capital transfer tax has been so eroded by the scope for gifts and the easements for the small businesses and farmers that it seems set to fail in much the same way as estate duty failed to bring about a significant change in the ownership of wealth.

Before long capital transfer tax will attract to itself the same serious criticism as did estate duty. It is now, and was probably always, unlikely to succeed in making a marked effect on the distribution of wealth. What is more, it makes no distinction between inherited wealth and the savings accumulated during a lifetime of work. Sooner or later (and the sooner the better) there will have to be an accessions tax – a tax which is based upon the cumulative total of gifts received from all sources and paid by the donee, not by the donor, as is the case with capital transfer tax.

## Tax avoidance

On the basis that prevention is better than cure, it probably pays to try to avoid taxes in the first instance rather than to evade them. The most constructive recent approach to the problem of tax avoidance is that by Professor Cedric Sandford (1973). Professor Sandford sees three types of avoidance.

(i) avoidance which governments find acceptable but which they have not specifically sought, for example when a man takes a wife;

(ii) avoidance which governments welcome and, indeed, deliberately seek by tax concessions, for example capital allowance on agricultural buildings;

(iii) avoidance which governments deplore because although it is in accord with the letter of the law, it is not within its spirit.

Whilst there is plenty of room for the view that much of the 'avoidance' of the first two types is of questionable merit because of the extent to which the tax base has been so seriously eroded, here we are concerned with avoidance 'which governments deplore'. In other words avoidance when the principal motive or purpose of a transaction or of an arrangement is to reduce tax.

Traditionally British governments have sought to deal with 'deplorable avoidance' by waiting until some abuse is identifiable and then introducing a law to stop it. A Canadian Commission called this 'the sniper approach', but a more homely view might be to suggest that it is really shutting the stable door after the horse has bolted. Indeed, as Sir Alexander Johnston, a past Chairman of the Board of Inland Revenue, pointed out, the Royal Commission on Taxation (the

Radcliffe Commission) which had been reported in the early 1950s had been against general anti-avoidance legislation largely because they were assured by the Inland Revenue that their powers to deal with avoidance were adequate. 'Yet,' said Sir Alexander in a paper read to the Institute of Fiscal Studies in 1974, 'this was the beginning of the golden age of dividend stripping – 1954 to 1963' (dividend stripping was a lucrative method of taking dividends without paying tax, which was finally killed by a sniper's bullet).

A great part of the trouble is that no one, least of all the Inland Revenue, may even know there is a horse in the stable until, well fed, he has bolted – except the parties to an avoidance scheme and its inventor, that is. After all, as soon as the Revenue does find out what is going on they may load the rifle. But what is more, avoidance arrangements are a valuable marketable commodity. Today they are making some very clever men very rich indeed.

Credit where credit is due: the *Sunday Times* has done more than most papers to expose what is going on. On 6 June 1976 the *Sunday Times* published the first of a number of articles by Lorana Sullivan on the methods of tax avoidance. Under the heading 'How a £60 million tax dodge works', they quoted an example based on the fact that companies claim tax relief for interest paid on loans. The loophole arose because, before the 1976 Finance Act (we trust) closed the gap, these loans did not have to be used for specific business purposes. As a result, a number of tax avoidance specialists were selling complex loan arrangements to clients anxious to cut their tax bills. The scheme was not restricted to legitimate companies. Individual high tax bracket taxpayers were easily transformed into paper companies if they wished to adopt this method of tax avoidance.

The 'packaged programme' involved the interchange of money between a number of banks and what the *Sunday Times* called '£100 off the peg' finance companies often on an international basis – 'to Guernsey and back again with side trips to Switzerland, Gibraltar and the Isle of Man'.

A typical arrangement outlined by Lorana Sullivan worked something like this:

> Company A expected record pre-tax earnings, and was anxious to minimise a large tax bill.
>
> Under the guidance of their tax adviser they 'borrowed' a large sum of money from a friendly bank and immediately paid the bank a year's interest on the loan.

> The company then deducted this interest payment from its pre-tax profits, significantly reducing the tax liability.
>
> However, the company was then left with a large unnecessary loan on its books: it therefore assigned its liability to repay the loan to one of the 'paper' finance companies, which charged a fee for accepting the transaction.
>
> The outcome was that the company had briefly borrowed and repaid the loan without actually using the money for anything. In fact it probably remained in the same finance group throughout the transaction. The finance company received a fee for officially passing the money through its hands and the company made a net saving in tax relief running into many thousands.

With similar avoidance deals for other companies in progress, the banks and finance houses specialising in such transactions had a vast flow of 'monopoly' money constantly flowing between them. What is more, close investigation of the personnel who run these banks and finance houses reveals a small interlinked network, with the same names re-appearing within different organisations throughout the system. The paper discovered two finance companies less than two years old but which in that short time had between them accumulated approximately £600m in charges against deposits and promissory notes held or issued by members of one of the leading bank groups in this field.

As the *Sunday Times* concluded, if the £600m held in the registers of these finance companies represented the total of dozens of individual deals, 'the amount of corporation tax quite legally avoided, at least this time, was probably close to £60m.'

On 29 May 1977 the *Sunday Times* published the second of Lorana Sullivan's articles. The article exposed the major tax avoidance scheme adopted by a large international contractor. It is estimated that the deal may have saved the company the greater part of its 1976 tax bill. The method used to reduce the tax bill of £24.4m involved charging an annual annuity against it. This worked in the following way:

> The contractor purchased an annuity contract from an investment company which was one of the contractor's subsidiaries. A £35m annuity was paid by the investment company to the contractor. There then followed a series of complex side deals which ended with the contractor charging £35m against its own profits.
>
> At the standard corporation tax rate of 52 per cent it was estimated that the cntractor's tax bill would be lowered by the amazing sum of £18.2m.

The cost to the contractors for this advice was about £2.8m paid to a company of whose shares 98 per cent are held by a charitable trust whose objects are 'the relief of poverty, the advancement of religion and other purposes beneficial to the community as are charitable at law'. This method of charging an annuity payment against taxable income was perfectly legal until the 1977 Finance Act eliminated tax benefits in similar transactions, or at least once again we hope so.

On 9 October 1977 the third of Lorana Sullivan's *Sunday Times* articles appeared. The latest scheme she brought to light involves commodity trading, otherwise known as the 'Commodity Carry Scheme' for the high rate individual taxpayers. The 'Commodity Carry Scheme' uses real commodities' future transactions to obtain a tax loss. The scheme involves the use of 'straddles', in other words buying and selling different delivery months in the same commodity.

The risk is minimal as the contracts tend to balance eventually; but in the intervening period one side of the straddle will be in profit while the other side shows a loss. The great advantage is that the losses are realised before the profits; put another way, a technical loss for tax purposes is created but before any profits are realised.

For the taxpayer with £50,000 of taxable income wanting to create a £50,000 tax loss, the scheme would work something like this:

> The taxpayer enters into a commodity trading partnership with two dealing companies in this field and with one of the associates of the tax avoidance specialists. The taxpayer contributes 90 per cent of the partnership's capital. A loan facility for four times the tax loss needed by the taxpayer would then be granted to the partnership by one of the inter-connected banks.
>
> The partnership then starts trading in commodity futures aiming for losses of £55,555 (the taxpayer needs 90 per cent of this loss or £50,000) on one side of the straddle. When this point is reached the taxpayer leaves the partnership, selling his interest to another associated subsidiary company controlled from the Isle of Man.
>
> The taxpayer takes his £50,000 loss with him, leaving behind an equivalent unrealised profit.

Obviously, the taxpayer is paid for his 90 per cent interest in the partnership, and however much the partnership makes is taken away once the profit side of the straddles is realised.

The *Sunday Times* reports that it is estimated that the use of the scheme to offset £50,000 of taxable income costs between £7,580 and £12,980. However, this must be compared with the £43,700 that the taxpayer would have to pay the Inland Revenue on unearned income of £50,000.

On 25 November 1977 the Chancellor was asked whether he intended to amend the law so as to prevent schemes of the kind which we have just described (*Hansard*, 1977e). In reply the Chief Secretary stated:

> I have read the *Sunday Times* article and I am aware of these schemes, under which arrangements are made for a partnership to be formed with the definite intention that a tax loss should arise and that the person for whose benefit the arrangements are made should then leave the partnership. The Revenue tells me that it does not recognise the ensuing claims as valid under existing law. However, its refusal to accept them will doubtless be contested and it could be some years before certainty is reached through the judicial process. To put the matter beyond doubt, therefore, the Chancellor will introduce appropriate legislation in next year's Finance Bill. He will be considering from what date legislation against a claim to loss relief contrived in this kind of way should be effective.

How do we meet this situation? Professor Sandford argues that a policy against avoidance should include 'the aim to make the letter of the law accord more closely with the intention'. Sandford quotes Philip Vineburg in support of the view that 'harmonisation of letter and spirit is much more a matter of policy'.

> Vineburg, writing of the Canadian situation, has deplored 'the failure of draftsmen notwithstanding their obvious prowess and ingenuity, to find a suitable way in tax matters to express what is really meant'. He continues, 'Evidently there are many occasions when tax legislation fails correctly to express the true intent of Parliament. In some measure, in all fairness, this may be inevitable. It is impossible for any single government official or team of officials to foresee the practical application of all the measures which they are drafting. Moreover the practices of tax planners who seem so quick to take advantage of any loophole bedevil their efforts and on occasion have made a mockery of what they intended to achieve. This is not an insuperable obstacle. Considering the resources of the tax department, their contact with the business and professional community which they could turn to their advantage to a much greater degree, the increasing prevalence

> of tax forums and tax literature where new ideas are freely bruited about, their ready ability to cause the law to be changed year by year and even more frequently, there is really no excuse for the currently prevalent situation where they appear to be the last to find out.
>
> We must learn anew to make the tax laws say what we mean. Because of past failures, all efforts at clear draftsmanship should not be abandoned entirely. Exposure of projected amendments to legal talents closer to the market place would be helpful. Errors should be corrected as soon as they are discovered instead of waiting to see what some court may make of it in five years hence. Just as businessmen must learn about the tax laws, the makers of tax laws must learn about business (Sandford, 1973, pp. 114-15).

The time has surely come for a fresh approach. Even William Davis in *Punch* as recently as 28 January 1978, commenting on the Revenue's drive on foreign journalists who have so far been evading income tax, quotes the President of the Foreign Press Association as saying 'My members have been surprised at how much forbearance and understanding the Inland Revenue has shown.'

In this particular circumstance 'reassuring gentlemen', as Davis kindly puts it, was right. Mostly this is the norm and right again. But where we are dealing with schemes which are being carried out with the sole objective of avoiding, postponing or reducing large sums of tax liability, it is folly. It is worse: it is grossly unjust to millions of individuals and to thousands of companies, all of whom, grumbling perhaps while they do so, pay their share.

What are now required are general anti-avoidance powers – the 'shotgun' approach, as the Canadian Carter Commission called it. We need a law which frustrates any scheme which is not one which would normally be entered into and the creation of any rights or obligations which, again, would not normally be created by parties dealing at arm's length, unless tax avoidance was the sole or main purpose.

There are many who oppose this proposition very strongly. It is argued that it would threaten the constitution. But would it? The Board of Inland Revenue (not the government of the day) would administer it. The Revenue, clearly, would have to provide a procedure whereby the taxpayers could clear, before entering into a transaction, whether it was deemed to be 'caught' or not. There would be a right of appeal to the Special Commissioners or, at the end of the day, the Courts. On balance this may be a more democratic method than retrospective legislation.

*The wisdom of being 'self-employed'*

If anyone doubts that, at least where tax is concerned, 'self-employed' is best, it is only necessary to ponder the successful outcry by Britain's North Sea divers. These divers had, for some years, been taxed wrongly by the Inland Revenue as self-employed. They had therefore been assessed under the regulations of Schedule D, which permit a much more liberal approach to 'expenses' than is the case with those who are employed and taxed, through PAYE under the rules of Schedule E.

Thus it was not surprising that £15,000 a year divers, faced unexpectedly with the correct Revenue view (that they were employed, not self-employed) financed an Action Committee with the object of restoring hemselves to this hitherto advantageous tax position. After all, it saved each of them from £3,000 to £5,000 a year.

They have won. The government announced that, notwithstanding the Revenue's correct interpretation of the present laws, they have decided to make an exception of the divers: from 1978 onwards they are once again to be regarded as 'self-employed'. To such depths of expediency has Britain's economic plight brought it.

In the *Guardian* of 10 February 1978 Raymond Gardner provided a rather more colourful example of the benefits not only of being an actress of some repute, but of having good advisers as well. 'Powder blue bankrupt' concerned Miss Diana Dors:

> Of course she's broke. That is official. The bankruptcy court says so. Gone, alas, are the Yankee cars and even the white Rolls-Royce. But that's only because she swapped her white one for a blue one seven months ago. 'Well' says Diana, as though it will serve as an explanation 'It's usually blue or white'. Summing up my best foot-in-the-door manner, and with one eye on the exit, I suggested that she might tell us how you can be bankrupt and swan around in a blue Rolls-Royce, run a pad in Beverley Hills, and keep house in Sunningdale.
>
> Diana gives a cross between a knotty grin and an even knottier pout, and says that everyone would like to know the answer to that. So get on with it. 'Let's put it this way. When you're in this business, in the position I'm in, somehow, somewhere, along the way you acquire advisors, managers, agents, tax consultants,

> accountants and somehow between them they manage to kind of roll you along. More times than not it's all there for the publicity. It all looks much better than it is. But one has got to keep up some sort of style, because it's no use saying that Diana Dors goes to the film studios on the Tube. You've got to have style.'

Quite: but at least Miss Dors has stayed in Britain. She could, probably more profitably, have set herself up in Guernsey or Switzerland.

The fact is that, leaving deliberate evasion entirely on one side, if the self-employed (with a little help from their accountants) are interpreting the rules just 10 per cent too liberally, about £200m a year is staying in the pockets which should go to the Chancellor.

## Tax evasion

If you cannot avoid tax, or the Schedule D rules are not liberal enough for you, then there is tax evasion. Tax evasion is illegal. Nevertheless it is taking place on a very large scale indeed. By definition, its extent is not known, and, in truth, is not open even to reliable estimation. Evasion is not confined to any one classification of taxpayer though, hardly surprisingly, some are in a better position to engage in it than others. The law which provides for the employed to claim deductions from income is a good deal tighter than that under which the self-employed compute taxable profits. That is why 600,000 or so building workers left employment for 'the lump'.

Justice requires it to be said that there is evasion among the employed, either directly, as it were, through false expenses claims, or undisclosed benefits, or indirectly through so-called 'moonlighting' jobs (for example, painting, decorating, playing in bands, and serving in public houses) the rewards for which are never declared. Most particularly, among those technically employed are directors of private companies whose practical control over the financial affairs of their business is really no different from that of the self-employed. For them there is considerable scope for manipulation of their tax bill if they are so minded.

In their report for the year ended 31 March 1976 the Board of Inland Revenue said:

> In the nature of the case it is not possible to know the extent of undetected evasion. There are, however, a number of indications that its scale is increasing. One of these is that the amount of tax recovered in major cases as a proportion of the total tax yield is

> only about one-fifth of what it was 15 years ago, and there is no reason to suppose that the standard of compliance is any higher than it was. As the Chancellor of the Exchequer explained to the House of Commons during the debates on the Finance Bill, the conclusion from such figures seems to be that there has been a significant decline in the success of the Inland Revenue in detecting and countering tax evasion. It was against this background that the Chancellor put forward proposals to strengthen our investigation powers (Inland Revenue, 1976b, p. 7).

Beyond this, in August 1977 the Board announced that Inspectors of Taxes would, on a selective basis, continue in-depth investigation of business accounts with the exploration of circumstances which suggest that tax has been underpaid for some previous year due to fraud, wilful default or neglect on the part of the taxpayer. It is too soon to judge the results of this fresh approach but early signs are that the amount recovered by way of tax and, where appropriate, penalties, is increasing. In the year ended 31 March 1977 Inspectors settled just over 14,000 investigations involving under-assessment in past years gathering in £27m, including penalties and interest. The number of investigations is not related in any way to the number of cases calling for examination: it represents the limits of Revenue resources which are available.

The methods used to evade tax are legion. They range from complicated frauds to simple understatements of takings, or overstatements of outgoings. More often than not the common feature is cash transactions. It is cash which clouds the moonlight operation. But how to assess the scale of it? The gross receipt of Income Tax is £18,500m. Even if the volume of evasion is low overall, at a rate of even a modest percentage it is clearly big money in any Chancellor's book. If we were all suddenly to become as honest as we should be, the next Budget could include much more in the way of tax relief.

Though the highly controversial Finance Act 1976 justifiably gave the Revenue powers to call for documents of a taxpayer and others which, in an Inspector's opinion, are likely to contain information relevant to any tax liability to which the person is or may be subject, the tax laws are still strangely lacking some seemingly elementary features.

Almost a quarter of a century ago the Royal Commission on the Taxation of Profits and Income said:

> We recommend that every person who carried on a trade, profession or vocation (for brevity, we will refer to him as a 'trader')

should be placed under a statutory duty to keep records of his transactions. Unless he does so how can he ever be in a position to state at the end of the year what the figure of his profit has been? The records that we regard it as essential to require are of the simplest kind: a record of all the receipts that have accrued to the trade during the year and of all the payments or other outgoings that are to be set against them, and a record of the opening and closing stock and of outstanding debtors and creditors. . . .

. . . if accounts are submitted in support of a return, the legal significance of the accounts should not be in any way different from that attaching to a return itself. A false return involves liability to a monetary penalty: it must be so, since so much of the efficient administration of the Income Tax Acts depends on the accuracy of the taxpayer's own statements. But accounts submitted in support are not in law themselves a return, although in many cases the words that the taxpayer uses in referring to them have the effect of incorporating them in and so making them part of a return. We think that there is no place for fine distinctions on this point and we recommend that the law should be amended so as to provide that whenever a taxpayer submits accounts to an assessing authority, either in support of a figure tht he has returned or in lieu of a formal return, the accounts should rank as a return for the purposes of the assessment and penalty provisions of the Acts. . . .

. . . Considering how much turns upon the accuracy of the records of cash takings and of the stock sheets, we decided to adopt a suggestion made to us by one of our witnesses, that a trader submitting accounts should be required by law to attach to them a certificate signed by himself verifying the completeness of the underlying records. We do not think that anything elaborate is called for or ought to be required: but we do think that it is only reasonable that he should be asked to put his signature on a positive statement covering such major points as (i) that all cash takings have been recorded in the books, and (ii) that all stock has been included in the stock figure, taking that stock at some stated method of valuation (Royal Commission, 1955, pp. 120 and 322).

It is perhaps unfair not to give sufficient weight to the extent to which the preparation of business accounts is the bread and butter of accountants. The accountant is not the inspector. It is not easy for either to tackle a strong-minded and determined man bent on paying as little as possible. Thus a further recommendation might well be that there should be a statutory requirement, when an accountant is acting for a taxpayer, for the accountant to give a proper certificate including an opinion on the quality of the records produced to him.

But at the end of the day, as with race relations, all the laws in the world will not alter things entirely. There has to be a marked change for the better in public attitudes. We have the most dreadful double standards which, sadly, many politicians support. Regularly we witness a quite disgusting hue and cry over 'welfare state scroungers' – over fraudulent claims to various benefits. In December 1977 the Department of Health and Social Security said it expected 25,000 prosecutions in the year for fraud (the Inland Revenue brought proceedings against 194 people for all offences including 22 for stealing GIRO cheques) and announced it had increased its fraud specialists by 385 over the previous eighteen months. All to combat £2.6m lost through false claims out of the £13,000m paid out. Would that people and Parliament willed the Board of Inland Revenue to be as zealous.

## Postscript

Since this paper was prepared the Chancellor of the Exchequer has announced in the Budget of 11 April 1978 four schemes to counter tax avoidance:

(i) artificial avoidance by some partnerships dealing in commodity futures;
(ii) avoidance through land sales with right to repurchase;
(iii) devices to avoid CTT charges on discretionary trusts and through the use of associated endowment and term life policies.

In his Budget speech, Mr Healey said:

> Lastly, tax avoidance. This has emerged recently in a new form which involves marketing a succession of highly artificial schemes – when one is detected, the next is immediately sold – and is accompanied by a level of secrecy which amounts almost to conpiracy to mislead. The time has come not only to stop the particular schemes we know about but to ensure that no schemes of a similar nature can be marketed in future. So the provisions I shall be introducing this year to deal with artificial avoidance by certain partnerships dealing with commodity futures will go back to 6 April 1976, that is, before the date when the intention to legislate was announced in a Parliamentary Answer.

> My proposed measures against avoidance by means of land sales with the right to repurchase will go back to 3 December 1976, the date foreshadowed in a Parliamentary Answer; and I will from today counteract devices for avoiding the CTT charges on discretionary trusts and avoidance of CTT through the use of associated endowment and term life policies.

What was interesting about the Chancellor's approach was that, instead of moving towards general anti-avoidance powers, he has clearly sought to discourage avoidance schemes by seeking to cancel them out retrospectively. Retrospective legislation is always controversial and presumably we are unlikely to see schemes being negated from a date earlier than some announcement in Parliament. Thus there could still be profitable gestation periods. However, it seems more likely to me that the avoidance counsellors will in future concentrate on rather less grand schemes designed to sell to a smaller group of clients. Chancellors of the future are unlikely to want to find time in Finance Bills to deal with loss of revenue through avoidance of a comparatively minor nature. Individually, of course, the tax saved may be very substantial.

5

# Private capital's blood transfusion

Frank Field

The economic views of those on the far left of British politics are not usually taken seriously by the establishment. An exception to this rule has been the debate revived by two Marxists on the collapse of UK profits. In this chapter we will look critically at this thesis as well as showing how it has been used to spear-head a massive redistribution of resources towards the corporate sector. We will then examine the extent of the tax and price code concessions won by campaigners who promised that higher profits would lead to greater investment. The chapter concludes by judging how successful this policy has been in helping to regenerate British industry.

## Profits collapse

Writing in 1971 on 'the critical condition of British capital' Andrew Glyn and Bob Sutcliffe presented 'some startling facts about the recent decline in the rate of profit on capital and the share of profits in the national income'. While a number of aspects of Britain's recent economic performance are well known, e.g. the rise in unemployment at the same time as an unprecedented high rate of price inflation and money wage increases, 'What is not so well realised, and especially by the left, is the extent to which these trends are eating into the profits of capital' (Glyn and Sutcliffe, 1971, p. 1).

This theme is developed by Glyn and Sutcliffe in a more substantial work published under the title *British Capitalism, Workers and the Profit Squeeze* (Glyn and Sutcliffe, 1972). Here they analysed what they claimed to be the fall in the *share* of profits in the national income as well as a decline in the rate of profit as a proportion of capital employed. It is important to our discussion that we look in more detail at the case put forward by these two writers.

In the first part of their analysis of UK profits, Glyn and Sutcliffe measure profits as a percentage of national income for 'this is the outcome of the process or struggle by which the national income is distributed between classes' (ibid., p. 54). In doing so they deducted stock appreciation – on the grounds that this 'is that part of the profits which derives from the fact that stocks of raw material and finished goods have gone up in value due to price increases. It is thus only a nominal profit . . . (for) the firm has earned nothing which can be used to buy new capital. . . . Stock appreciation thus distorts profit figures upwards and (as) . . . it has been of increasing importance, so the deduction makes an important difference to the figures' (ibid., pp. 57 and 58). Later on we will question more carefully the basis upon which most commentators have calculated stock appreciation.

The initial result of this analysis shows a steady downward trend in the *share* of profits since the early 1950s – falling from 25.2 per cent in 1950–4 to 21 per cent in 1960–4. 'But since then the steady fall has become an avalanche. The share of profits has fallen from 21.2 per cent in 1964 to 12.1 per cent in 1970' (ibid., p. 58).

Glyn and Sutcliffe go on to consider a number of reasons which might account for this dramatic decline in profitability and in doing so they highlight two main causes. In the first place they find a significant correlation between the more recent large increases in money wages and the fall in the share of profits. Linked to this is another reason why British industry has been unable to pass on the higher wages in higher prices; competition has increased in the home market.

Glyn and Sutcliffe then turn to consider the falling *rate* of profit over the past few years. By looking at the profits of only quoted companies (although recently their profits have been a declining proportion of total profits in the corporate sector), by excluding profits earned overseas, and by valuing capital at current prices, they showed that the rate of profit fell from 11 per cent in 1965 to 8.8 per cent in 1967 and 5.8 per cent in 1970. 'This shows very clearly that the rate of profit before tax has fallen enormously since 1967, and just how misleading are the figures from company accounts if not interpreted carefully' (ibid., p. 67). Likewise, the rate of profit after tax on quoted industrial and commercial companies has fallen from 7.1 per cent in 1964 to 4.1 per cent in 1970. 'So the fall in the rate of profit after tax is much greater than the fall in the pre-tax rates' (ibid., p. 67).

Even though Glyn and Sutcliffe believe that these results underestimate the true fall in the rate of profit, they are able to conclude on the basis of their research 'that since 1964 the rate of profits in the UK has collapsed' (ibid., p. 68). Their findings have been given support by academic writers and the economic establishment and we now turn to examine how they have built on the Glyn/Sutcliffe foundations.

In a review article G. J. Burgess and A. J. Webb look at the data not only presented by Glyn and Sutcliffe but by John Hughes (Hughes, 1974) and Mervyn King (King, 1975). After analysing these data they conclude: 'it would appear that, regardless of the approach employed or the company grouping considered, there is agreement that the pre-tax share of profit has been experiencing a significant secular decline over the past two decades. The observed post tax position ranges betwen a near maintenance and a small decline in profit share until the middle 1960s, with a marked fall taking place since then' (Burgess and Webb, 1974, p. 2). These two authors present a similar conclusion on the rate of return on capital. 'All the series indicate that the rate of return on capital has experienced a secular decline, at least throughout the 1960's, whether profitability is measured before or after tax. Although different conceptual approaches may slightly modify the results obtained, the marked downward trend is apparent regardless of the method adopted or the company grouping considered' (ibid., p. 17).

Falling profitability, and its consequential effect on investment and employment, has now become a regular theme in public pronouncements from the economic establishment. A significant contributor to the debate is the Bank of England, and the source of much of the Bank's comments is the work of J. S. Flemming and his colleagues. (See, for example, Flemming, 1976.) Flemming's work is different from most other contributions in that he considers the effects of taxation on the real return on capital over the years since 1960. Account is also taken of the 1974 tax relief on increases in the value of stocks which were in excess of 10 per cent of trading profits. After the data has been reworked to take account of these two factors, the real return on capital is shown to fluctuate around 7 to 9 per cent in the early 1960s, falling to a little over 3 per cent by the end of the decade. The post-tax real return on capital remains fairly stable until 1974. It is at this point that the value of stock appreciation in gross trading profits rises dramatically – from an average of 5 per cent in the 1960s to 44 per cent in 1974. 'This lowered the post-tax real rate of return almost to zero in 1974. Tax relief on stocks, announced in November 1974, has subsequently raised the rate to 3½ per cent but anticipation of this relief is likely to have been small, and for most of 1974 the managers of companies would have thought that, on average, their real rates of return were negligible' (ibid., p. 42).

Similar findings have appeared in *Trade and Industry*, the weekly magazine produced by the Departments of Industry, Trade, and Prices and Consumer Protection. In presenting more up to date figures than were contained in Flemming's research, a recent review article concludes that the latest estimates show that, when measured on replacement cost basis, the profitability of industrial and commercial companies in 1976 was little changed from the previous year. But the rate, after providing for stock appreciation, remained below 3½ per cent, 'an historically very low level. The figures for 1975 and 1976 were well below half the rate for 1970, the low point in the previous cycle' (*Trade and Industry*, 1976, p. 519).

The declining rate of profit in the private sector of British industry is also a subject to which the Treasury has given attention. Commenting in one of its *Economic Progress Reports* on the different profitability surveys, the Treasury wrote, 'The profitability of British Industry has been declining in recent years and needs to be revived' (*Economic Progress Report*, 1977a). Citing the *Trade and Industry* survey it observed that 'all these figures involve assumptions and judgements; the results should not be taken as a precise measure but as an indication of the order of magnitude and the broad trends.' But do all the figures point to a general trend? We now turn and look critically at the foundations upon which most of these studies have been built. There are four major reservations which, when added together, suggest that the unanimity of left/right views on the collapse of UK profits is not only misplaced, but has diverted attention away from what may well prove to be the most important trend in redistribution since 1974.

## Profit crisis?

In the first place the way in which inflation is taken into account in all the calculations could lead to a considerable over-estimation of the effect of rising prices on profit levels. All the series of data quoted have emphasised the importance of taking the current replacement costs rather than the historic costs of capital equipment. But how accurate a picture is presented by current cost accounting? Although it is important to take depreciation into account, this figure presented in company accounts is not an accurate guide to new investment requirements. There are a number of reasons for this. First, it is difficult for any accounting procedure to reflect the fact that, usually, new investment will be more productive than the plant that it replaces. This is just one reason why firms may not replace exactly the same volume of old capital. Moreover, while current cost accounting measures the inflation rate for the replacement of capital goods by an index constructed to measure price rises of capital goods, no allowance is made for real capital gains on fixed assets or stocks, and this is a key assumption in the calculations showing a collapse of UK profits. Thus one body in its submission to Sandilands Committee observed that the 'depreciation provision is so complicated that a single simple adjustment for inflation cannot be expected to produce a "true" figure' (TURU, 1974, p. 1).

The rate of stock appreciation is also similarly calculated in rather crude terms. As we have seen, the argument is that much of British industries' profits are paper profits in that they have been brought about by increases in the value of stocks, which themselves have to be replaced in time at an even higher price. But present calculations of stock appreciations are, like economics, an inexact science. First of all there is evidence that some firms have been able to anticipate the increased price of stocks in their pricing policy which are then taken into account for calculating 'allowable costs' and therby for price increases under the price code. Further, the calculation for stock appreciation is based on the general rise in prices. Again, the price of stocks can and does rise at a lower level. (Although it is equally true to say that at the time of the oil and commodity price boom in 1973–4 the opposite was true.) Also, as the Trade Union Research Unit's (TURU) submission to the Sandilands Committee shows, 'adroit purchasing policies' may well add to real profits. In this submission the Unit looked at the rise in the price of raw cotton. Taking 1972 as 100, the direct import price in the first quarter of 1973 was 97, rising to 106 in the second quarter of 1973. The index for home sales of imported cotton shows a rise from 115 in the first quarter to 242 in the last quarter of 1973. Clearly the timing of any purchase of stocks during that year, as well as whether they were bought direct or from home merchants, would affect the real profits of the particular company concerned.

An additional factor which is ignored in inflation accounting procedures is the extent to which it pays to borrow in periods of inflation. Over the past few years the real rate of interest has been negative and to some extent firms have been able to put the cost of inflation on to lenders. Of course there are limits to such a policy. But in Table 5.1 data are presented on the undistributed income of companies as a percentage of fixed capital, and reworked data are presented on bank lending as a percentage of fixed capital. This shows a dramatic fall in the percentage of fixed capital being financed from undistributed income but a rise in the percentage financed from bank lending.

TABLE 5.1 *Percentage of capital financed from undistributed income and bank lending 1965 to 1974*

| Year | Undistributed income as % of fixed capital | Bank lending as % of fixed capital formation |
|---|---|---|
| 1965 | 114.8 | 20.3 |
| 1966 | 105.3 | 7.6 |
| 1967 | 107.0 | 13.9 |
| 1968 | 109.4 | 21.6 |
| 1969 | 87.4 | 21.9 |
| 1970 | 63.5 | 33.3 |
| 1971 | 74.3 | 21.1 |
| 1972 | 90.6 | 78.3 |
| 1973 | 92.1 | 86.9 |
| 1974 | 44.9 | 74.2 |

(*Source*: *The Times*, 16 June 1975, reworked data)

A further factor which is not taken into account fully in many of those analyses which purport to show a dramatic decline in the profitability of British capitalism is the effect of inflation on the tax burden of companies. In periods of rapidly rising prices it pays to postpone tax payments for as long as possible. And while companies are required to pay advanced corporation tax (which is in effect the payment of income tax on shareholders' dividends), other corporation tax only becomes due after a period of up to two years – that is for those companies which are paying mainstream corporation tax. The Treasury has gone on record as suggesting that after capital allowances and relief of stock appreciation have been deducted, and allowances made for advance corporation tax on dividends, 'the residual "main stream" corporation tax bill can be nil' (*Economic Progress Report*, 1977a).

## Tax and inflation

The second reason why the sweeping statements about the collapse in UK profits should be viewed with some caution is that if the role of the tax system, and its interaction with the rate of inflation, is taken into full account then 'A closer examination of the facts . . . demonstrates that the reality of the situation has not been quite as dramatic or simple as has been claimed' (King, 1975). In a study of UK profits which specifically looked at the effect of company taxation in a period of rapid inflation, King came to three main conclusions. He found that over the period 1950 to 1973 there was an underlying downward trend in the share of conventional gross profits before tax. The experience of conventional gross profits after tax 'was rather different. . . . The results suggest that however profits are defined, there was no long run or *secular* decline in the share of profits after tax.' However, King shows that if stock appreciation is deducted from profit 'then the profit share did fall sharply in the period 1969 to 1971 with a slight recovery after that.' This fall is accounted for by two factors. First, by the cyclical position of the economy during that time but also, and more importantly, the real tax burden on companies increased because tax was charged on a very high level of stock appreciation. It is important to note in this context the significant tax reductions made for stock appreciation in the November 1974 Budget, as well as the various revisions of the price code (allowing stock appreciation to be calculated as it is for tax purposes when calculating allowable costs for price increases) which were made after King had completed his analysis.

## Economic cycle

A third reason why the studies quoted earlier may not accurately reflect the same level of profits earned on private capital is that many of them have not fully taken into account the effect of the cycle of economic activity on the profitability of British industry. The difference this makes to the calculations is stressed by M. Panić and R. E. Close (Panić and Close, 1975). These two authors note that there is still immense disagreement about the most appropriate way of adjusting company accounts to take account of rising prices. For their analysis they use the historic cost estimates, adding that work by NEDO 'shows that the use of the available replacement cost series would not invalidate the main conclusions' (ibid., p. 21).

The Panić/Close findings are in agreement with the other data cited in that over time, pre- and post-tax data show a secular decline in the profitability of UK manufacturing industry since the early 1950s. But they observe that the decline in pre-tax profitability was concentrated mainly in the first nine years of the period, in contrast to the decline in the post-tax rate which took place chiefly in the 1960s. To this they add one important rider: 'It is no coincidence that, over the period analysed here, the highest rates of return were achieved in 1955, 1960 and 1964 – all peak years of economic activity; or that sharp increases in profits reported over the last year occurred during the period of rapid recovery. In fact, we have estimates that most of the decline in the pre-tax rate of return between 1964 (14.2 per cent) and 1970 (12.1 per cent) could be accounted for by the difference in capital utilisation' (ibid., pp. 23–4).

There is also an additional reason why the widely held belief about the collapse of UK profits should be viewed with caution. A careful reading of some texts suggests that some academics may have preferred to abandon scholarship in order to become campaigners, drawing conclusions from the data which do not stand up to careful scrutiny. Earlier we cited the work of Burgess and Webb, and in particular their conclusion, 'It would appear that, regardless of the approach employed or the company grouping considered, there is agreement that the pre-tax share of profit has been experiencing a significant secular decline over the past two decades. The observed post-tax position ranges between a near maintenance and a small decline in profit shares until the middle 1960s with a marked fall taking place since then.' In fact their own series of figures shows a peak share of 13.1 per cent in 1960 and 13.5 per cent in 1965. But their analysis begins in 1956 with 10.9 per cent as the share of post-tax profits. This falls to 10.2 per cent in 1972, the last year in their table – hardly the secular decline which the authors claim in the text.

While these reservations suggest that any claims on a falling or negative rate on return of capital should be viewed with healthy scepticism, the campaign emphasising the need to redistribute to the private sector continues under different guises, aided and abetted by the influential sections of the media. For example, *The Economist* has put its special pleading for private capital in terms which tries to forge a common interest between workers and their industrial bosses. 'Britain will average over a million unemployed for the rest of the 1970s unless profits are doubled' (*The Economist*, 1976). In response to this and similar campaigns the government rightly points to a number of concessions which aimed 'to improve the flow of company finance', while adding 'the Government now looks to Industry to take advantage of the conditions created to expand and prosper' (*Economic Progress Report*, 1977a). How important have these concessions been in redistributing resources to the private sector and to what extent has British industry responded by increasing investment?

## Government concessions

During 1974 Mr Healey presented three Budgets which are relevant to our theme. In his March 1974 Budget he drew attention to the liquidity crisis in British industry which he viewed as a temporary difficulty resulting from the three day week. However, the Chancellor added, 'We shall watch the situation closely and adjust our policy flexibly to insure that the banks have sufficient resources to meet these (i.e. companies') needs' (*Hansard*, 1974a, col. 284). The Chancellor noted, however, that 'profits last year reached a very high level. . . . There was, in fact, a significant increase in the share of total national income going to companies'. Partly as a result of this increase in profits, corporation tax was set at 52 per cent for tne financial year 1973 and companies were requested to pay advance corporation tax which was offset against their tax liability for the year ending 1974. As we have already noted, advance corporation tax is in effect the payment by companies of income tax on dividends to shareholders.

Two small measures aimed at helping companies were announced in the Chancellor's July 1974 Budget. In the first place the regional employment premium of £1.50 per week per male employee was doubled. This took effect from the first week in August 1974 and it was calculated that it would add £118m in a full year to company liquidity. Second, in order to help firms raise finance, the 1973 5 per cent limit on dividend increases was raised to 12½ per cent.

These two changes were insignificant in value compared with the concessions made to the corporate sector in the November 1976 Budget. In presenting these measures the Chancellor commented that inflation was forcing thousands of firms to restrict their output and lay off workers 'not because of lack of demand for their products . . . but simply through lack of working capital' (*Hansard*, 1974b, col. 258). He noted that firms were being hit in two particular ways. In the first place inflation 'has increased the cost of replacement stocks to a degree which, under the present tax rules, impose burdens which industry was never meant to carry.' The Chancellor therefore introduced changes 'so as to avert the real and immediate danger of cuts in investment, stock building and employment'. Tax rules were implemented so that the maximum profit represented by the increase in the value of stocks on which tax is payable was limited to 10 per cent of trading profits. The value of this concession in a full year was put at £800m.

The second way in which firms were being affected was that the price code was operating more severely 'than was originally intended by the last Government'. Two changes were therefore simultaneously made to the code. Companies were permitted to recoup increased prices over a period of a year up to 17½ per cent the cost of their investment programmes for that year in plant and machinery and industrial buildings. Also, safeguards in the code were clarified so that profit margins of manufacturers were not reduced to below the levels of April 1973. These concessions were also valued at £800m during 1975. By 1976 the Trade Union Research Unit (TURU) estimated that these two concessions have 'transferred something of the order of £2bn a year to reinforce the depleted level of company incomes' (TURU, 1976, p. 1).

In the same Budget the Chancellor announced an increase in funds for investment. Finance for Industry was to receive £1bn over the following two years so as to ensure a necessary supply of funds for investment, particularly amongst small firms.

In his April 1976 Budget the Chancellor set on a more permanent footing the concessions made to the corporate sector in his November 1974 Budget. Because some businesses claimed that they needed to create balance sheet reserves against the possibility of stock relief being withdrawn, and this was in fact reducing their ability to borrow, Mr Healey stated that stock relief would continue 'in substantially its present form for two more years' but with one change. The purpose of giving stock relief in the first place was to strengthen the incentive to invest. 'There has been increasing criticism that the profit deduction operates unfairly against companies investing in fixed assets, because the profits base to which it applies is calculated before deducting depreciation allowances . . . I therefore propose that in future profits for this purpose should be calculated after deducting allowances for depreciation.' In addition the Chancellor stated that there was no question of clawing-back the tax relieved under this scheme in the case of all those companies whose stock valuations and rates of investment are maintained or increased. 'This means that for the great majority of companies stock relief really implies a deferral of tax not only for some short or limited period but into the indefinite future' (*Hansard*, 1976, col. 248).

In the same Budget Mr Healey recalled that the Committee on Inflation Accounting (headed by Mr Francis Sandilands) has recommended that the present system of 100 per cent capital allowances should be continued and suggested that the commitment to the system established in 1972 should be continued. This proposal was accepted which, together with the stock relief, has had an important effect on the amount of corporation tax paid by companies. The Chancellor put it in the following words. 'The continuation of stock relief and the present system of capital allowances means that substantially the whole of any profits which a manufacturing company re-invests in its business, whether in fixed or working capital, will effectively be relieved from corporation tax.'

One other important announcement made in the Budget concerned revision of the price code. In announcing that there would be changes the Chancellor said that the government 'will take full account of the needs of industry, and in particular of the need to allow sufficient recovery of profits to encourage the new investment we need and the new jobs which the investment will bring.' Behind this short statement were government plans to transfer a potential additional £5bn to the company sector. We therefore turn to examine in a little more detail the 1976 changes in the price code, and in doing so we will draw upon the work completed by the Trade Union Research Unit on the value of the concessions (for full details see TURU, 1976).

## Price code changes

The first change involved that part of new investment which could be passed on in price increases during the year in which the investment was made. Prior to the 1976 changes the rate since May 1975 had been 20 per cent. The consultative document on the price code raised this to 35 per cent, which was further revised to 50 per cent when the new code came into effect. In addition, retailers, who were previously excluded under the scheme, were allowed to pass on 35 per cent of the new investment cost in the year during which the investment took place. This move was not the most cost-effective way of increasing investment for firms could still claim 50 per cent of investment cost against price increases even though their investment budgets had been reduced. Even so the TURU estimated that an extra £1.7bn to £2bn could be passed on to consumers in the year following the revised price code under this heading alone.

However generous the offsetting costs of investment were, they were not the only changes brought about in the 1976 price code. Major changes were also made on the way depreciation and the treatment of stocks could be valued under the new code. Under the old code companies had to keep to the method by which they had valued depreciation in their accounts since the commencement of the code in 1973. This restriction was lifted and companies were allowed a general marking up of depreciation of 40 per cent to previous allowances. The TURU estimates that this change increased potential sales revenue by £1.2bn.

The third major change gave companies the option of calculating the cost of materials currently consumed on the basis of the latest contracted purchase price for those stocks. In addition companies when presenting net profits to the Price Commission could make a 70 per cent reduction of the increase in stock values in the relevant period to take account of stock appreciation.The TURU estimates that the first concession from stock pricing could have added £1bn to company revenue and that of the stock appreciation deduction was worth up to £2bn to corporate finance in the year following the price code changes.

Two other changes also increased the amount of revenue in the company sector. In the first place, the provision whereby increases in productivity were to be partly reflected in lower prices was abolished. Second, whereas under the previous code falls in unit cost had to be entirely reflected in lower prices, the new code specified that only half of the fall in cost need be reflected in prices. The TURU estimates the value of the productivity deduction around £0.4bn and the unit cost gains at £0.5bn.

Further revisions were made to the price code in the middle of 1977. The new code abolished the rule by which manufacturing and service companies' prices could only be raised in line with increases in 'allowable costs'. And while the other price control on the net profit margins was to continue, we have already seen that these rules suffered major modifications in June 1976, and it is doubtful whether the net profit margins now act as a constraint on price increases. Indeed, a survey carried out by the National Institute of Economic and Social Research showed that while two fifths of manufacturers reported that their current prices were about the same as if there had been no controls on prices and profits, one in five manufacturers 'thought that their current prices were higher than without the price code' (Everly, 1977).

The most important revisions of the code were therefore made in 1976. Potentially these changes could have increased profits by up to £5bn, although the TURU claims that 'our rough estimate is that companies may raise their profits on home market trade by between £3–£4bn.' Put another way, the 1976 changes alone meant a doubling of company profits if we follow the way Glyn and Sutcliffe, the Bank of England *et al.* have calculated the return on capital. But how effective have these major tax and price code concessions been in fulfilling the government's goal of raising appreciably the level of investment in British industry?

## Increasing the seed corn?

A cursory glance at the figures shows how important is the government's emphasis on increasing investment in manufacturing industry. If gross fixed capital formation since 1970 is presented as an index (1970 equalling 100) we see that investment fell in each year until 1974, only to fall again in subsequent years. What is noticeable is that the short boom in 1974 did not see a restoration of investment back to its 1970 position.

This fall in investment is seen most clearly if the data are represented minus capital consumption, i.e. the amount of capital used up in the process of production. From this we can see that the boom in 1974 saw the level of investment at only three quarters of the 1970 level. Since then investment has continued to fall and the 1976 figures show just how devastating the decline has been – a fall to almost one third of its 1970 position.

TABLE 5.2 *Gross fixed capital formation less capital consumption in manufacturing industry in 1970 prices (1970 = 100)*

| | |
|---|---|
| 1970 | 100 |
| 1971 | 82.6 |
| 1972 | 54.8 |
| 1973 | 53.1 |
| 1974 | 76.0 |
| 1975 | 45.6 |
| 1976 | 35.1 |

(*Source*: *National Income and Expenditure*, 1977, Table 10.7)

It would be wrong to think that the decline in UK manufacturing investment is bound up with the supposedly recent fall in company profits. The trend is much more long drawn and pre-dates the debate on the falling rate of profits. This can be seen from the recently released data on the value of net domestic fixed capital formation in manufacturing industry for each year since 1948. These have been reworked in 1970 prices thereby giving an index on the volume of investment over the same period. Again the results are deeply worrying. The volume of investment in manufacturing industry in 1976 was lower than any year since 1949 (*Hansard*, 1978, col. 639–40).

With these figures it would be more appropriate to talk about the collapse of investment in UK manufacturing industry than the collapse or crisis of profitability. As we have seen, both tax concessions in a number of budgets and quite major changes in the price code have increased company liquidity, and what is clear is that they have not been used for the regeneration of British industry. So what have companies been doing with their increased finance?

Some companies have issued new capital notes to shareholders. For example during 1977 GEC issued a £178m of new floating rate capital notes to shareholders in proportion to the value of their existing share holdings. Other companies have used their increased funds, not for capital investment, but for financial dealings. A slightly exasperated Treasury brief noted that managements were tempted (and presumably found wanting) 'to apply retained profits to reduce company debts or employ their funds to make financial investments where they will earn high rates of return' (*Economic Progress Report*, 1977b). However it is doubtful whether this is because of the supposedly low or negative rate of return on existing capital. In a report on a pilot survey of how companies do (or more precisely, do not) set profit objectives Panić and Close observed that 'there is no reason why the past rates of existing capital stock should exert great influence on investment decisions – unless they are taken to show certain clear and irreversible trends' (Panić and Close, 1975, p. 21). Rather the decision to invest is based on the expected rate of return on the new capital.

And it is at this point that the weakness of the government's free market strategy to increase investment becomes clear. While there is no doubt that companies have been given substantial additional resources to invest, what is also beyond doubt is the fact that the economy is running way below existing capacity. One estimate suggests that industry is currently working at 10 per cent below capacity. In other words output could be expanded significantly without increasing the capital base. For firms to invest in the market economy requires that they not only have the necessary funds to do so, but that the goods which are demanded cannot be produced from existing capacity. A policy to increase investment by channelling resources to the private sector is only half a policy. The other half is an expansion of demand with a commitment to a return to growth and full employment. While this is a path along which the government seems at present unprepared to tread, the redistribution of resources to the private sector continues.

To have increased investment over the past couple of years would have served well the long-term needs of the British economy. But it requires more than increasing profits of the private sector during a depression for the capital base to be renewed and extended. Even the accelerated capital projects approach, which has been highly cost effective, can only modestly redress the decline in Britain's manufacturing base which we have just detailed. The community, including the private sector, would have been better served if the government's promise to look carefully at establishing an investment bank had been pursued with only half the rigour of its free market approach to regenerating British industry (Hughes, 1976). Furthermore, any policy of increased investment, which was also part of the wider strategy of returning to full employment, would require another U-turn in government policy. Most new investment is capital intensive, allowing the same output to be produced with fewer workers. A policy of safeguarding Britain's manufacturing base needs to be accompanied by an expansion of jobs in the service and public sectors, if full employment is also to be restored.

## Conclusion

In this chapter we looked at the arguments put forward by Left and Right to support the view of a collapse in UK profits. It is on the basis of such a belief that the government's policy to regenerate British industry has been based. But we do not yet possess the expertise to measure accurately either the share of profits in national income or the rate of profit on capital employed in times of rapidly rising prices. What is beyond doubt, however, is that since 1974 one major governmental aim has been the massive redistribution of resources to the private sector. This policy of redistributing to the private sector has been one of the most important actions carried out by the present Labour government. But such a policy has not brought about the expected increase in investment; rather there has been an investment strike. It is this collapse of investment in manufacturing industry, rather than the plummeting rate of return on capital, which forms the basis of today's industrial crisis.

6

# The wealth tax debate

Cedric Sandford

This chapter is in two parts: the first traces the origin of a wealth tax in Labour Party thinking, the official Party commitment to such a tax, the discussion – centring on the green paper and the Select Committee – and the situation in 1978. The second part examines the constraints on the introduction of a wealth tax: economic objections, administrative problems and, not least, the policy-making failings of the Labour Party especially in the inability of the Party to develop any real philosophy about the distribution of wealth.

## Origin of Labour's wealth tax

The first public airing by the Labour Party of the idea of a wealth tax appears to have been in a speech by Mr Callaghan, then Shadow Chancellor, shortly before the 1964 General Election. But the idea of a wealth tax must have been around in Labour Party circles for some time before that. In 1956 Nicholas Kaldor (now Professor Lord Kaldor) had written a report for the Indian government in which he had advocated an annual wealth tax, basing his recommendations very much on the Swedish model. By then Kaldor had already established himself as the pre-eminent thinker on tax reform in the Party – a position dating from the previous year, when, to the Majority Report of the Royal Commission on the Taxation of Profits and Income (Cmd 9474, June 1955) he had appended a powerful Minority Report advocating a corporation tax and a capital gains tax (Royal Commission, 1955).

Despite such influential advocacy, the Labour Party did not include any reference to a wealth tax in their 1964 manifesto and when Mr Callaghan became Chancellor he shelved the idea in favour of other reforms, in particular the corporation tax and capital gains tax. Mr Jenkins, who succeeded Callaghan at the Exchequer, in his Budget speech in 1968 expressed his interest in 'the further exploration of the ways in which the taxable capacity of those who possess wealth should be differentiated from those who depend primarily on wages and salaries'; but congestion in the Inland Revenue precluded any bold new ventures in taxation and Mr Jenkins contented himself with the special charge on investment income.

Interest in a wealth tax in Labour Party circles continued to grow, however, supported by the TUC General Council which in its annual economic reviews since 1968 has regularly advocated a wealth tax. *Labour's Economic Strategy* (August 1969) contained specific proposals for a wealth tax 'with a starting point of £50,000, and with progressive rates of 1 per cent through to 5 per cent on wealth above £400,000'. The document added: 'A tax of this kind has already been successfully levied in a large number of countries including the whole of Scandinavia, Germany, Luxembourg, Holland and Switzerland and should present little difficulty here once the nettle has been grasped.' Even so, the Party's manifesto for the 1970 General Election, although emphasising the need to reduce inequalities of wealth by taxation, contained no explicit commitment to an annual wealth tax. However, the proposal continued to harden. *Labour's Programme for Britain* (8 July 1973) declared the intention of the Party to 'introduce a wealth tax consisting of an annual levy on the largest concentrations of private wealth . . . progressive on net personal wealth holdings in excess of £50,000 at present values'. The same document promised an increase in income tax on very high incomes and a reduction of the threshold for the investment income surcharge. Then, in the Labour Party manifesto for February 1974, the wealth tax at last became a Party commitment with the unadorned phrase, 'We shall introduce an annual wealth tax on the rich.' Along with the wealth tax was to be a new tax on major transfers of personal wealth, increased taxation on property speculation and an attack on 'tax dodging across the whole field'.

As the first stage in implementing this commitment, in the Budget introduced a few weeks after Labour had become the government in February 1974, Mr Healey repeated the same cryptic message of the manifesto: 'This government intends to introduce an annual wealth tax on the rich'. He continued, 'Such a tax is an accepted feature of many other countries' taxation systems. But it will be a new departure in this country, and I believe it should be introduced only after a thorough public discussion about the precise form it should take, the rate at which it is levied, and its relationship with other forms of taxation. My first step towards this reform will, therefore be the publication of a green paper during the summer' (*Hansard*, 1974a). The green paper, entitled simply *Wealth Tax*, appeared on 8 August 1974 and included the suggestion that there might be a Select Committee of the House of Commons to examine the possibilities (*Wealth Tax*, 1975). In the October election of 1974 the Labour Party, besides promising to proceed with legislation for the introduction for the capital transfer tax, reaffirmed its intention to introduce an annual wealth tax and specified that it would be 'on wealth above £100,000'.

### *Why tax wealth?*

A wealth tax (or more accurately an annual personal net wealth tax) is a tax levied each year on the total value of an individual's stock of assets less liabilities. In principle it covers assets of all kinds, except any specifically exempted and is normally subject to to some *de minimis* limit. Thus it includes personal possessions such as house, boat, car, furniture, jewellery and other personal chattels; financial assets like stocks and shares, and bank balances; and also the value of land and agricultural and industrial assets owned by individuals. In principle it takes no account of how the possessor acquired the wealth or how he uses it – though special reliefs may, of course, be introduced for particular kinds of assets like farms, such concessions usually taking the form of favourable valuation procedures.

Apart from administrative advantages, which may result from the increased knowledge of a taxpayer's wealth which can be checked against income or gift tax returns, a wealth tax has, in general, been advocated on three main grounds. First and most widely it has been proposed on grounds of what the economist calls 'horizontal equity'. The argument is that wealth gives its possessor advantages over and above the income, if any, derived from it. Thus the possessor of wealth has security, independence, and the opportunity of advantageous purchase. In so far as wealth yields income, he acquires this income without having to sacrifice leisure. These advantages give the owner of wealth additional taxable capacity. If the tax system is to be fair between individuals this additional taxable capacity should be taken into account and an income tax should be supplemented by an annual wealth tax.

It was recognition of these kinds of advantages of wealth which led to the introduction in the United Kingdom early this century of differentiation in the income tax between earned income and investment income; but such differentiation is an imperfect way of taking account of the additional taxable capacity of wealth, since it excludes wealth which yields no income in money terms, though it may carry many of the other advantages, and only lightly taxes wealth yielding low income. Hence, for this purpose, it is better to have a wealth tax. The essential point was made vividly by Nicholas Kaldor. He compared a Maharajah with a large stock of gold and jewels but no income with a beggar who had neither income nor gold and jewels. If income tax alone were imposed each would pay the same – zero. But there is no doubt as to who has the higher taxable capacity.

The second argument for imposing an annual wealth tax is to use it as an instrument to reduce inequality in the distribution of wealth. The objective may be a radical or a limited one. The radical objective is achieved by imposing wealth tax such that, taken in conjunction with income tax, the wealthy are unable to pay both without parting with some of their assets; thus, each year, the wealth of the wealthiest is reduced. A more limited objective is a milder wealth tax which it is possible for the wealthy to meet along with income tax, but which does ensure that those who have avoided progressive income tax by moving into assets which yield capital gain and little or no income, are none the less heavily taxed. Whilst such a tax would not positively reduce inequality each year, it would check accumulation by the rich.

The third motive for an annual wealth tax has been more a subject of academic discussion than a practical motivation of policy-makers – namely that a wealth tax, especially if imposed in partial substitution for income tax, might stimulate the more efficient use of resources. Because a given value of wealth incurs the same liability to tax irrespective of its yield, then it is argued that a wealth tax would encourage transfer from nil-yielding assets to yielding assets: for example, a man with a plot of waste land would pay wealth tax on it even though it yielded no income and would thus be encouraged to develop or cultivate it; and a businessman would have a particular inducement to minimise unnecessary stockholding, and low-yielding idle balances, and apply resources more productively. At the same time, because the wealth tax was in substitution for income tax, higher yields would be more attractive as carrying less income tax. Incentive to effort would be increased by the decline in income tax; nor would a substitutive tax of this kind necessarily reduce the incentive to save, for, although additional saving would add to the wealth tax base, the fruits of saving would carry a higher return. In practice, however, as we shall see below, high yield and efficiency are not precisely equatable and there are other economic disadvantages of a wealth tax, even of the substitutive kind.

The appropriate form of a wealth tax varies according to its purpose. Thus the horizontal equity objective implies a proportional or mildly progressive wealth tax with a low threshold. In the UK the logic would clearly be to impose the tax at a threshold low enough to enable it to replace the investment income surcharge. The objective of radically reducing inequality of wealth would imply a progressive tax with a threshold which might be higher than that for the first purpose: in determining the threshold it would be necessary to decide who constituted the rich. As to the efficiency objective, this would imply a tax structure similar to that for horizontal equity: if efficient use of capital were required then the tax should apply across the board to all capital, and depending on the nature and extent of the accompanying income tax reductions, the purpose would be more likely to be achieved with a proportional or mildly progressive wealth tax than with a highly progressive one.

Of these motives, the only one to appear in official Labour Party literature has been the desire to tax the rich in order to reduce inequality of wealth. The radical objective seems to have been implied, because none of the Labour Party documents suggested any income tax reduction accompanying the introduction of a wealth tax – indeed, some had linked a wealth tax with proposals for increasing income tax.

## *The green paper and the Select Committee*

The green paper on a wealth tax was a remarkable document. A careful reading reveals that it carried only two hard commitments: that there would be a wealth tax and that the tax base would not include the value of pension rights. The cynic might be excused for believing that the cunning politicians had inserted the first and the crafty civil servants the second. In contrast to Labour Party literature the green paper stressed two objectives of a wealth tax, namely both horizontal equity and the reduction of inequality, but gave no indication of the relative importance to be accorded to them. It argued, however, that a threshold sufficiently low to enable the investment income surcharge to be completely eliminated, was not administratively feasible 'in the foreseeable future'. The possibilities outlined in the green paper were so various that any wealth tax resulting from it was compatible both with a reduction in the taxation of the wealthy or with a very substantial increase. Thus, there was a hint of possible income tax reductions; there might (or might not) be a ceiling provision limiting the total paid by an individual in income tax and wealth tax combined; the investment income surcharge might (or might not) be allowed as an offset against wealth tax; two possible rate structures were outlined, each with a threshold of £100,000, though with scale B much heavier than scale A – but it was stressed, in bold type, that the starting point and rates had 'been taken merely for illustrative purposes'; and so on and so on.

The green paper was unique amongst green papers on taxation. Other green papers, like that on *Local Government Finance* and on *A Possible Inheritance Tax in Place of Estate Duty* had left as many options open. Other green papers, like that on VAT or the Tax Credit Scheme, had committed governments to a particular tax. But none had, at the same time, committed a government firmly to the principle of a tax whilst leaving virtually everything else open. If we assume that the government was sincere in its desire for a wealth tax, the position it took up in the green paper was essentially illogical. If the government was so vague about the desired objectives and methods of achieving them, it should hardly have been prepared to commit itself to the principle. The structure of a wealth tax depends essentially on the purposes it is intended to fulfil. There is not really one wealth tax, but a number of possible wealth taxes with very different implications and structures.

The green paper is notable also for omissions. Two of the most important were the failure to analyse the possible economic consequences of a wealth tax, save for a cursory reference to possible difficulties for agriculture and the small business; and the complete omission of any reference to the capital transfer tax, though the white paper on this tax appeared the same day as the green paper on the wealth tax and both taxes ostensibly had a common purpose of reducing inequality in the distribution of wealth.

It is clear that the House of Commons Select Committee on a Wealth Tax, set up in December 1974 to make recommendations on the form and structure of a wealth tax in the light of the green paper and on evidence submitted to it, had no easy task. It deliberated and took written and oral evidence during the first half of 1975; then, after the summer recess, reconvened to agree a report. In the event the Committee could agree only to publish each of the draft reports considered, together with the Minutes of Evidence and Appendices containing written submissions.

An examination of the voting pattern and the main contents of each report reveals both the reasons for disagreement and the degree of support for particular proposals; indeed, it becomes clear that, despite the lack of a majority report, a large majority of the Committee shared certain principles in common. When the Committee resumed its meetings in the early autumn of 1975 it had before it a draft of a report prepared by the Chairman. Many of the Committee members disliked the draft and three alternative drafts were prepared. The deliberations of the Committee took the following form. The Liberal Report (submitted by the sole Liberal member on the Committee, Mr John Pardoe) was first proposed in place of the Chairman's draft. The Conservatives supported it and it was lost only by the casting vote of the Chairman. Next a report submitted by Dr Jeremy Bray was considered – but it received only the support of two of his Labour colleagues and was rejected by the large majority of fifteen to three. Then Mr Maurice Macmillan presented a report for the Conservatives; it was supported by Mr Pardoe and defeated only by the casting vote of the Chairman. Finally the Chairman's draft was put to the vote and carried – but only by the Chairman's casting vote. This report was then considered at a series of meetings, paragraph by paragraph. Finally in its amended version it was put to the vote – only to be rejected. In the vital last stages two Labour members were abroad at a conference. The best the Committee could do was to publish all five reports: the Chairman's report both amended and unamended, the Liberal report, the Conservative report and the report of Dr Jeremy Bray.

Although ending almost on a note of farce it would be wrong to discount the work of the Select Committee. It fulfilled a vital educational role: its own reports and the oral and written evidence amounted to some 2,000 pages of closely-packed print. Moreover, there was a logical consistency about each of the reports which the original green paper had conspicuously lacked. The disagreement on principles between the reports stems primarily from differences of objectives. The Chairman's draft report made horizontal equity its main objective but also sought to make a limited contribution to reducing inequality. The Conservatives' report was concerned almost wholly with horizontal equity. The Liberal report accepted horizontal equity as the main objective, and wished a wealth tax to make a limited contribution to reducing inequality, but its distinctive feature was the proposal to use a heavy wealth tax as a means of making big reductions in income tax to stimulate effort and enterprise – the efficiency objective. Finally, Dr Bray's report was concerned only with reducing inequality. The differences in the proposals of these reports in respect of rates of tax, allied changes in income tax, and ceiling provisions, all stem logically and consistently from these differences of objective.

It is convenient to talk of the Chairman's reports, the Conservative and the Liberal reports as constituting the 'main' reports, for each of these received the support of around half of the Committee, in contrast to that of Dr Jeremy Bray which lacked substantial support. Despite their significant differences all the main reports had much in common in matters of detail, often differing substantially from the suggestions of the green paper. Detail apart there was one very important common element to the main reports. All saw horizontal equity as the major objective of a wealth tax, and all accepted the conclusion which logically followed, namely that the investment income surcharge ought to be completely replaced by a wealth tax. This in turn implied that the threshold should be brought down from the £100,000 proposed by the green paper to a figure more like £30,000. The odd one out was the report of Dr Jeremy Bray where the sole concern was reducing inequality, and which proposed to retain the £100,000 threshold, together with the highest of the illustrative scales contained in the green paper, with no ceiling provisions and no proposals for reducing income tax, save that investment income surcharge should be set off against wealth tax. Such proposals were completely out of line with those of the large majority of the Committee.

In December 1977 (*The Times*, 20 December) the TUC/Labour Party Liaison Committee, with the Prime Minister present, made a firm commitment to a wealth tax of the kind outlined above and agreed that 'work should be set in hand immediately on a white paper and draft clauses with the clear intention to legislate in the first session of a new Parliament.

## *The present position*

In a written answer to a Parliamentary Question the Chancellor of the Exchequer announced on 18 December 1975 that, in consequence of the delay of the Select Committee in producing its report, which 'took a good deal longer . . . than the Government had hoped' and because of 'the many issues involved', he did not feel able to introduce a wealth tax that session. However, he indicated that the Inland Revenue would continue its preparatory work and that he would consider publishing draft clauses for public discussion during 1976. No mention was made of a wealth tax in the Queen's Speech in 1976 and not long afterwards the Chancellor announced that he was not proposing to introduce a wealth tax in the present Parliament. However, this was too much for Mr Jack Jones and, in the words of *The Times* of 7 December 1976 the TUC 'wrung from Cabinet Ministers a joint initiative to revive the Left's cherished idea of a tax on wealth.' The TUC/Labour Party Liaison Committee agreed to set up a working party consisting of two government Ministers, two Trade Unionists, two members of the NEC, and two of the PLP, in the words of Mr Murray, 'to look at ways in which we can find a practical way of getting a wealth tax in, hopefully within the lifetime of this present government.' Not one member of the TUC/Labour Party Liaison Committee nor of the working party had been a member of the Wealth Tax Select Committee.

The first fruits of the working party's activities appeared in the Social Contract mark III, *The Next Three Years and Into the Eighties*, the document drawn up by the TUC/Labour Party Liaison Committee and approved by the TUC General Council and the National Executive Committee of the Labour Party in July 1977. It said:

> The government should press on and publish detailed proposals for a wealth tax in the next Parliamentary session. The option which the Liaison Committtee are considering in detail would entail a threshold of £100,000 at present values with rates rising progressively from 1 per cent of net assets to 5 per cent for fortunes over £5m.

The paragraph went on to indicate that relief would be given along the lines of capital transfer tax for owners of productive assets such as farms and small businesses and to make a somewhat optimistic estimate of yield. The particular version of wealth tax which the Liaison Committee was thus considering in detail was the Scale B of the original green paper, rejected by all but a handful of the Select Committee.

This essay is being written just four years after the election of February 1974 which the Labour Party won on the basis of a manifesto containing a firm commitment to introduce a wealth tax – a commitment reasserted in the second election of that year. Yet no wealth tax has been introduced, nor is it conceivable that it will be in the lifetime of the Labour government elected in October 1974. Why is this and what lessons can be learnt from Labour's wealth tax saga? The answers will be discussed under three heads: economic considerations, administrative constraints and the failings of Labour Party policy-making.

## Economic considerations

The whole thrust of Labour Party policy statements on a wealth tax was the advocacy of an 'additive tax' (one imposed on top of income tax which the wealthy could only have met by disposing of assets), with the object of reducing inequality in the distribution of wealth. Such a tax carries economic dangers, which must have been pointed out to ministers by Treasury officials, which were apparent from the evidence submitted to the Select Committee and which gained force from the state of the economy.

The combined rate of income tax and wealth tax can be measured by converting a wealth tax into an income tax equivalent. Thus a 5 per cent wealth tax is equivalent to 100 per cent income tax on wealth yielding 5 per cent, to a 50 per cent income tax on wealth yielding 10 per cent, and to a 25 per cent income tax on wealth yielding 20 per cent. If a taxpayer's marginal rate of income tax and wealth tax combined is in excess of 100 per cent, then his only advantage in trying to save (i.e. reducing his consumption) is to slow down the rate at which his wealth diminishes. With a combined marginal rate over 100 per cent no income benefit can be derived from saving and to most people it must seem futile. Not only does such a tax situation carry a big disincentive to save, it also carries a strong incentive to dissave. In other words such a tax is a very positive encouragement to the rich to go on a spending spree, since the expenditure would be almost wholly at the expense of the revenue authorities. Additionally, a tax of this kind must be a strong incentive for the rich to emigrate if they can get their wealth out with them; and not only the rich, but also those who see themselves becoming rich in the future as a result of inheritance, saving or enterprise. Thus a heavy wealth tax unaccompanied by reductions in income tax gives a strong incentive to avoidance by emigration.

The effects of such a wealth tax on the private business could also be considerable. A public company with readily marketable shares suffers little or no economic disadvantage as a result of a wealth tax levied on individual shareholdings. But where a business is owned by a single proprietor, by a group of partners, or closely held in a private company, then a wealth tax could have serious consequences for the growth and continuance of the business. The position in agriculture is similar, but accentuated because of the very low yield on agricultural property. Whilst a wealth tax may aid agriculture in the long run by bringing down the value of agricultural land, at best the industry would face a difficult transition period and debilitating uncertainty; at worst its efficiency would be seriously impaired carrying the danger of farm fragmentation reducing the efficiency of the agricultural unit.

Clearly the significance of these consequences depends on the precise rate structure, but in some measure they would result from any wealth tax unaccompanied by reductions in income tax and even a substitutive tax carries some dangers to the growing points of industry. It is a characteristic of a wealth tax that tax is paid whether the taxable assets yield income or not. Thus a new business, which has not yet had time to become profitable would be hit by a wealth tax even though it paid no income tax; similarly an old established business going through a bad patch arising, say, as a result of a loss of markets from no fault of its own, would find problems of readjustment made more difficult because of the continuing liability to wealth tax.

A wealth tax of the additive variety would almost certainly have an unfavourable effect on business confidence and, in general, an unfavourable effect on investment in privately owned businesses, including agriculture. It is in this respect that the economic circumstances of the British economy in the mid-1970s are so relevant, for a time of high unemployment and low investment could scarcely be considered opportune for the introduction of a new tax on wealth. The state of Britain's economy in the 1970s is relevant in another way also. A high rate of inflation is unfavourable to the introduction of a wealth tax. Inflation accentuates valuation problems, upsets the relationship between values of different forms of wealth, makes it more difficult to design a meaningful rate structure for a wealth tax (which should take account of prevailing rates of return) and brings the threat of rapidly reducing thresholds and increasing tax rates in real terms. A period of high and fluctuating rates of inflation is an inappropriate time to introduce a wealth tax intended to be a stable and permanent feature of the tax system.

These economic dangers of a wealth tax must have given Labour Ministers cause to pause.

## Administrative constraints

The economic objections apply mainly (though not solely) to an additive wealth tax aimed at reducing inequality. The administrative difficulties, on the other hand, apply particularly to a wealth tax aimed at horizontal equity. Horizontal equity is concerned with the taxation of those advantages of wealth which generate additional taxable capacity. These advantages are conferred by wealth as such and are not dependent on its being held in large amounts. As we have seen, the logic of the horizontal equity argument is a threshold sufficiently low to replace the investment income surcharge.

Whilst the argument for a wealth tax on these grounds did not appear in official Labour Party policy documents, it is none the less clearly set out in Mr Denis Healey's foreword to the green paper. He wrote: 'Income by itself is not an adequate measure of taxable capacity. The ownership of wealth, whether it produces income or not, adds to the economic resources of a tax payer so that the person who has wealth as well as income of a given size necessarily has a greater taxable capacity than one who has only income of that size.' The green paper, in fact, recognises the logic of this horizontal equity argument; in paragraph 30, it refers to the wealth taxes on the continent, characterised by low thresholds, points out that the continental countries had generally introduced their wealth taxes at about the same time and for much the same reasons as the United Kingdom had introduced its differentiation between income from property and income from earnings; and continues: 'One logical possibility would therefore be to substitute for the investment income surcharge a wealth tax with a low threshold; but the administrative difficulties, both for tax payers and the Inland Revenue ruled this out in the foreseeable future. It will therefore be necessary to retain the surcharge as a means of collecting tax . . . from those with moderate amounts of wealth.'

But if fairness between taxpayers at higher levels of wealth requires the replacement of investment income surcharge by a wealth tax, should such fair treatment be denied at lower levels of wealth holding? The main reports of the Select Committee recognised the illogicality of the government's position and urged it to bring down the wealth tax threshold from that proposed in the green paper to make possible the elimination of the investment income surcharge as soon as possible. However, 'as soon as possible', in the view of the Inland Revenue meant a very long time indeed and, they suggested in evidence to the Select Committee, involved a very substantial increase in operating costs. The Inland Revenue arguments do not carry complete conviction. Why can continental countries manage low thresholds for wealth tax and not the UK? Partly the answer lies in the administrative structure proposed for the UK wealth tax which is quite different from that of continental wealth taxes. Whereas they are closely geared to income tax, in the UK it was proposed that the wealth tax should be administered from regional offices and be linked not with income tax but with wealth transfer taxes.

The main Inland Revenue objection to a lower threshold was the additional costs of valuation which they felt would be incurred. Since then the Layfield Report has proposed that domestic house property should be valued for local tax purposes on a capital rather than an annual basis – a recommendation accepted by the government. The application of this proposal would fundamentally ease the valuation problem for smaller wealth holdings, for the value of private housing is currently over 40 per cent of total personal wealth and represents a much larger proportion of the wealth of small and medium sized wealth holders. To use the same valuation procedure for both local taxation and an annual wealth tax would enormously simplify the administrative problem and reduce the costs of a lower wealth tax threshold. However, it must be recognised that a capital valuation of domestic property would take a number of years to complete. Thus, administrative constraints put a limit to the speed of introduction of a consistent wealth tax seeking to promote horizontal equity.

The wealth tax debate, as conducted through the Select Committee, revealed one other serious administrative difficulty about the introduction of a wealth tax aiming at horizontal equity. The green paper had proposed to omit the value of accumulated pension rights from the wealth tax base. But, as the Select Committee pointed out, such an omission would create considerable injustice as between persons. As an extreme example consider the civil servant, with a non-contributory inflation-proofed pension and the businessman who put his savings into his business and relied for retirement income on selling the business and buying securities. If pension rights were excluded then the civil servant would pay tax neither on the accumulating pension funds during his working life nor on any capital sum from which his pension was derived in retirement. Conversely, the businessman would be paying wealth tax on the savings put back into the business and on the securities from which his retirement income came. Yet to tax the value of pension rights could also create inequities. Such rights are not realisable or transferable like most other assets and, indeed, the civil servant who died before retirement would derive little or no benefit from them. It is possible to estimate values for pension rights which recognise their particular characteristics; but such valuations are necessarily somewhat arbitrary; it is clear that the capacity of a wealth tax for achieving horizontal equity is at best imperfect.

A further administrative consideration emerged from the work of the Select Committee. Whatever the form of wealth tax adopted, the method of administration proposed by the Inland Revenue would carry a high cost in relation to yield, even apart from the compliance costs imposed on the tax payer. High administrative costs are not a recommendation for a tax at any time. In a period of widespread concern about the growth of the Civil Service they are even less attractive.

## Failings in Labour Party policy-making

Analysis of the wealth tax saga raises many issues about the processes of policy-making in the Labour Party. Many democrats will be concerned at what they see as the excessive power of the TUC in extorting from the government the joint working party to implement a wealth tax and flouting, in the process, the work and views of the Select Committee of the House of Commons. Others, reading between the lines, will not find it difficult to discern in the vacillations over a wealth tax the perennial conflicts between the Left and Right of the Party. But the features most relevant to the question why a wealth tax has not been implemented are probably three, all interconnected: lack of research and preparation; apathy amongst many Labour MPs; and, above all, the failure of the Party to develop a coherent philosophy on the distribution of wealth.

The kind of statement in Labour policy documents, like that quoted above from *Labour's Economic Strategy*, which proposed a wealth tax with top marginal rates of 5 per cent, and stated that 'a tax of this kind' was levied in a large number of European countries and 'should present little difficulty here' was fundamentally misleading. The generous interpretation must be that the assertions were made from ignorance, both of the details of wealth and income taxes abroad and the difficulties of introducing such a tax here. The wealth taxes abroad are predominantly for purposes of horizontal equity, taking the place of our investment income surcharge and intended to be paid from income. None of the European countries has a marginal rate of wealth tax more than half that proposed in the Labour Party document and in about half the European countries wealth taxes are proportional at rates under 1 per cent. In addition, apart from the investment income surcharge, the top rates of income tax in such countries are generally lower, often much lower, than in the United Kingdom; whilst those countries with the highest wealth tax and income tax rates limit by ceiling provisions the proportion of income that can be taken in wealth tax and income tax combined. There are other relevant differences, notably on thresholds. The kind of wealth tax proposed in the Labour Party document may or may not be desirable, but it is a very different animal from continental wealth taxes. As to the problems of introduction and operation, we have already touched on some of them. The lack of research and lack of preparation by the Party are likewise revealed by the vagueness of the green paper; although the Labour Party had been publicly advocating a wealth tax for something like ten years, when it came to implementing it they apparently had very little idea of what they wanted or what the implications might be.

In a number of ways the Labour Party showed a lack of interest in the Select Committee on wealth tax which is in marked contrast to that of the Conservatives. The initial membership of the Select Committee appears to have been chosen with less care on the Labour than on the Conservative side, where it is clear to see that members with special and relevant interests had been chosen (Sandford and Robinson, 1975). It is possibly a reflection of this casualness of choice that there was more turnover of Labour members during the life of the Committee than of Conservatives. An analysis of the meetings of the Committee shows that the attendance of Conservatives in the public sessions was very much higher than that of Labour members, the Conservative members averaging 78 per cent to Labour's 57 per cent. As to participation, measured by the number of questions asked per member in evidence sessions, apart from the chairman, who was a Labour member, the participation rate of Conservative MPs was 10.3 as against 2.8 on the Labour side. It should be remembered, also, that the failure to obtain a majority report probably resulted from the absence of two Labour members abroad at a conference at the vital time. It is a characteristic of the Select Committee that they often tend to include more able and active members of the Opposition than of the government side because one expects the best MPs of the ruling party to be members of the government. But this can hardly account for, or justify, the poor showing of Labour MPs. On the two Select Committees on taxation during the life of the Conservative government, i.e. corporation tax and tax credit, the Conservative members managed an attendance which was in fact somewhat higher than that of the Labour Opposition and the participation rates, taking the two committees together, were much the same for both Parties.

The reaction of Labour MPs to a wealth tax is perhaps an accurate reflection of public attitudes, or more specifically, of the attitude of Labour Party supporters. A recent survey of 400 electors, drawn equally from the constituencies of Hayes and Harlington and of Bath, showed less than 30 per cent who thought a wealth tax a good idea; perhaps more significantly, as these two constituencies may not be a typical cross section of the electorate, of the 126 self-acknowledged Labour supporters in the two constituencies together, only 37 per cent thought a wealth tax a good idea (Sandford, Lewis and Fleming, 1978).

The fundamental flaw in the Labour Party policy-making is the absence of a clear and coherent philosophy on the distribution of wealth. Even within the field of taxation (and that is by no means the whole relevant area of policy) there are a number of different ways of reducing inequality of wealth; but the appropriate tax package depends very much on defining the objectives clearly. This requires answers to a number of questions of which the most crucial are probably the following: how far should tax be related to the source of the wealth? How far to its use? Which forms of tax are the most effective for reducing inequality? What kind of society do we seek? How important is speed of attainment? What economic price is it reasonable to pay to promote equality? Who are 'the rich'? There is no evidence that the Labour Party has asked most of these vital questions, let alone furnished itself with satisfactory answers.

It is not possible in the short space of a chapter to do full justice to all these issues nor to consider all the possible tax packages; but we can say something on each question and thus give some idea of its relevance.

The characteristic of an annual wealth tax is that it taxes wealth irrespective of how it is acquired and irrespective of how it is used. Thus, under a wealth tax, wealth acquired by hard work and enterprise is taxed equally with wealth acquired by inheritance or winning the football pools; many people would consider such lack of discrimination both unfair and unwise. Similarly it can be held that wealth used in certain ways, for example, in the maintenance of an historic home open to the public, or in the form of productive assets in the hands of a frugal owner-occupier in agriculture, should be treated differently from wealth in the hands of the playboy. If these distinctions are considered important, then the emphasis of the tax package should be discriminating. Thus a combination of inheritance tax, capital gains tax extended to include gambling winnings and an expenditure tax to catch the playboy's extravagance might better accord with many people's ideas of a sensible and fair policy to reduce inequalities than a heavy wealth tax; this would not exclude the possibility of a wealth tax, but one which was aimed primarily at horizontal equity.

The particular form of reform of death duty rushed into law in the first year of the Labour government illustrates the same lack of philosophy and bears on two of the questions. The capital transfer tax, by closing the gifts loophole and by levying a periodic charge on trusts is, in principle, a more effective way of reducing the concentration of wealth in the hands of the rich than the old estate duty. But, although it seems to have been briefly considered in a private working party of the Labour Party, no public discussion was sought by the Party on the respective merits of a capital transfer tax and an accessions tax, i.e. a tax in which the rate is determined by the receipts of the donee and heir rather than by the total gifts and estate of the donor. These taxes differ in several important respects. Many observers consider an accessions tax is in principle fairer than a capital transfer tax: because it taxes in relation to the amount received by beneficiaries, because it is easier under an accessions tax to take account of the circumstances of the heir (e.g. to give a special threshold or concessionary rate to the minor or disabled child of a deceased parent) and because it bears less heavily on large families than an equivalent capital transfer tax. But, most relevant here, it is also likely to be more effective in reducing inequality of wealth. It is large receipts not large estates (or a large aggregate of gifts) that *perpetuate* inequality and an accessions tax strikes at the heart of the matter by taxing in relation to the cumulative amount received by inheritance and gift from whatever source. An accessions tax also provides a positive incentive to the wealthy to disperse their wealth by gift or at death to those who have received little by way of gifts and inheritances, for by so doing their tax bill is reduced (Sandford, Willis and Ironside, 1973, especially chapter 17).

This feature of an accessions tax highlights another philosophical difference between a capital transfer tax and an accessions tax. Capital transfer tax reduces inequality in one way only – by reducing the wealth of the rich and transferring it to the state sector. An accessions tax works partly in this way, but also it promotes a transfer of wealth within the private sector. For those who seek state socialism the capital transfer tax is the more appropriate weapon. For those who wish to see a reduction of inequality within the private sector of a mixed economy, the accessions tax is the more suitable.

Consider the question of speed and economic cost. Broadly speaking, a death duty is a way of taxing wealth heavily which minimises the economic cost: whilst there may be some detrimental effects on some private businesses and possibly some disincentive to save as a result of heavy death duties, unlike an annual wealth tax death duties do not prevent the building up of a flourishing business, nor affect the incentive to save other than for the motive to bequeath. The most successful businesses can, indeed, be expected to 'go public' within the creator's lifetime or, at least, be capable of so doing at his death. Moreover there is nothing in the process of inheritance *per se* which ensures that the heir of a successful businessman is a suitable (let alone the most suitable) person to carry on the business. Perhaps the essential point about a death duty is that it is levied at a time when the former owner has to part with the wealth anyway. Especially as inheritance is probably the most powerful force making for inequality in the distribution of wealth and is likewise a way of acquiring wealth which is generally unrelated to the merits or efforts of the recipients, there seems much to be said for making a wealth transfer tax the dominant instrument in a policy to reduce inequality of wealth. However, death duties have one drawback from the viewpoint of the egalitarian. They only apply to any particular property, on average, once in a generation. Some might therefore feel that death duties are too slow a way of reducing inequality of wealth.

A heavy annual wealth tax would speed up the process – but it would also carry very serious economic disadvantages such as those already outlined above. To the author the cost outweighs the gain. Whilst a society with a much less unequal distribution of wealth would probably have few economic disadvantages and some advantages compared with the present UK society, the process of getting there could be enormously damaging. If speed of attainment is held to be supremely important, then there is a case for considering a capital levy – a short sharp move rather than the continuing adverse effects of an annual wealth tax. To say this is not to advocate such a drastic remedy, but it might prove less damaging in the long run than continued heavy annual taxation of capital.

Finally the question, what is the target? Who are the rich? All the emphasis of the government seems to be on taxing those with wealth above £100,000. The proposed wealth tax threshold in the green paper, and mentioned in the October 1974 manifesto, was £100,000. This is the form of wealth tax on which the TUC/Labour Party Liaison Committee has agreed. Similarly, the most recent modifications to the capital transfer tax, which have raised the threshold to £25,000, mean that over a ten-year period something like £100,000 can be passed on by a married couple to one member of the next generation without any tax being paid. Because transfers are free between husband and wife it is possible, at death or even by gift, for each of the married couple to pass £25,000 to the same child without tax. If over the previous ten years they each use the annual £2,000 exemption for the same purpose, then £40,000 can be passed over in this way, quite apart from the use of the £100 gift exemption, the exemption for gifts from normal expenditure and the special relief on marriage gifts. The figures on the distribution of wealth show that anyone with £100,000 is well into the top 1 per cent of wealth holders. (For example the Royal Commission has reported that all persons in the top 1 per cent of the distribution possessed wealth valued at £46,000 or more (Royal Commission, 1975, p. 68). The figures relate to 1975 and refer to the total population of the United Kingdom. The series assumes that those people not figuring in the Inland Revenue figures have no wealth.) Is no one below that to be regarded as rich? There is indeed some evidence to suggest that this is the wrong target. It is clear from the statistics of the Royal Commission that there has been a substantial decline in the proportion of wealth possessed by the very top wealth holders throughout this century and in the past decade or so; but there is much more doubt about how far the wealth of the top 20 or 50 per cent has declined. The capital transfer tax could prove to be more subject to avoidance than estate duty (if in different ways) and fail to hit the right target.

## Conclusion

It may be argued that it is unreasonable to expect any party to undertake the detailed thinking and research necessary to answer the sort of questions outlined above. But surely on such a matter it should have a philosophy? And if the Labour Party itself had not the resources to embark on an analysis of the effectiveness of alternative ways of reducing inequality, one would have at least expected that when the Party assumed government it might have asked the civil servants to conduct such an inquiry. It is clear it did not do so. When the Select Committee on Wealth Tax was taking evidence from members of the Board of Inland Revenue Mr John Pardoe MP, having indicated some of the possible alternative ways of reducing inequality, put the question to Mr W. H. B. Johnson: 'Have the Board of Inland Revenue ever done a study to show which of these methods would achieve the fairer distribution of wealth that is apparently desired?' Reply: 'Not a study in that sense. These are questions that are always under examination, of course. You cannot study the effects of a particular tax until you have it.' Mr Pardoe repeated the question with a particular reference to the alternative effects of a donor and a donee based tax and put the specific question 'Have you actually been asked for this study?' Answer: 'Not a formal study, no.'

It is indeed typical of the Party's haphazard and topsy-turvy approach that it committed itself to a capital transfer tax and a wealth tax before, as a government, it set up the Royal Commission to find out the facts on the distribution of income and wealth; and that it determined the wealth tax threshold before receiving the first report from the Commission.

To those, like the author, who wish to see inequality of wealth in the United Kingdom reduced (albeit gradually) the Labour Party and government are a profound disappointment. The Party has always proclaimed its concern for equality. Yet it has evolved neither philosophy nor strategy to reduce inequality and some of its proposals are positively misguided. Wilsonian ad hocery is just not good enough.

7

# Family and kinship in Eaton Square

Ceri Thomas

If there was ever any substance to the claim that governments have 'soaked the rich' with their taxation policies, there is infinitely more truth in the view that social research has soaked the poor. In reviewing the work that has been carried out on the rich we shall demonstrate that, with a handful of exceptions, academics have totally ignored the affluent end of the social spectrum and concentrated for a variety of reasons on the poor. The benign neglect with which the rich have been treated is seen not only as a remarkable oversight of what is in any case a tantalisingly interesting subject, but, more damningly, is an acid test of the ideology of our social science.

By looking afresh (bearing the rich very much in mind) at orthodox explanations and descriptions of, for example, family and kinship patterns which have been held to be particular to the poor, this chapter will cast serious doubts as to the continued relevance of these orthodoxies as well as scrutinising the paths taken by social scientists to arrive at their conclusions. Perhaps most of all this chapter is a plea for a sustained effort to produce a sociology of the rich and by looking at one small area of London we suggest the ground is fertile for research and that even the briefest glance at the cycle of affluence implied there is more than sufficient to tell us that the rich are indeed a suitable case for treatment.

## The poorer brethren

Before turning to our 'target group' however let us remind ourselves of some of the mainstream post-war studies of working-class communities and, having been transformed by the rediscovery of poverty in the mid 1960s, the new forms which this work adopted in the poverty industry.

Twenty-five years ago Michael Young and Peter Willmott embarked on a study of the social fabric of Bethnal Green which came to be regarded as the grandfather of them all – *Family and Kinship in East London* (Young and Willmott, 1957). It followed in the traditions of the school of community studies which, with the help of Conrad Arensberg and Solon T. Kimball (Arensburg and Kimball, 1940), Alwyn Rees (Rees, 1950) and the like, had already traced the inner workings of communities in rural Britain. Young and Willmott, however, perhaps for the first time, succeeded in conveying the concept of an urban village as a place where town dwellers lived and died in the same comforting intimacy which hitherto had been the preserve of the pastoral idyll. But the authors saw the basic unit of this fabric, the institution of the family, being threatened by an aspect of social policy, the institution of the housing estate:

> This book is about the effects of one of the newest [institutions] upon one of the oldest of our social institutions. The new is the housing estate, hundreds of which have been built since the war. . . . The old institution is the family. It has been official policy to move people out of the cities, and we felt it would help in the assessment of this policy if more were known about its effects upon family life (Young and Willmott, 1962, p. 11).

The scenario of the post-war rehousing schemes in outer boroughs of London and the parallel development of new towns need not concern us here. What is of interest is the fundamental purpose of the work; in addition to describing or modelling working-class urban communities it sought further to evaluate policy and indeed highlight the degree to which the family (institution) was being threatened by the housing estate (policy). There would seem here to be a direct parallel with the alleged threat to the rich (institution) from a whole battery of policies. The media regularly report the break-up of family estates in the struggle to pay death duties, the stately home thrown open to the public to pay the repair bills, and the mass emigration of our most qualified and talented 'professionals', managers and custodians of the City to escape the apparently intolerable burden of taxation and pay restraint. From time to time studies of the pay and attitudes of Britain's top paid have been carried out, and their findings do not support those rather crude assertions. For example, Chris Pond has already quoted in Chapter 3 the recent survey by Political and Economic Planning (PEP) of members of the British Institute of Management which found that over half of the respondents were fairly or very well satisfied with their levels of earnings, and the level of earnings in this country compared to those in some other countries was given as a cause of dissatisfaction by only 4 per cent of the respondents. *The Times* (20 February 1978) interpreted the report to say that 'Anxieties are indeed present but apparently not to anything like the extent which is sometimes suggested.' The position of wealth holders, however, remains a mystery. We are told that the wealthy as a group are at least under great stress (or have disappeared from Britain altogether).

If this is true then it follows that the institutions which tend to govern the lives of the wealthy must themselves be under attack and in a state of transformation, which is itself a justification for academic interest; if the proposition is false then social science has a duty to expose and reject the fallacies. Furthermore the likely appearance of a wealth tax in the next Labour Party election manifesto gives the wealthy an added priority in the bidding for research resources. In effect we know almost nothing about the family and kinship patterns of Britain's ruling class, we can know even less about the effects of a wealth tax – it could be construed as sheer callousness to allow this stage of ignorance to prevail.

## *Local networks*

Returning to the side of the social coin for which there is an accepted body of knowledge let us look again at the family and kinship of the working classes. An important component of such studies has been that they are 'locality based' – indeed the names of the places where the communities were examined are almost synonymous with the studies themselves: Young and Willmott's Bethnal Green, Rowntree's York and Coates and Silburn's St Ann's, Nottingham. The small volume of work which has been undertaken on élites has tended to ignore this component and it is an oversight which we will emphasise in our own brief examination later in this chapter. To those of us educated to think of the rich, or certainly professional classes, as originating from, and operating within, a large scale and non-continuous geographical area (i.e. the jet set) this emphasis may seem very strange. Locality based studies have tended to represent the patterns of the working classes more clearly than for any other groups. Elizabeth Bott noted this in 1957.

> It is only in the working class that one is likely to find a combination of factors all operating together to produce a high degree of connectedness: concentration of people of the same or similar occupations in the same local area, jobs and homes in the same local area, low population turnover and continuity of relationships, at least occasional opportunities for relatives and friends to help one another to get jobs; little demand for physical mobility, little opportunity for social mobility.

In contrast Bott points to the 'non-place' nature of the professions.

> Homogeneous local areas of a single profession are very rare; a man's place of work and his home are usually in different local areas; professional training leads him to make relationships with people who do not know his family, school friends and neighbours; in most cases getting a job depends on skill and training rather than on the influence of friends and relatives; many professional careers require physical mobility. Almost the only factor associated with high class status that tends to increase connectedness is ownership of shares in common enterprises by relatives – and this is less likely to occur among professional people than among wealthy industrialists and commercial families (Bott, 1957, pp. 112–13).

Similarly Young and Willmott discovered the effects of the working-class family in the housing market and were particularly concerned with the ability of kith and kin, especially mothers, in helping to procure homes for young couples. They stressed that where property was rented privately the relationship between the mother and the rent collector was crucial in determining whether a young couple would find a home nearby. A housing society official was quoted as saying 'We prefer sons and daughters. They know all the rules through having lived there. They know what has to be done. You don't get no trouble with them' (Young and Willmott, 1962, p. 40). The onward march of the council house sector however was beginning to threaten such cosy arrangements which at county hall were to be branded as 'nepotism'.

The idea of tight networks of family and relatives operating to improve or preserve the welfare of individuals is, however, not particular to manual groups only. In any case as John Westergaard and Henrietta Resler in their comprehensive attack on such orthodoxy noted in relation to the manual working class 'such ties are rather ineffective buttresses against insecurity' (Westergaard and Resler, 1976, p. 377). Furthermore these writers, in contradiction of their predecessors, point out that family ties operate more and more potently 'the higher up the scale of privilege one goes, though they take a different form from the characteristic of the manual working class' (ibid., p. 378). Children benefit from inheritance of wealth, parental influence on their future, from marriage settlements, covenanted gifts (to avoid tax) and loans and gifts (to avoid death duties). Wealthy families rely on professional agents such as family solicitors and accountants and may express themselves financially through family trusts for example. 'An intricate network of ties by blood relationship and marriage within and between the élites of business, conservative politics, senior civil service, and high professions strengthens the unity conferred by common wealth and power' (ibid., p. 376).

Unfortunately, however, there has been little in the way of empirical confirmation of these characteristics of the rich. Two publications in particular have pulled together the rare strands of our knowledge from the past twenty years of work (Stanworth and Giddens (eds), 1974 and Urry and Wakeford (eds), 1973). Richard Whitley's contribution made use of elementary network analysis to measure the degree of connectedness of the directors of our largest companies. Its fundamental purpose was to examine the proposition that these individuals constitute an 'élite' through manifesting a high degree of cohesion and showing a common culture. In an earlier paper (Whitley, 1973) Whitley had shown a culture to exist among the directors of twenty-seven large financial institutions. His results showed that while the educational background of the industrialists was less restricted than that of the financiers 'they are still predominantly based on wealth and a substantial number enjoy membership of an exclusive social institution, prestigious London clubs' (Whitley, 1974). He also reaffirmed the conclusions of Michael Barratt Brown who stressed the important focal position of merchant bankers and the role of interlocking directorships among merchant banks, commercial banks, trusts, insurance companies, and domestic and overseas industrial companies in knitting the fabric of power together (Brown, 1973). Yet such studies are very rare and, as we demonstrate later, it is an elementary exercise to uncover contemporary evidence of these networks – in fact with the added component of locality or proximity.

### *The poverty industry – the dangers of overkill*

In seeking answers to our questions about poverty we have all too often searched only in the places where poverty comes to the surface. This tendency combined with our dodging of the issue of where poverty is created has inadvertently lent credibility to the notion that the causes of poverty lie with the characteristics of its victims. As a society we seem to require a constant reminder of Tawney's observation 'The problem of poverty is not a problem of individual character but a problem of economic and industrial organisation. It has to be studied at its source and only secondly in its manifestations' (Tawney, 1913).

But unfortunately structural explanations of poverty are far more intangible and much less sensational or newsworthy than the symptoms of poverty which are regularly exposed in newspapers and television reports. Why do the features of inequality prove so elusive? Certainly inequality is stoutly defended on many sides to the point where Tawney suggested it had been elevated to the level of a religion, but he offered hope to all those concerned with its devaluation.

> It may well be the case that capricious inequalities are in some measure inevitable, in the sense that, like crime and disease, they are a malady which the most vigorous precautions cannot wholly overcome. But when crime is known as crime, and disease as disease, the ravages of both are circumscribed by the mere fact that they are recognised for what they are and described by their proper names, not by flattering euphemisms. And a society which is convinced that inequality is an evil need not be alarmed because the evil is one which cannot wholly be subdued. In recognising the poison it will have armed itself with an antidote. It will have deprived inequality of its sting by stripping it of its esteem (Tawney, 1964 p. 56).

How much has this esteem remained intact or been stripped? Even given the motivation the examination of inequality of property ownership and income distribution in Britain is a hazardous affair.

In an introduction to a mammoth text on America's wealth – *The Rich and the Super Rich* – Peter Wilsher suggests that the American author in reviewing British sources of data might be forgiven for suspecting 'a deliberate intent to confuse and obscure' (Lundberg, 1968, p. 2). Indeed he stresses that the absence of a wealth tax itself shrouds the question of 'who owns what' in mystery, simply by ensuring that no regular survey of assets can thereby be produced.

The poverty industry for its part has tended to steer well clear of scrutinising the processes which create inequality and has for this very reason been frequently surprised when liberal policies have failed to result in radical improvements. Roger Lee criticised the naïveté of those who were disappointed by the Community Development Projects' modest achievements. If poverty were diagnosed as part of the normal structures of British capitalism by the researchers themselves, how could they expect to abolish poverty 'when the removal of the normal structures has been ruled out' (Lee, 1976, pp. 11-14)?

Another radical geographer, David Harvey, has pointed out 'If we "urban renew" we merely move the poverty around; if we don't, we merely sit by and watch decay' (Harvey, 1975, p. 143). It was perhaps the misconception that poverty was an entity in itself combined with frustration that renewal policies so consistently failed, that eventually led to the popularity of 'benign neglect' in America. Harvey warned of the excesses of sociological inquiry by those whose hearts are doubtless well positioned but whose sympathy makes them blind to the causes of grievance and to their possible remedies.

> In fact, mapping even more evidence of man's patent inhumanity to man is counter-revolutionary in the sense that it allows the bleeding-heart liberal in us to pretend we are contributing to a solution when in fact we are not. This kind of empiricism is irrelevant. . . . Our task does not lie there. Nor does it lie in what can only be termed 'moral masturbation' of the sort which accompanies the masochistic assemblage of some huge dossier on the daily injustices to the populace of the ghetto, over which we beat our breasts and commiserate with each other before retiring to our fireside comforts. This too is counter-revolutionary for it merely serves to expiate guilt without our ever being forced to face the fundamental issues, let alone do anything about them. Nor is it a solution to indulge in that emotional tourism which attracts us to live and work with the poor 'for a while' in the hope that we can really help them improve their lot. This, too, is counter-revolutionary – so what if we help a community with a playground in one summer of work to find that the school deteriorates in the fall? These are the paths we should *not* take. They merely serve to divert us from the essential task at hand (ibid., p. 145).

There are, however, pitfalls to this line of argument if the genuine exploration of the processes of inequality and the examination of the institutions which maintain and generate these processes is ignored in favour of a preoccupation with 'simplistic manifestations of class conflict' (Harrop and Kirby, 1975, p. 24).

### *The easy option?*

Perhaps at this point we should consider the attractions inherent in poverty and the poor as subjects for social research; these considerations may go some way at least in explaining how the imbalance has occurred. It is convenient to divide our attention towards the characteristics of, first, the researchers, which involves the researcher's perception of the target group and, second, the grant-giving bodies.

The researchers as individuals tend to have a radical rather than conservative viewpoint for various reasons. Typically they are aware or adopt the view that the images of society portrayed by television, radio, drama, films, novels and newspapers are focused more often than not through ruling class or wealthy lenses. With this in mind it is up to the individual researcher to positively discriminate in favour of the poor and ensure that any alternative views of the world are reported. Perhaps a classic example of this positive discrimination was the collection of essays, *Working Class Images of Society* (Bulmer (ed.), 1975). It could be argued for instance that ruling-class images of society would be redundant because of course the ruling class has created society in its own image. The bases for this outlook may be found deep in the sociological literature stemming both from Marx (alienation) and Durkheim (anomie) and may be followed through the literature in the 'rediscovery of kinship' in working-class communities and the intrinsically parochial outlooks of such communities as revealed by Bott and others and finally to Runciman's development of reference group notions to explain the acquiescence of the poor in the face of stark inequality (Runciman, 1966).

Having made an initial decision to concentrate on the poor there is a vast array of more pragmatic considerations to maintain the researcher on this course. It is no secret that in terms of the collection of primary data through questionnaires and doorstep or fireside interviews the working-class respondent is in the main infinitely preferable to the wealthy. He will, for example, be more accessible, both by being at home more often and unprotected by screening devices such as butlers, maids, personal secretaries, appointment systems and so on. Having been contacted, the respondent will be more passive during the interview than his wealthy counterpart, who may be aggressive towards the researcher or his quesitons or the 'intrusion of personal privacy' itself. The poorer respondent will by this time in his life be accustomed to being on the receiving end of interviews – for jobs, houses, flats, supplementary benefit, exceptional needs payments and so on and therefore not object to 'just one more questionnaire' which may in any case be a welcome relief to the isolation or loneliness of perhaps a pensioner living alone. In contrast the affluent respondent has a busy timetable; as we know from NHS waiting rooms or DHSS offices, the time of the poor person is treated as infinitely less valuable than the time of a rich person. Having himself interviewed applicants for jobs or contracts, the affluent person will be more assertive and likely to beat the interviewer at his own game. More important he is more likely to assert his position and refuse to answer certain questions or terminate the interview altogether. (Empirical documentation of this is hindered, of course, by the impossibility of classifying the refusals in questionnaire surveys.)

A crucial advantage which the poor person has over the rich is that he will in fact have less to disclose, particularly if questions about ownership are being posed. A question relating to the tenure of houses, for example, will cause no embarrassment to a family in a council house who most often live in one house only, but in contrast could cause embarrassment to the wealthy who own several. Bound up with this is the problem of accuracy; it is, for example, with a much higher degree of certainty that one derives the income of an individual on supplementary pension than the family with a combination of earned and unearned income – even if the respondents are equally willing to divulge the information, which is unlikely.

At the end of the day a researcher often has the onerous task of attempting to codify respondents, and given a pyramidal structure of society with many similar people at the bottom and few at the top it is no surprise that coding poor people is considerably easier than coding a rich person whose circumstances are more likely to be financially eccentric. Given the information that the only wage-earner in the household is a local authority manual worker it is no great effort to verify an earnings figure from secondary sources such as a summary of wage rates (*Time Rates of Wages and Hours of Work* – Department of Employment, HMSO) alongside an earnings survey (*New Earnings Survey*, Department of Employment, HMSO) – the margin of error is tiny. One may compare this with the problem of estimating a figure for the highest paid. 'For example, the £122.70 a week – £6,380 p.a. – average total earnings which the NES gives for the top managers of trading organisations does not exactly tally with the £14,299 and £11,509 p.a. average salaries for respectively, managing directors and general managers revealed by a recent survey of executive pay' (AIC/Inbucon, 1977). As the NES survey is based on PAYE numbers perhaps this tells us more about the basis on which top managers are paid than anything else. The complexity of the task for verifying *unearned* income does not bear thinking about for the average sociologist in the street.

Finally on the more pragmatic considerations, if numbers are important in arriving at a significantly large sample the resident on the densely populated council estate is far and away the more attractive proposition. Essentially when it comes to the wealthy the researcher is plagued with exactly the same occupational hazards as the dustman: long drives, gates to be opened and closed, dogs to be fended off and so on. Thus all other things being equal, which admittedly is unlikely in the extreme, the researcher at this low level of decision making is lured as if by sirens to diagnose the conditions of the poor – literally in their own backyard.

## The cupboard is bare

In the absence of an ability or desire to collect primary data we may seek published data on the extent of affluence, but indeed we shall be sadly disappointed. The TUC discovered this when submitting evidence to the Royal Commission on the Distribution of Income and Wealth – on the higher incomes from employment reference, indeed it spent 13 of its 49 paragraphs in describing the inadequacy of data and calling for the Commission to undertake new research of its own initiative. In particular the TUC called for 'detailed case studies of the circumstances of high income families' of the type so common among poverty studies. Furthermore they urged the Commission to examine 'the scale of self-employment incomes, fringe benefits, business expenses, consultancy fees, and share option schemes' in affecting the day-to-day lives of individuals or families. In underlining the inadequacy of published data on the rich the TUC also exposed how inaccessible the limited information is.

> A large proportion of the research into the top income earners is also restricted to private research and business consultancy organisations, and those who can afford to pay for such research. It is significant that the recent Child Poverty Action Group (sic) pamphlet on homeworkers costs 50p but the results of the British Institute of Management survey of executives pay costs £90 (Royal Commission, 1976d, p. 396).

Obviously such discrepancies in cost make the choice for the poverty stricken research student, embarking on a sociological line of inquiry, a fairly easy one.

What data are available are unfortunately the by-product of our system of taxation – the Inland Revenue Survey of Personal Incomes and the TUC considered that the size of the sample for incomes over £10,000 to be far too small at 375. The same problem also arises with the New Earnings Survey and ensures that the very wide dispersion in earnings known to exist at the top will produce meaningless average figures.

Since 1967 companies have been required to publish in their annual reports the salaries of their chairmen or their highest paid directors, but such a narrow requirement does not provide information for a sufficiently large number of directors for general statements to be made. Certainly we cannot deduce from the accounts the relative importance of such salaries compared to the unearned incomes and fringe benefits of those individuals. Even so it is interesting to note that Sir Frank McFadzean (Shell Transport and Trading) was the highest paid executive in 1975 at £91,842 (or £1,766 per week) (Labour Research, 1977a). Sir Kenneth Keith, a resident of Eaton Square, was shown to earn £62,000 in the year ending March 1976 as chairman of Hill Samuel. There were twenty five directors listed as receiving in excess of £50,000 per year. In addition of course are the fringe benefits and Labour Research again quoted the *Daily Telegraph* of 11 January 1974 on the subject of these perks.

> When it comes to number, standard and refinement of fringe benefits, few managements anywhere in the world can top the best of the carefully nurtured perk packages which somehow get overlooked when the British manager is comparing his lot (miserable, underpaid, misunderstood) with that of American, German, Italian, French and Japanese executives.

Certainly if our managers forget these perks there is little hope for the humble researcher in uncovering the facts and figures, perhaps even less for the Inland Revenue if it ever seriously tackled this important component of the make up of pay of our top paid.

## *Who pays the piper?*

Turning to the grant giving bodies the lack of current research on the wealthy is documented by SSRC's catalogue of research, only three projects in recent years even approached the subject.

1977 'Inheritance and the Creation of Personal Fortunes in Britain' (Professor C. D. Harbury) Grant 1974-7.
1977 'The Theory of Income Distribution' (Professor H. F. Lydall) Grant 1976-7.
1975 'The Distribution of Wealth in Britain' (Professor A. B. Atkinson) Grant 1971-4.

Certainly the contributions of these workers need no elucidation here, but it is only they, and perhaps one or two more, who have kept any broader views of the distribution of wealth afloat in recent years. This is of course in marked contrast to the amount spent on researching poverty. The third report of the DHSS/SSRC joint working party on Transmitted Deprivation (1977) which accounts for one small part of the SSRC's budget, lists twenty one major sub-contracts, six commissioned papers and four seminars along with regular workshops.

An additional source was provided each year by the Institute of Community Studies – *The Poverty Report* – and the 1976 version for example includes a brief resumé by Lucy Syson of research on poverty 'over the last five years or so' with a very useful reference list amounting to nearly seventy publications (Willmott, 1976). In contrast consider the problem which confronted John Urry and John Wakeford when in 1973 they published *Power in Britain* (Urry and Wakeford, 1973) which represented 'the most recent useful published material on the topic that we could discover.' It was with this criterion in mind that they included for example 'The Social Background and Connections of "Top Decisions Makers" ' by Tom Lupton and C. Shirley Wilson which was first published in 1959. Clearly the 'heady' days of the 1960s had left the weft and warp of our most notable family trees totally uncharted by social science.

But what are the attractions for grant giving bodies like the SSRC and DHSS in concentrating on poverty? Clearly in political terms it is currently adviseable to appear socially responsible in the research field with an in-built bias towards the problem-solving approach. This concern in combination with a larger scale policy of positive discrimination ensures that research monies are concentrated on the poor. Thus while many fieldworkers on projects like the Transmitted Deprivation Programme of the DHSS/SSRC may have their reservations about its ideology the message is fairly clear: study deprivation at the lowest or most reduced scale of analysis – the family – and study the worst first – the problem families. The SSRC/DHSS however seem particularly worried that the work will be misinterpreted: 'Although in broad terms the main emphasis in studying causal mechanisms has so far been upon what can be described as "familial influences" it should be recognised that the studies being supported are not exclusively concerned with familial processes. In virtually all of them, the researchers are examining the interrelationships between familial factors and social ones, such as occupational status and housing conditions. Thus the approach is less narrow than it might appear.' Nevertheless one gains the distinct impression that the fundamental reason for such intensive study of, in some cases, small numbers of families, is not just that they are poor families – but that they are 'problem' families – problems either for the social services departments, headmasters, housing departments or police authorities.

The 'problem' ideology has been implicit in terms of the positive discrimination approach to area research, although areas are usually euphemistically termed according to 'stress', 'priority' or 'action'. Following the recommendations of the Seebohm Report (Seebohm, 1968) the twelve experimental Community Development Projects were established in areas of special need. The aim was to help people to 'assume an increasing measure of control over their lives' to 'use constructively the services which exist' and 'to take some of the load off the statutory services' (Holman, 1970). It was a trio of geographers who expressed their dissatisfaction with such action/research projects in terms which the reader of this chapter may now find familiar. 'But our main reservation is that present methods of positive discrimination are insufficiently radical, since they fail to come to grips with the basic processes responsible for the manifestations of inequality *that we know exist*' (my emphasis) (Coates, Johnson and Knox, 1977, p. 236).

It is perhaps a truism that individuals and organisations tend to perceive problems as problems only in relation to their potential ability to solve or ameliorate them. Inherent in this perception process is the value statement dominant in the main research funding bodies, that the problem and cause of (and solution to) poverty all lie with the poor themselves. In addition the bodies are constrained in their policies by the knowledge that almost any other conclusion would meet head on with the interests of institutions where power in Britain is concentrated; thus research must always produce recommendations which are 'realistic', that is, acceptable and piecemeal. In fact simply by stating the level at which research is conducted – the individual and the family – the findings of the research are almost assured as being liberal rather than radical in tone. Having decided on the lowest level of analysis it is impractical to draw conclusions about higher order processes. Conclusions about 'problem families' will therefore logically (i.e. consistent in scale) say very little about the higher order societal and institutional processes, which determine the distribution of resources and which may determine that one particular family becomes 'a problem', or, in David Harvey's terms, 'The substantive interpretation of an element is not independent of the scale at which we envisage the system's operating' (Harvey, 1969, p. 452).

The relative importance of the attitudes of research workers on the one hand and research funders on the other in guaranteeing that the rich are, in effect, left in peace is more difficult to gauge, and we do not choose to surmise whether the problem is that of no one knocking at the door, or of the custodians within being deaf to the applications which are made.

Perhaps there is something intrinsic in the academic make up which demands an interest in 'how the other half live'. Given the status of prominent academics until recently, this has usually ensured an interest in the poor. But a fortuitous by-product of the self-proclaimed financial demise of such workers may indeed result in a diametric swing towards the rich as this predetermined target – it would be no bad thing.

### *Downward visibility*

The poverty industry is manned not solely by academics but by an assortment of journalists, lobbyists, and pressure group researchers and it is at them that Westergaard and Resler may have been directing their criticism of false diagnosis.

> The spurious equation that identifies characteristics of the poor with causes of poverty then leads to the conclusion that poverty is in large part the result of old age, physical and mental handicaps, high fertility, family dissolution and child bearing outside marriage. (Westergaard and Resler, 1976, pp. 123–4).

To these groups may be coupled the respective voluntary organisations whose primary purpose is to bring the problems of their clients to the public's notice, to act as advocate in the public arena and to bargain for resources to be devoted to their particular cause. It is this multiplicity of causes which unintentionally leads to the false diagnosis.

> Subsistence poverty is indeed common among old people, the sick, the handicapped, and so on, but only because the majority of the old, sick and handicapped have previously been dependent on jobs

> that provided them with few or no other resources to fall back on than meagre benefits from public funds. Rank and file wage earners – manual and routine non-manual – live with the risk of poverty over their heads. They face a likely prospect of poverty on retirement. And they face a threat of poverty even before that: on redundancy and if forced to work short-time, on transfer to low paid work in the later years of working life; in sickness, in widowhood, and through loss of subsidiary household earnings (Westergaard and Resler, 1976, pp. 124–5).

It is the false diagnosis of all these apparently discrete categories of poor as abnormal and separate from the mass of the wage-earning population that, in Westergaard's view, leads inevitably to false prescriptions. Typically these come in the form of doses of incomes and prices policies meted out by governments of both parties. Written prior to the last three years of pay restraint under the present Labour administration Westergaard's conclusions appear almost prophetic in hindsight.

In his *Relative Deprivation and Social Justice* W. G. Runciman reminds us of Durkheim's dictum that 'What is needed if social order is to reign is that the mass of men be content with their lot. But what is needed for them to be content, is not that they have more or less but that they be convinced that they have no right to more' (Gouldner (ed.), 1959, p. 200). Runciman suggested that we could expect a period of prosperity and economic change effectively to rock the boat 'by making people aware of the possibility of a higher standard than it would otherwise have occurred to them to hope for'. But he also noted what would happen during a period not unlike the past three years when real incomes have fallen; 'Conversely, a decline in prosperity, if not too violent, can restrict the sense of relative deprivation by inhibiting comparisons with more fortunate groups' (Runciman, 1966, p. 25). It is this likely response which has in some ways been exploited, for example in convincing the Labour Movement to look to the poor and low paid during a recession in attempts to secure periods of restaint in collective bargaining. W. W. Daniel in July 1975 produced a repeat of Runciman's study and uncovered similar patterns of reference group behaviour. He further discovered implicit support for a potential flat-rate pay policy provided that the flat amount was respectably large – with £6 generally considered to meet this demand (Daniel, 1975). As a study its significance to this discussion is that a proposed national scale pay policy was gauged for acceptibility via the reductionist (micro scale) device of a questionnaire of individuals, and the results were of some use in selling the policy despite the fact that the respondents could not have anticipated the operation of such a policy or the level of inflation which was to continue despite its eventual adoption. In short this sociological exercise succeeded in reinforcing a pattern of downward social comparisons which, as Runciman suggested above, would accompany a period of declining prosperity.

The media have certainly performed their role adequately in this respect by convincing large sections of wage-earners that the low paid have benefited from a policy that ostensibly favoured them – even though the policy itself was purely permissive and despite considerable evidence to the contrary. Similarly mass unemployment is portrayed by those with property to defend as the great leveller; the pseudo-logic being that true equality is reached after a series of inflationary wage claims which eventually finds the miner, the car assembler and the hospital porter alongside each other in the dole queue. The combined effects of pay restraint, mass unemployment and falling real incomes according to the Runciman diagnosis is most likely to increase the frequency of comparisons with those who are worse off and in effect to reduce senses of relative deprivation – with the possible exception of the Sproat/Media 'better off on the dole' syndrome.

The voluntary groups and pressure groups unfortunately participate in this process. Lacking direct access to government they are forced to convey their message publicly via the media, and the negative spin-off from this may be the increased 'downward visibility' of significant numbers of working people. It is doubly unfortunate that the propertied cabals remain for the most part socially myopic at such times and perhaps could benefit from G. K. Chesterton's famous aphorism 'The honest poor can sometimes forget poverty. The honest rich can never forget it' (Chesterton, 1908). In any event a reminder to the poor of the facts of affluence is long overdue.

## Cycle of privilege

How do the rich maintain their hold on the country's most powerful and valuable institutions? Why are these institutions so resistant to change? How do small groups of individuals come to form an élite and by what mechanisms does their influence become all pervasive?

From a review of the scant literature on the sociology of the rich the interested reader immediately becomes aware that what he is studying is a cycle of privilege. One only needs to strike into the cycle at one point – perhaps at education to find oneself automatically dealing with

Party (Conservative), Position (The City), Varsity (Oxbridge) and so on. M. B. Brown (1973) took the controllers of British industry as his starting point. Lupton and Wilson (in Urry and Wakeford (eds), 1973) examined the backgrounds of six particularly élitist occupational groups, Glennerster and Pryke (in ibid.) began at the public schools, Philip Stanworth and Anthony Giddens (1974) at the careers of company chairmen. Westergaard and Resler (1976) found it convenient to begin with the Conservative Party and finally C. D. Harbury and P. C. McMahon have investigated the importance of inheritance and the passing on of family fortunes either at death or *inter vivos* (in Stanworth and Giddens, 1974).

The *leitmotif* which runs through all these studies of the different aspects of our élite is that of 'connectivity and network'. It is this which makes redundant any explanations in terms of a conscious conspiracy by the ruling class. It is the easy intimacy nurtured over generations of close family contact and its ramifications in the handful of public schools, universities, financial institutions and prestigious clubs which ensures that any positive effort to conspire is seldom necessary. Similarly the financial and commercial muscles of this group are very rarely flexed, for indeed while major decisions may sometimes be inevitable the reality of privilege lies in the overwhelming majority of non-decisions.

> The power of capital . . . is revealed much less in positive acts of decision-making – involving conflict and choice between alternative policies – than in the everyday, for much of the time unquestioned, application of those assumptions which give priority to private capital accumulation and market exchange in the use and distribution of resources. Power is to be found more in uneventful routine than in conscious and active exercise of will (Westergaard and Resler, 1976, pp. 143–4).

Lupton and Wilson found confirmation of this in the published proceedings of the Parker Tribunal (appointed to investigate allegations that information about the raising of the bank rate had been leaked). In evidence Lord Kindersley demonstrated what we forget all too often: that business at all levels, but especially at the very top, is conducted not by individuals acting as nameless two-dimensional automatons, but as personalities whose individual characteristics, aptitudes, perceptions and beliefs not only influence important decisions, but in addition are familiar to other decision makers who take such knowledge into account when backing their own hunches. This view of the City was used to explain how Lazards (the merchant bank) came to sell gilt-edged securities. The lesson, sociologically, is not whether a leak of information in fact took place but simply that a leak would signify the same degree of informality and social connectivity as does the reliance on hunches and trusting 'horses for courses' which develops out of the same close social proximity.

Lupton and Wilson further demonstrated the interchange of roles which may take place and the potential for conflicting interests to arise when an individual occupies several roles. On the issue of the bank rate the Attorney General in cross examination had apparently thought it strange that it was not the Governor of the Bank of England who approached Lord Bicester (of Vickers) about the possible consequences of a change in the rate on the Vickers issue, but Lord Kindersley, Chairman of Lazards Bank as well as Director of the Bank of England. Indeed one is comforted by the obviously chummy atmosphere in which top business is conducted. Lord Kindersley: 'Look here, Rufie [Lord Bicester], is it too late to stop this business or not?' and 'I have discussed this with Jim – with the Governor – and I am coming on to see you' (Bank Rate Report, 1957).

Of course at the end of a gruelling day at the City such workers might be forgiven for wanting to get away from it all but we would be mistaken as Richard Whitley (in Stanworth and Giddens, 1974) shows in his review of the people (and companies) you might bump into in a handful of our top clubs. The Carlton came out the best place to meet fellow directors of industrial companies, but Brooks's was undoubtedly 'where it's at' as far as the directors of the large financial institutions were concerned. Almost half (46 per cent) of the financiers were members of at least one of the top nine clubs; the Carlton, Boodle's, Brooks's, Buck's, the Beefsteak, Pratt's, The Turf, St James's and White's.

## Eaton Square

The fairly modest literature of the affluent has thus furnished us with a knowledge of some of the principal components of privilege. We turn now to examine one component which has always been of primary importance in studies of working-class communities but usually ignored in any discussion of the rich – proximity. To what extent do the rich hide themselves away in unobtrusive urban enclaves or scatter themselves widely to their crumbling country seats? Clearly it is always easier to find large concentrations of any element by reducing the scale of analysis than by adopting the macro view.

In this short case study we have adopted the street as our scale – a street providing shelter for approximately 230 households in about 118 houses, most of which are subdivided into flats. While converted flats are considered a poor risk by building societies we are fairly confident that the prospective buyer of one such property would allay the manager's anxiety as soon as he mentioned the name of this particular street – Eaton Square, S W 1. It is no exaggeration to say that to tiptoe through the names of the natives of this most select part of London is tantamount to negotiating a whole minefield of references in *Who's Who*. Indeed with over 50 households represented in *Who's Who* a researcher would have a one in four chance of knocking on the door of someone whose biographical details are more a matter of public knowledge than of questionnaire data. In the absence of any national average for the number of VIPs per British street we may only tentatively suggest that one in four is probably rather on the high side.

While we shall concentrate on the information provided by *Who's Who* for individuals on the electoral register it is also true that this compendium of well-known persons is far from comprehensive. Individuals such as Beryl Reid, the actress, Harry T. Hyams the millionaire property developer, Prince and Princess Galitzine, along with sixteen ladies with the title 'Lady' or 'Hon. Mrs', a Countess and the Honourable Charles Cayzer all failed to impress sufficiently the compilers of the 1976 volume, or indeed chose not to be included. But in keeping with the best traditions of social sciences this exercise concentrates on those areas ripe with an abundance of ready data – and so could justifiably be subtitled 'Who's Who in Eaton Square'. It is also known that the electoral register itself does not include all who are presently resident in the square such as Robert Carrier the restaurateur, Bernie Cornfeld, the industrialist, and the Duke of Westminster.

### *The model estate*

Not unlike our post-war towns and housing estates the Grosvenor estate, of which Eaton Square is the heart, was built with a clear sociological model very much in mind. Thomas Cubitt, the master builder, was commissioned by the Duke of Westminster to develop the estate, and its eventual shape is witness to the hierarchy of the day. The large town houses of Eaton Square were built to accommodate the servants in the top floors, the masters on the middle floors and the working quarters in the basement. The mews properties were allocated mainly for the coachman and his family close by while further out in roads like Chester Square the rich middle class were provided with smaller 22 room houses. Moving down the social scale, a Victorian census enumerator would have found the craftsmen at the border of the estate nearer Sloane Square in the properties now affording so many trendy *pieds-à-terre.*

The most obvious physical change to overtake Eaton Square has been the sub-division of the houses into totally self-contained and serviced flats. Indeed only three houses remain undivided. The flats vary in size but are often no more than eight or ten rooms, though the rooms are never of modest dimensions.

The factor of overriding importance to a face-to-face researcher is the universal adoption of the entry-phone – a device perhaps even more effective than the traditional butler for keeping callers at bay. This may also considerably inhibit the development of community or neighbourhood in the area and any ideas of door-to-door collecting activities – so popular among the charities for working-class estates – may best be shelved as far as the square is concerned.

The square forms part of the Grosvenor estate administered by the Duke of Westminster, and the estate itself stretches for 100 acres into Mayfair and 200 acres in Belgravia. Appropriately, both the Duke of Westminster and his son Earl Grosvenor maintain residences in Eaton Square.

## *Social fabric*

The square is composed mainly of ageing English families and a high percentage of aged widows who live alone, often with their offspring spending most of their time in different continents. The traditional residential pattern has more recently been threatened by the take-up of flats for use by the executives of, in the main, multinational and American companies. Such flats would tend to lie empty for extended periods of the year, although remaining serviced by housekeepers. These residents of the square, who tend not to be represented in the electoral register let alone in *Who's Who*, are typically Portuguese or Filipino in origin and would perhaps offer different images of the square and society in general in the course of a first-hand social survey.

The English butler, part of our most treasured heritage, seems to be a dying race even in these quarters – possibly more a victim of technology and the answer-phone than of stringent economies within the household; certainly chauffeurs remain as conspicuous as the coachmen of the last century. Whether these offer a service as company agents or family agents is a question that may merit investigation, although the distinction may prove quite arbitrary.

Unfortunately evidence of community spirit is particularly elusive and especially so from a distance. A residents' association was recently established as a result of local initiative, and it was reported that people resident for fifteen or twenty years were finally meeting for the first time although, as we discover later, other establishments regularly provide the inhabitants of Eaton Square with more points of contact. Inquiries revealed that the oft quoted allegiance of the wealthy to the Conservative party is no thing of the past.

In addition to stalwarts of the Conservative party such as Lord Thorneycroft and the Rt Hon. Julian Amery, there is no doubt that Eaton Square is most overtly Conservative in its politics, although this is generally a Conservatism of the paternalist consensus variety rather than the aggressive, even confrontationalist type which political scientists sometimes ascribe to the present leadership. The possibility that in their dotage the aristocracy revert to their Liberal political roots more akin to the politics of their ancestors is one of the hypotheses which could benefit from empirical research.

The church of Eaton Square suffers from the inevitable Friday migration patterns of the residents. While in fact many of them will be active in the church in the rural estates, they are rarely to be found in the pews of St Peter's (Belgravia) on Sunday. Direct initiatives from the Church are similarly hampered by the metallic negatives of the entry-phone which almost invariably report that 'Lady . . . is not receiving visitors this afternoon.'

While Ray Pahl (1965a) in particular has examined the social patterns of commuter villages and dormitory towns like 'Dormersdel', the question of the weekday city village has been totally overlooked, to our knowledge. Is entertainment confined to the weekened at the country estate or on the grouse-moor, or do less grandiose meetings occur during the week, involving perhaps the women of Eaton Square, at which decisions of more subtle intent than financial mergers take place?

## *The family*

In striking resemblance to the picture painted by Michael Young and Peter Willmott in Bethnal Green, the extended family in Eaton Square continues to act as a second stage support system. One of the prime elements of the education of Eaton Square children is the comprehension of their ancestral roots and an awareness of distant twigs in their family trees, for the simple reason that contacts of this sort so often come in handy. Perhaps the main difference between the functions of the families is that in Eaton Squre connections may be traced in history, irrespective of actual contact patterns of the present day, and that these very findings are sufficient to warrant co-operation. Again, however, we may only emphasise that this field has remained fallow for many years and may turn out all the more productive if considered now.

While the individuals of a family may well spend most of their time apart or outside the country, many of them maintain residences in Eaton Square and still consider it as 'the hearth'. Perhaps confirming some preconceptions about the jet set, a recent baptism of an infant attracted kin from all corners of the globe – the last relative arriving in Heathrow an hour before the ceremony on the Saturday morning; the family was to remain intact for the duration of the reception, but by 1 p.m. relatives were once more boarding their aircraft.

Despite such signs of almost unconstrained mobility, there is also evidence of close family networks within the square – without delving into long ancestral lines to trace second and third cousins. The Dowager Duchess of Devonshire, for example, ex Mistress of the Queen's Robes, was a Cecil by birth, but married the 10th Duke of Devonshire, whose sister married the Rt Hon. Harold Macmillan and it is their daughter who is now the wife of the Rt Hon. Julian Amery – who lives in Eaton Square. The present Duke and Duchess (youngest of the Mitford sisters) of Devonshire live close by in their town house in Mayfair. It was the Duchess who was recently quoted by the *Sunday Express* (4 December 1977) during the opening of new council houses in Derbyshire: 'You are extremely lucky to have a new house. I have only ever lived in second hand houses'.

Some would argue that the most appropriate first step would be an analysis of the inheritance patterns of our sample, but unfortunately this awaits the examination of more detailed and unpublished data than available at present. Harbury and McMahon however described the necessary investigations: first, trace the father's name, second his date of death, third, trace the probated value of his estate at death. 'Methods of tracing involved the use of published directories, such as *Who's Who*, *Burke's Peerage*, etc., searching in the General Registry of Births, Deaths and Marriages at Somerset House, the probate calanders of wills and letters of administration in cases of intestacy and divers other means' (in Stanworth and Giddens, 1974, p. 124). They discovered that the VIPs in their sample – that is people mentioned in *Who's Who* or *Kelly's Handbook of the Titled, Landed and Official Classes* – had an even chance of having a father who left more than £250,000 at 1956-7 prices. In fact this probability of inherited wealth was significantly (statistically) higher than that for wealthy people in general (1 in 3). From this it is plausible that Eaton Square's VIPs – and obviously the individuals on which this study focuses – have been more fortunate in inheriting wealth than most wealthy people in general. Harry Hyams, excluded from the VIP listing in *Who's Who*, perhaps serves to support the point made by Harbury and McMahon, that the self-made millionaire is less likely to be found in *Who's Who* than the old established wealthy.

### *Education*

Moving on from inheritance to public school we find that 'Eaton' might almost be synonymous with 'Eton': no less than eighteen of our sample passed their well spent youth there – from the Rt Hon. Julian Amery down to Sir Charles Villiers; Harrow came a poor second with three, and Winchester, Charterhous and Rugby had two each.

| | |
|---|---|
| Eton: | Rt Hon. Julian Amery, Lord Boothby, Lord Campbell of Eskan, Sir William Cayzer, Sir Roger Chance, Ralph Dutton, Sir Seymour Egerton, Sir James Gault, Hon. Vere H. Harmsworth, Thomas Hohler, Viscount Hood, Viscount de L'Isle, Neil L. Mclean, Daniel L. Meinertzhagen, Lord Reigate, Lord Rotherwick, Lord Thorneycroft, Sir Charles Villiers. |
| Harrow: | Peter Allen, Earl of Bradford, Earl Grosvenor. |
| Charterhouse: | Sir Osbert Lancaster, Harold Oppenheimer. |
| Rugby: | Sir Alex Cohen, Sir Kenneth Keith. |
| Winchester: | John Beevor, Lord Broughshane. |

Given their excellent start in life it is no surprise to discover that of our twenty-seven young men groomed for greatness only six failed to continue their studies at Oxford, Cambridge, or Sandhurst. The six 'drop-outs', however, seemed not to have suffered unduly from this break with convention. Lord Thorneycroft moved to the Royal Military Academy at Woolwich, from there into a career in politics and is now to be found at the right hand of Mrs Thatcher herself. Earl Grosvenor also apparently benefited from certain compensations if the *Daily*

*Mail*'s description of him on 9 August 1977 is at all accurate:

> Poor Earl Grosvenor. Since he wrecked his Piper Apache plane in April (it cost £12,000 ten years ago) he has found it most difficult to find a replacement. However with an inheritance of £16 million – making him the richest young man in Britain – he can no doubt afford to buy more little playthings.

The *Daily Mail* pulls no punches but is probably sure of its facts when we realise that the Chairman of Associated Newspaper Group (which includes the *Daily Mail*) is of course the Hon. Vere H. Harmsworth – son of Lord Rothermere who was the *Daily Mail*'s proprietor in the 1930s. (Now resident in South Africa Lord Rothermere became famous for his patriotic writings particularly in support of Sir Oswald Mosley: 'Hurrah for the Blackshirts' ran the headline in January 1934.) That the *Daily Mail* has never been the most sympathetic of organs to the Labour Party is no secret and this may indeed be cause for neighbourhood troubles in the square because Harmsworth's next door neighbour is none other than the Rt Hon. Harold Lever MP.

Three other rebels from the Oxbridge convention Sir Kenneth Keith, Sir Seymour Egerton and Thomas S. Hohler, as we will discover later, also seemed to progress quite satisfactorily in spite of this apparent drawback.

Finally, perhaps a phenomenon which merits attention is the converse of another of Ray Pahl's notions 'Urbs in Rure'. To what extent are the residents of Eaton Square 'Rus in Urbe' (Pahl, 1965b) or rural folk living in town? Most of them have been educated in a rural setting and draw much of their status from their position in what is commonly a rural estate, where, we may argue, systems of status are more clearly defined than in urban contexts. A recent funeral service in London took place to commemorate the life of a man never known inside the Belgravia church but, unknown to the local clergy, had been a pillar of his local church at his country home.

## *Jobs for the boys?*

The City plays a prominent role in the economic activity of the square and in the provision of jobs for its inhabitants. Certain individuals emerge quite clearly as pillars of this community. Daniel L. Meinertzhagen, for example, is managing director of Lazard Brothers, the merchant bank. M. B. Brown has stressed the influence of these banks and illustrated the interlocking directorships in banking, insurance, industry and commerce which link together groups of major British companies.

> Any industrial company can be expected to do all its banking through one of the Big Eight commercial banks, and if it is a large company the chairman or other leading director may well be asked to sit on the board of the bank. At the same time, any company that wishes to issue shares in the Stock Exchange will do this through an issuing house (merchant bank) which underwrites the issue and takes a commission, and may wish to take up some of the shares (at a premium) even if there is no difficulty in disposing of them on the market.
>
> The insurance companies according to the Radcliffe Report of 1959, abide by an unwritten law that they will not hold more than 5 per cent of the equity of any one industrial company and that they avoid entanglement in management. This does not prevent them from taking a great interest in the dividend that any company in which they have invested is likely to declare, nor from encouraging their directors to sit on the boards of the larger industrial companies. A happy solution is where a merchant banker sits on the boards of an associated commercial bank, an investing insurance company and one or more industrial company (Brown, 1973, pp. 97-9).

Brown listed thirteen major industrial and financial groups, but we were concerned only with such groups containing representatives from Eaton Square. Unfortunately the groupings represent the situation in 1960 and the *Who's Who* information refers mainly to 1976 directorships. The annotated table does, however, give an indication of the potential influence of Eaton Square residents.

It is a fairly easy thing to demonstrate that to register the interests of Eaton Square one has to include eleven of Brown's thirteen groupings. Thus it is heartening to know that the voice of little Eaton Square is being heard, from the City throughout our industry, and in fact to all corners of the globe via overseas companies. In another table Brown provides information about the boards on which the top merchant bankers had seats in 1966. Again we examine just the Eaton Square representatives and list them according to their respective merchant bank.

This information referring to 1966 reveals new lines of connections, for example Seymour Egerton and Daniel Meinertzhagen have by this time directorships of Alexanders' and Phoenix in common. More up

TABLE 7.1

| Group | Merchant bank | Big 8 commercial banks | Other banks and trusts | Insurance companies | Home industrial companies | Companies operating overseas |
|---|---|---|---|---|---|---|
| 1 | Lazards de Steins | Lloyds | Cowdray Trust<br>Whitehall Securities<br>S. Pearson[1]<br>Merc. Credit[1]<br>BOLSA | Royal Exchange<br>Commercial Union | Gallaher<br>Eng. Electric<br>EMI<br>Rolls-Royce[5]<br>British Match[6]<br>Wm Cory | P & O<br>Dalgety |
| 2 | Rothschilds<br>Sassoons (assoc with Barclays | | Shield Unit | Sun Alliance | | De Beers[2]<br>Anglo-American[2]<br>RTZ<br>Rand<br>British South Africa |
| 5 | Fleming | National Provincial | Coutts[4]<br>Ottoman<br>Union Discount | Sun Alliance | Imp. Tob.<br>Gallahers<br>Boots<br>TI | British American Tobacco<br>Tanganyikan Concessions |
| 6 | Phillip Hill[6]<br>Higginsons<br>d'Erlangers<br>Samuels | Midland | City Centre | Eagle Star | Assoc. Eng.<br>Elliot Auto<br>Beecham<br>Hawker Siddeley<br>Rank Org. | Cons. Goldfields<br>Shell<br>Antofagasta<br>Channel Tunnel |

| | | | | | | |
|---|---|---|---|---|---|---|
| | | | | | Stone-Platt<br>Reddifusion<br>Utd Drapery<br>Brt. Elect. Traction<br>Sears Hlds | |
| 8 | Schroders-Helbert Wagg | Lloyds | City Properties | Atlas<br>Legal & Gen. | Pressed Steel<br>Babcock & Wilcox[3]<br>T. Tilling<br>Tate & Lyle | |
| 9 | Jardine Matheson | Martin's | Hong Kong & Shanghai<br>Chartered Commercial Bank of Australia | London Royal[1] | Cunard<br>Furness<br>Withy | Hudsons Bay<br>BP |
| 10 | | District | | Liv. London & Globe[1] | Lancs Cotton<br>Lancs Steel | Turner & Newall |
| 11 | | Barclay's[2] | Barclays DCO<br>UDT<br>Halifax Bdg<br>Yorkshire Penny<br>British Linen | Norwich Union<br>Phoenix | Barclay-Courage | |

[1] Meinertzhagen
[2] Oppenheimer
[3] King
[4] Egerton
[5] Fraser
[6] Keith

(*Source*: Brown, 1973)

TABLE 7.2

| Merchant bank and banker | Banks and trusts | Insurance co. | Home industrials | Overseas companies |
|---|---|---|---|---|
| LAZARDS | | | | |
| D. Meinertzhagen | Mercantile Credit<br>Alexander's Disct | Liverpool<br>London<br>Globe<br>Royal<br>Phoenix | Rootes<br>Trollope & Colls | |
| MORGAN GRENFELLL | | | | |
| Sir George Erskine (Lord Erskine of Rerrick) | | | GKN<br>(ex Harrods) | British Commonwealth Shipping |
| SCHRODER'S-HELBERT WAGG | | | | |
| C. H. Villiers | Banque Belge<br>Standard Bank (South Africa) | Sun | United Premium Oil and Cake | |
| HILL SAMUEL | | | | |
| K. A. Keith (d.ch.) | | Eagle Star | Beecham's<br>Utd Draperies | Consd Trust |
| R. E. E. de Trafford | Williams Deacon's<br>Electronic Trust | Royal Exchange<br>Atlas | Elliot Auto<br>Berger<br>Jenson | |
| COUTTS | | | | |
| S. J. L. Egerton (ch.) | National Prov.<br>Alexander's Disct | Phoenix | (ex *The Times*) | |

to date information from *Who's Who*, 1976 also shows Charles Villiers to have moved from Schroder's-Helbert Wagg to the chair of Guinness & Mahon, merchant bank, but of course has since then been appointed as head of the British Steel Corporation, and Sir Kenneth Keith to have become chairman of Hill Samuel, chairman of Rolls-Royce (1971) Ltd and director of The Times Newspaper Ltd.

The merchant bankers of Eaton Square are not the only ones to have their fair share of influence in the running of industry. Anthony Hepper, for example, was formerly chairman of Upper Clyde Shipbuilders and Industrial Adviser to the DEA (1966-7) and is now a director of Cape Industries. Ian Fraser is chairman of Rolls-Royce Motors, director of BOC International as well as being deputy chairman of Lazard Brothers. Lord Thorneycroft is chairman of Trust House Forte, Pye and a director of Securicor, Sir Rex Cohen is chairman of Barclaytrust Property Management Ltd. Sir William Cayzer and Herbert Robin Cayzer (Lord Rotherwick) are chairman and deputy of British and Commonwealth Shipping Co. Ltd. Finally, of course, the Rt Hon. Harold Lever is not totally without influence and interest in the running of our industrial economy.

### *Clubs*

In keeping with the community concepts of close proximity of home, work and social life we find that the residents of Eaton Square do not care to travel too far in the leisure hours; indeed their sources of relxation may be found just the other side of Buckingham Palace – in the clubland of St James's. White's is by far the most popular of the nine clubs previously mentioned and may boast ten of our VIPs in its membership.

| | |
|---|---|
| Beefsteak | Rt Hon. Julian Amery, Lord Campbell of Eskin, Sir Seymour Egerton, Sir Osbert Lancaster, Sir Charles Villiers. |
| Boodle's | Sir Seymour Egerton, Hon. Vere H. Harmsworth. |
| Brook's | John Beevor, Sir William Cayzer, Ralph Dutton, Viscount Hood, Harold Oppenheimer, Lord Reigate. |
| Buck's | Rt Hon. Julian Amery, Neil L. Mclean. |
| Carlton | Rt Hon. Julian Amery, Ronald H. Senior. |
| Pratts | Sir Seymour Egerton, Sir Kenneth Keith, Sir Osbert Lancaster, Neil L. Mclean. |
| St James's | Sir Osbert Lancaster. |

| | |
|---|---|
| The Turf | Earl Grosvenor, Thomas Hohler, Lord Rotherwick. |
| Whites | Rt Hon. Julian Amery, Lord Boothby, Lord Broughshane, Sir Rex Cohen, Sir Rudolph De Trafford, Sir James Gault, Sir Kenneth Keith, John L. King, Neil L. Mclean, Daniel Meinertzhagen. |

## Conclusion

This brief glimpse at one square in London suggests that many of the patterns discovered by sociologists and anthropologists in post war working-class communities may not in fact be so particular as has been made out. When we align close geographical proximity alongside occupational contact, shared leisure pursuits, identical educational backgrounds, similar levels of wealth holding and affluence we should begin to suspect that this community may also manifest the sort of quaint parochialism, limited horizons, and constrained reference group behaviour that has been so important in the plethora of sociological literature surrounding the poor. What significance should we attach to this assertion? First, it sets up a whole range of hypotheses which have yet to be tested in any rigorous way – the exercise outlined hitherto merely poses the questions, it does not attempt to supply answers. The hypotheses themselves, once tested, could provide a sociological framework for explaining the wider scale phenomena of change and stasis in British society. It suggests perhaps that the continuance of degrees of inequality almost unparallelled in the industrial world may be explained by the considerable powers of resistance which the privileged may call upon to defend their property and position. A sociology of the rich would uncover the structure and mechanisms of their resistance in the same way that the sociology of the poor has explained the process of acquiescence. Second, the realisation that the institutions of family and kinship and the processes of aspiration, self-assessment and relative deprivation may be just as significant (or irrelevant) among the rich as among the poor may go some way in stripping inequality of its esteem in response to Tawney's long forgotten call. The rich, given the way our society is structured, tend to benefit from a combination of benign neglect, inertia, mystique and ignorance – in effect the rest of society treats them in the way that befits the Golden Goose.

Therefore shall we now begin to cease asking ourselves, and in particular the majority of people in this country, why gross inequalities are allowed to persist? Such questions may be seen to be purely hypothetical because our respondents, particularly when confronted as individuals, have few real alternatives to those policies and processes that determine the status quo. A more realistic approach may be to ask questions of the rich and powerful in order for them to explain why they are wealthy, and will remain so, and why most other people own next to nothing. At least in adopting that policy we may, like the iconoclasts, shatter the image that poverty is the child of the poor and begin to search elsewhere for its parenthood, though a few doors may be slammed in our faces along the way.

8

# Holding a mirror to inequality: the review body on top salaries

David Jordan

If the government of the day hoped that the appointment of the Review Body on Top Salaries (or the Top Salaries Review Body (TSRB) as it is commonly, and perversely, known) would remove the degermination of those salaries for which it is responsible from the choppy waters of political controversy, it and its successors must have been severely disappointed. Far from dimming the lights on the debate about the remuneration of those entrusted with the management peaks of the public sector, the reports of the Top Salaries Review Body have provided an opportunity for the examination of the principles used to determine top pay in the public sector under the full glare of public scrutiny. As such they have proved political hot potatoes, particularly for the Labour administrations who have had to handle the most fundamental reviews produced by the TSRB (usually at the same time as advocating pay restraint as part of a package of measures designed to combat Britain's economic ills).

While the TSRB's reports have provided powerful ammunition for those concerned with the distribution of earned incomes and for the political and media discussions of the issue, their content represents, as yet, a fallow field in which academic interest has still to plough a furrow. Despite the constant deluge of academica on the general problems of wages and salaries, no one has yet 'turned the spotlight on the interrogator' and reviewed the Review Body. This is an omission which we can only take the first steps to rectify in the following few pages. We take a look at the work of the Top Salaries Review Body to date and the underlying reasons for its recommendations as well as the fate of its proposals amidst the political hue and cry which has accompanied them. We look at some of the specific sources of argument and recrimination as between public and private employees – factors like job security and the level of pensions available to each. And, finally, we pose the question of whether the methods used by the TSRB to determine salaries in the higher echelons of public service have, in effect, led to its becoming a focus for a wider disenchantment with the overall distribution of gross earned incomes in Britain.

## In the beginning

The Top Salaries Review Board was appointed in May 1971. Under the Chairmanship of Lord Boyle its terms of reference were 'to advise the Prime Minister on the remuneration of the chairmen and members of the boards of nationalised industries; the higher judiciary; senior civil servants; senior officers of the armed forces, and other groups which may be referred to it'. Though its primary reference was to the remuneration of the higher echelons of the public sector the majority of the nine reports produced by the TSRB between May 1971 and the end of 1977 have been concerned with the salaries, allowances and expenses of government ministers, MPs and peers. Despite this we intend to focus primarily on its main reference.

The formation of the Top Salaries Review Body appeared to bring to an end an uninterrupted period of ad hoc determination of top salaries in the public sector. Summarising the pay history of one of the groups brought together under the umbrella of the TSRB one commentator has noted that 'the post-war history of higher civil service remuneration has been characterised by a progression from one short-term crisis to the next' (TSRB, 1974a, p. 113). For this group salary determination in the post-war years echoed previous eras – a succession of ad hoc committees each reasserting, though with occasional variations in emphasis, the underlying principles of comparability on which top civil service pay was based. But the long time intervals between reports combined with inflation and the periodic crises of the British economy depressed top pay in the civil service. The differentials squeeze, by no means a new phenomenon, gathered momentum. 'The differential between a Permanent Secretary and an Assistant Secretary was 222% in 1956 but had fallen in 1969 to 169.5% (Assistant Secretary = 100%)' (ibid., p. 113)

The relative rewards of the higher judiciary followed a similar pattern. In fact the decline in the salaries of judges was even more pronounced and was largely attributable to institutional inertia. The salaries of the judges of common law courts remained unaltered for almost a century after being fixed in 1851 and 'the history of judicial schemes since 1954 has consisted of a series of piecemeal increases, more or less in conjunction with salary movements in the higher civil service and changes in the cost living.' At the same time 'the early history' of senior officers in the armed forces 'shows many resemblances to the civil service and judiciary, the outstanding characteristic being a static salary structure over long periods of time' (ibid., p. 119). Just as with the judiciary, the salary levels of the higher ranking officers in the armed forces came increasingly, in the post-war era, to be linked to pay in the civil service – 'an implicit relationship gradually became an increasingly accepted convention.' So much so that the 1960 pay review felt able to state that in future 'pay would be governed broadly by the relative changes in pay of comparable grades in the home civil service' (quoted in ibid., p. 121). And when the government prompted the last report of the National Board for Prices and Incomes (NBPI) on the pay of the armed forces it was 'in the light of' the increases awarded to higher civil servants.

By comparison with the long histories of pay determination in the civil service, the judiciary, and officers of the armed services, that of the chiefs of nationalised industries is short. Public enterprise in Britain is largely a post-war phenomenon. As well as being new, salary settlements at the top of the nationalised industries posed particular problems. On the one hand, appointments to the chairmanships and boards of the nationalised industries unavoidably represented public appointments (chairmen report direct to ministers); on the other the structure, and increasingly the goals, of nationalised industries had far more in common with private companies than public service. Moreover the skills required of their managers were also directly comparable. Perhaps unsurprisingly, therefore, pressure quickly built up for a more direct comparison with equivalent salary scales in the private sector than had hitherto been practised in the public sector, though all top public sector pay owed something to direct comparison by this time. Indeed, as early as 1931 the Royal Commission on the Civil Service (the Tomlin Commission) had accepted that civil service pay should be based on 'broad general comparisons between classes in the service and outside occupations' reflecting the long term trend, both in wage levels and in the economic conditions of the country, and this theoretical approach had not been seriously challenged since. None the less the determination of salaries for the top jobs in nationalised industry presented a special difficulty of balance between public sector service and private sector incentives. In its report on Top Salaries in the Private Sector and Nationalised Industries the NBPI elected to jump firmly between these two stools. 'The public undertaking . . . reflects the traditional characteristics of the public service, one of which is that financial rewards at the top are not outstandingly high' but despite this 'it is certainly not self-evident that pay in the public sector should entirely match whatever is paid in the private sector' because 'any attempt in the public sector to match pay in the private sector might push up pay still further in the latter' even though the report cites evidence of promotion and rewards difficulties arising from differentials being squeezed at the top and problems of recruitment from outside arising from relatively low pay (NBPI, 1969). The failure of the NBPI and of either of the other two previous reviews of top salaries in the nationalised industries to grasp the nettle and sever the connections between public service pay and salaries in public enterprise, served only to secure the bonds already existing between the two. The Top Salaries Review Body took up the reins offered them by the NBPI (not long before its demise at the hands of an incoming Conservative government in 1970). The NBPI had proposed 'that ministers should have the help of some outside agency . . . when it becomes necessary to review top salaries in the nationalised industries' (ibid., p. 33). By the time this proposal was put into practice it had become clear that, in the words of the TSRB, 'de facto relationships have evolved between their respective pay structures. Over a period of time some of these horizontal relativities have become generally accepted, although they do not result from any measured evaluation of responsibilities' (TSRB, 1972, p. 1).

## The report stage

The TSRB's second report was its first on its standing reference (the first report had dealt with the pay and allowances of ministers and MPs) and was the first review of top salaries in the nationalised industries since the NBPI's report in 1969. The NBPI's recommendations had been implemented in three stages ending in January 1971 (though, in common with other members of the highest grades of the four groups covered by the TSRB, both deputy chairmen and chairmen deferred their final increase until July 1971 'in the nationl interest'). The most recent salary review for the higher echelons of the civil service, the armed forces and the judiciary had taken place in 1969, 1970 and 1969 respectively. The TSRB's first interim report (TSRB, 1972)

TABLE 8.1 *Salaries and salary reviews of the Higher Civil Service, the Judiciary, the Senior Officers of the Armed Forces and the Chairmen and Members of Boards of the Nationalised Industries from January 1971 to January 1978*

| | January 1971 salary at £ | January 1972 increase £ | April 1973 increase £ | January 1974 increase £ | January 1975 salary increased to £ | January 1976 | January 1977 increase | January 1978 increase |
|---|---|---|---|---|---|---|---|---|
| HIGHER CIVIL SERVICE | | | | | | | | |
| Head of the Home Civil Service | 15,000[6] | 1,750 | 250 | 350* | 20,175 | No increase (salaries in excess of £8,500 frozen under incomes policy) | Increase of £208 across the board | |
| Permanent Secretary to the Treasury | 15,000[6] | 1,750 | 250 | 350* | 20,175 | | | |
| Secretary to the Cabinet | 15,000[6] | 1,750 | 250 | 350* | 20,175 | | | |
| Permanent Secretary | 14,000[6] | 1,750 | 250 | 350* | 18,675 | | | |
| Second Permanent Secretary | 13,000 | 1,750 | 250 | 350* | 17,175 | | | |
| Deputy Secretary | 9,000 | 1,500 | 250 | 350* | 14,000 | | | |
| Under Secretary | 6,750 | 1,500 | 250 | 500* | 12,000 | | | |
| JUDICIARY | | | | | | | | |
| Lord Chief Justice[4] | 16,750[6] | 1,750 | 250 | 350* | 23,050 | | | |
| Lord of Appeal in Ordinary[4] | 15,500[6] | 1,750 | 250 | 350* | 21,175 | | | |
| Master of the Rolls[4] | 15,500[6] | 1,750 | 250 | 350* | 21,175 | | | |
| President of the Family Division[4] | 15,500[6] | 1,750 | 250 | 350* | 20,175 | | | |
| Lord Justice of Appeal[4}<br>Puisne Judges[4] | 14,000[6] | 1,750 | 250 | 350* | 19,425 | | | |
| Circuit Judge | 8,300 | 1,450 | 250 | 350* | 13,500 | | | |
| Metropolitan Magistrate[5] | 6,850 | 1,500 | 250 | 350* | 11,750 | | | |
| ARMED FORCES | | | | | | | | |
| Admiral of the Fleet<br>Field Marshal<br>Marshal of the Royal Air Force | 13,998[6] | 1,750 | 250 | 350* | 19,675 | | | |
| Admiral<br>General<br>Air Chief Marshal | 12,501[6] | 1,750 | 250 | 350* | 17,925 | | | |
| Vice Admiral<br>Lieutenant General<br>Air Marshal | 9,253 | 1,500 | 250 | 350* | 14,000 | | | |

| | January 1971 salary at £ | January 1972 increase £ | April 1973 increase £ | January 1974 increase £ | January 1975 salary increased to £ | January 1976 | January 1977 increase | January 1978 increase |
|---|---|---|---|---|---|---|---|---|
| Rear Admiral<br>Major General<br>Air Vice Marshal | 7,245 | 1,500 | 250 | 350* | 12,000 | No increase (salaries in excess of £8,500 frozen under incomes policy) | Increase of £208 across the board | Increase of 'up to' 10 per cent for those earning less than £13,000 and 5 per cent for those earning in excess of £13,000 |
| NATIONALISED INDUSTRIES | | | | | | | | |
| *British Steel Corporation* | | | | | | | | |
| Chairman | 25,000 | 2,500 | 250 | 350* | no increase | | | |
| Deputy Chairmen | 20,000–24,000 | 1,000–2,000 | 250 | 350* | no increase | | | |
| Board Member | 15,000–19,000 | 1,000–2,000 | 250 | 350* | no increase | | | |
| *Group A Boards*[1] | | | | | | | | |
| Chairman | 20,000[6] | 2,500 | 250 | 350* | no increase | | | |
| Deputy Chairmen | 16,000[6] | 2,500 | 250 | 350* | no increase | | | |
| Members | 10,000–15,000 | 2,000 | 250 | 350* | no increase | | | |
| *Group B Boards*[2] | | | | | | | | |
| Chairman | 17,000[6] | 2,000 | 250 | 350* | no increase | | | |
| Deputy Chairmen | 13,500[6] | 1,500 | 250 | 350* | no increase | | | |
| Members | 8,000–12,000 | 1,500 | 250 | 350* | no increase | | | |
| *Group C Boards*[3] | | | | | | | | |
| Chairman | 10,000–15,000 | 2,000 | 250 | 350* | no increase | | | |
| Deputy Chairmen | 7,500– 9,500 | 1,500 | 250 | 350* | no increase | | | |

Notes

*Plus threshold payments from June 1974.

[1] Group A Boards comprise: British Airways, British Gas Corporation, British Railways Board, Central Electricity Generating Board, Electricity Council, National Coal Board, Post Office.

[2] Group B Boards comprise: Commonwealth Development Corporation, National Bus Company, National Freight Corporation, UK Atomic Energy Authority.

[3] Group C Boards comprise: Area Electricity Boards England and Wales, British Airports Authority, British Transport Docks Board, British Waterways Board, Cable and Wireless Ltd., Civil Aviation Authority, North of Scotland Hydro-Electric Board, Scottish Transport Group, South of Scotland Electricity Board.

[4] Increases paid 26 July each year.

[5] Increases paid 17 July each year.

[6] January 1971 increase voluntarily forgone for six months. July 1971 therefore effective date.

(*Source*: TSRB, 1974a; *Hansard* 1975a, cols 81–5; *Hansard* 1977a, col. 631; *Hansard*, 1977f, cols 305–6)

recommended substantial increases for all its charges while at the same time emphasising that 'further study of each group is essential, both to ensure that salary levels are adequate, and to test the pattern of relativities within and between groups' (ibid., p. 1). The omission of the possibility that the salaries might be too high reflects the substance of the report which, citing concertinaed differentials, the rising cost of living, the substantial increases in earnings and comparable salaries, and the effect of declining real salaries on pensions for those retiring (regarded as 'particularly serious'), recommended large increases. These are set out alongside the recommendations of subsequent reports in Table 8.1. Even though the recommended increases were substantial, however, they fell short of the rises in both the Retail Price Index and the general level of salaries (derived from the Department of Employment's monthly index of wage and salary earnings). Prices increased by 20 per cent between July 1969 and January 1972 and salaries by 29 per cent between July 1969 and December 1971. Average earnings, by comparison, rose by 29.4 per cent in the latter period. According to the TSRB, 'on an annual compound basis since 1 July 1969, these amount to an overall average increase of 6.8 per cent, with a range from 3.9 per cent for the highest salaries to 8.4 per cent for the lowest. On the same basis inflation . . . has increased prices by 7.7 per cent a year, while average salaries have risen by 11.1 per cent a year' (ibid., p. 11). Even so, the recommended increases ranged between £1,000 and £2,500 in some cases back-dated to the beginning of the year (1972) and, in the light of subsequent events, it is a little surprising that the recommendations were implemented in full despite 'comment by Members of Parliament and the public that because of the problem of growing inflation, it was most unsuitable that such big increases should be given just at a time when restraint was being advocated for other sections of the public' (IDS, 1977a, p. 13).

Despite its pledge to complete an in-depth review on their standing reference 'within a year' the next two TSRB reports were of an interim nature. Both reports were inhibited by the terms of the then current incomes policies and were, in effect, constrained to recommend the level of increases deemed appropriate under the pay restraint measures. For 1973 this amounted to an across the board rise of £250. The TSRB indicated that, in percentage terms, 'this represents an increase of 3.0 per cent of the lowest level (£8,250), diminishing to 0.9 per cent at the highest level (£27,500), within our terms of reference' whereas 'the index of retail prices and average earnings . . . have moved by 9.1 per cent and 15.6 per cent' (January 1972–March 1973) (TSRB, 1973,

p. 1). The TSRB encountered a similar restriction on its freedom when it reported in 1974. Under the operable pay code increases were limited to £350 across the board though the TSRB took advantage of the 'flexibility margin' arrangements to bump up the salary of under secretaries in the civil service by an additional £150. This measure was justified by reference to the erosion of the differential between under secretaries and assistant secretaries. The TSRB also recommended the introduction of threshold increases for all those covered by its standing reference. Again these increases amounted to a decline in real income. 'The index of retail prices has risen by 6.5 per cent and average earnings by 10.2 per cent (April-December 1973). £350 . . . represents an increase of 1.3 per cent at the upper end of the range with which we are concerned (£27,750) and 4.1 per cent at the lower end (£8,500)' (TSRB, 1974b).

It was not until its sixth report that the TSRB was finally able to give unrestrained attention to its standing reference. Its report, issued in December 1974, not only fully reviewed the salaries of those within its terms of reference and recommended increases accordingly but also made an attempt to define the principles of pay determination which had governed its decisions. In addition, studies of the historical development and the interrelationship of the salaries in question, which had provided the background for the principles outlined, were made public as part of the report.

Leaving aside the statement of principles for the moment, the main thrust of the report was to recommend very large salary increases, averaging 28.8 per cent overall. Once again the TSRB was anxious to point out that the proposed rises by no means compensated the prospective recipients for the increase in the cost of living over the period concerned. At the time the TSRB could only estimate the likely relationship between the recommended increases and movements in prices and average earnings. Table 8.2 shows how these relationships worked out in practice. None the less the sheer size of the proposed increases in cash (shown in full in Table 8.1) and percentage terms proved wholly indigestible to a government recently committed to the social contract and urging the nation to exercise 'restraint' in wage settlements. For example, the chairman of British Steel was to have his salary boosted to £40,000, an increase of £11,900 or 42.3 per cent, the head of the civil service was recommended to receive a rise of 32.6 per cent and the highest officers of the armed services 40.7 per cent. One of the prime architects of the Social Contract, the leader of the Transport and General Workers' Union, Jack Jones, was forthright in his condemnation of the proposed rises and the then Secretary of State

TABLE 8.2 *Percentage increases in recommended salaries compared with average earnings and retail prices, July 1969–January 1975 (group averages)*

| | % |
|---|---|
| Civil Service | 71.9 |
| Armed forces | 65.0 |
| Judiciary | 56.9 |
| Nationalised industries | 58.5 |
| Overall | 64.1 |
| Average earnings | 116.1 |
| Retail prices | 74.0 |

(*Source*: TSRB, 1974, p. 186)

for Employment, Mr Michael Foot, stated that he considered himself 'overpaid' on £13,000 a year (a salary also set by the TSRB) and that £6,000 was enough for anyone to live on. Faced with this kind of weighty opposition it came as no surprise that the government elected not to implement the report in full. Instead a compromise deal was worked out to be phased in in two parts. Salaries which, under the proposals, would rise to less than £13,000 were to be increased immediately (i.e. from January 1975) by the full amount. Those rising to over £13,000 would receive the whole amount up to £13,000 plus half the additional amount over £13,000 with the balance paid in January 1976. To those already in excess of £13,000 would be added half the recommended increase with the balance to be paid twelve months later. These increases applied to the higher civil service, senior officers in the armed services and to the judiciary but *not* to the chairmen and board members of nationalised industries. Moreover the first of these groups was to have its pension rights based on the TSRB recommended rates and not on the actual rates paid. The rationale for this distinction, outlined by the Prime Minister, is worth quoting in full.

> The increases recommended for chairman and board members of nationalised industries raise wider questions about the levels of incomes at chairman and board level in private industry, with which those nationalised industry salary levels are compared. The Government accepts the Review Body's judgement that the chairmen and board members of the major nationalised industries are at present earning substantially lower salaries than their counter-

> parts in private industry. In the Government's view, however, the social justification for some of the very high incomes paid in private industry would be questionable, whatever the economic circumstances of the country, and however great the responsibilities the individuals concerned are asked to bear; and this is particularly so when regard is had to fringe benefits and benefits in kind which many of those concerned enjoy, to a greater extent than their counterparts in public service. In current economic circumstances, when the great bulk of the employed population, on much lower income levels, are being asked to accept increases within the guidelines set by the TUC in accordance with the Social Contract, it would be particularly difficult to justify the sort of increases that would result from applying to these incomes a percentage increase even as large as that of the rise in prices. It is of the essence of the Social Contract that, if those who are least well paid are to be enabled, within available resources, to improve their relative position, those who are most highly paid should accept the need for restraint (*Hansard*, 1974c, cols 653-50).

The terms of the compromise understandably created suspicion of the part played by the civil service in determining its own salaries. Indeed *The Economist* commented that it 'reinforces unkind suspicions that the civil service, like the devil, is most adept at looking after its own' (4 January 1975). Subsequent revelations have hardened this impression. According to Joe Haines, Harold Wilson's Press Secretary at the time, the implementation of the TSRB's sixth report was 'an outstanding example in my experience of the civil service attempting to influence the Cabinet.' Their efforts, in his view, included the deliberate manipulation of the timing of cabinet papers (Haines, 1977, pp. 18-22).

As well as announcing the levels of pay increases to be implemented, the Prime Minister also stated that the government intended to ask the TSRB to review the salaries of higher civil servants, senior officers in the armed forces, and members of the judiciary on an annual basis in future. And the position of the nationalised industries' chairmen and board members would be reviewed in the light of the Royal Commission on the Distribution of Income and Wealth's report on higher incomes.

The Royal Commission's report appeared in January 1976 but supplied little material which could be of practical use to the TSRB in determining top salaries. The TSRB itself had, by the end of 1977, not reported since its sixth report was issued in December 1974. In a sense there would have been little point. A succession of incomes policies had done the TSRB's job for it. Consequently no salary increase was awarded in 1975–6 when salaries in excess of £8,500 per year were frozen. In 1976–7 the government awarded the maximum possible increase of £208 per year. For 1977–8, while awaiting the next report of the TSRB due in April 1978, the Prime Minister announced a pay award which gave those nationalised industry chairmen and board members earning under £13,000 a rise of 'up to' 10 per cent, limited to 5 per cent for salaries in excess of £13,000.

This may be interpreted as something of a sop to those most affected by the standstill on pay – the chairmen and board members of the nationalised industries – who had lost no chance of emphasising their 'plight'. Frequent media reports highlighted the disgruntlement felt in nationalised industries, the anomalies experienced by board members paid less than executives with less responsibility (but with the good sense to have their wages fixed by collective bargaining), the squeezing of differentials, the drop in real income and the difficulty of persuading suitable candidates from outside to accept the top jobs in state industry. The 'less pay for more responsibility' problem was highlighted in November 1976 by the refusal of five directors of Cable and Wireless Ltd to accept renomination to their board – a problem overcome by the crisis expedient of adjourning the annual general meeting of the company before their resignations had been accepted. But the seeds of managerial collective action had obviously been sown because, in March 1977, an announcement was made of the 'formal establishment' of an Association of Members of State Industry Boards. The association has been actively lobbying for the removal of the 'unfair discrimination' against the staffs of nationalised industries since that date.

They would appear to have a case. The singling out of the nationalised industries remains inexplicable despite the Prime Minister's statement reported earlier. The reservations expressed about pay determination for this group can equally be applied to all those covered by the TSRB's reference. Despite its search, in its sixth report, for fresh underlying principles on which to base top pay in the public sectors, the TSRB came up with nothing new – in fact the traditional comparisons with the private sector and the maintenance of the *de facto* relationships which had evolved between the groups under consideration emerged as the prime determinants of top pay once again. The logic of allowing one group of public employees but not the others the salaries calculated and recommended on this basis is mystifying to say the least. And far more so than a refusal to pay salaries of such magnitude to anyone, whether on moral, political or pragmatic grounds.

By accepting the recommendations of the TSRB's sixth report, the Government implicitly accepted the logic of the arguments used to justify them. But the methods used by the TSRB and, indeed, the practice of using an independent pay review body to determine top salaries in the public sector, have not been universally accepted. We now turn our attention to the methods used by the TSRB, their appropriateness and the rationale underlying the TSRB's reports.

## A question of principle?

> A public body examining questions of pay determination has the responsibility and additional burdensome task of making its decisions overt, and based on clearly set out and justified choice of priorities and value judgements on which those claims are made (Written evidence from Mr Derek Robinson, in Royal Commission, 1976b, pp. 344–5).

The TSRB appears to believe that this is what is done in its sixth report, but if the priorities and value judgments of the TSRB are made clear it is in a fashion more akin to the 'revealed preference' of demand theory than in any explicit fashion. For example, to judge by the TSRB's initial discussion of job comparability with the private sector it would appear that the review body has considerable reservations about the applicability of the approach.

> We have made it clear that in our view comparability with the private sector must be the overriding factor for assessing pay levels for the top posts in nationalised industries. The difficulty comes when one tries to apply this same principle to the other groups covered by our terms of reference; while we are clear that in the future as in the past it will continue to have a part to play, we feel bound to introduce a note of caution . . . It appears to us that reliable assessments of comparability between different forms of occupation become increasingly difficult the nearer one approaches the top. Furthemore, the groups within our terms of reference differ so widely that comparison between them at the higher levels or, indeed, between them and the outside world, is, in some cases, of questionable value (TSRB, 1974a, p. 8).

None the less, when it comes to actually assessing levels of recommended pay the TSRB finds it impossible to break the chains of history and their report abounds with meaningless comparisons for their own sake. The TSRB saw 'no special merit in principle in the present equivalence between the salaries of a high court judge and of a permanent secretary in the higher civil service; but . . . considered it would be wrong in practice for the pay of a high court judge to fall behind that of the permanent secretary, and therefore regarded the maintenance of at least the existing parity as a safeguard' (ibid., pp. 6-7). And the TSRB was 'satisfied that the existing relationship between the senior grades of the higher civil service and senior officers of the armed forces remained appropriate, and we accept that it should be continued, subject to reviews from time to time, since circumstances may change and we do not consider that any horizontal relationship should be allowed to become rigid' (ibid., p. 23). Apparently the review body was unaware of any irony in this statement. The *de facto* relationships that had grown up between the groups covered by the TSRB's reference are allowed to continue largely by default – the review body being basically unable to think of any other way of determining pay given the difficulties of job comparison at the top end of the salary structure. We have to take these difficulties for granted because they are discussed only in the broadest generalisations – no explicit comparison of a public sector job with a particular position in private industry is ever made (with the exception of the chairmen and board members of nationalised industries). Instead we have to be content with repeated statements that the review body is satisfied that comparisons of a broad and general nature can be made. Ironically the one area where relatively straightforward comparisons were possible, in the nationalised industries where the common-sense comparison of level of salary with size of assets controlled can be made, provided the single instance of the government's rejection of the TSRB's sixth report.

This irony was compounded by the fact that the nationalised industries are also the most affected by another of the underlying principles thought by the TSRB to be important in determining top pay – the ability to recruit and retain staff. The TSRB provides precious little evidence to suggest that recruitment to the public sector would decline if top salaries were allowed to drop. Nor does it provide a basis for suggesting that large numbers of civil servants or senior officers in the armed forces would be forced to desert their posts. In fact no figures are produced on the rate at which those occupying top jobs in the public sector leave them to snap up private sector vacancies. The implied assumption, however, is that moves of this kind would be far more prevalent in the nationalised industries (although, again, figures are not provided) which, it is argued, also need to maintain comparability with the private sector in order to attract candidates for jobs filled from the private sector rather than via internal promotions. Here again the argument is not entirely convincing. In the first place the TSRB appears to be saying that nationalised industry top salaries should be set at a level sufficient to attract the best man for the job while at the same time rejecting the notion that public sector salaries should attempt to match the highest paid in the private sector. Implicitly the TSRB argues that those already paid the top salaries must be the best men – the traditional equation of salary and status noted by Barbara Wootton (see Wootton, 1962, p. 70). Even if this is true, it does not necessarily follow that there are not men available at considerably lower salaries capable or prepared to do the job. Or even, as in the case of a recent appointee to the chairmanship of British Rail, Mr Peter Parker, prepared to take a considerable drop in salary in order to do the job. The TSRB is, as has been pointed out by Mr Derek Robinson, setting a rate for the job and not for the man. It is certainly worth considering whether the latter approach might be more appropriate, particularly at the highest level, at least for the nationalised industries.

But setting a rate for the job is implied by the TSRB's attitude to salary structure. A 'factor of considerable importance, which bears directly on the salaries at all levels, is the maintenance of a national salary structure in which the assumption of greater responsibilities is matched by appropriately increased rewards.' As a direct consequence, the TSRB 'attach importance to adequate differentials within each pay structure. Compression of the kind that has existed since the time of our appointment bears unfairly on those who are promoted to the higher levels and, in some cases, on those immediately below' (TSRB, 1974a, p. 10). This attitude can be seen to stem directly from the TSRB's view of fairness. 'Whatever the spread of views as what is "fair", our discussions with representatives of staff associations who negotiate salaries of civil service grades up to the level for which we are responsible left us in no doubt at all that their members themselves feel that there should be substantial differentials between grades, in recognition of the greater responsibility involved. . . . Frankly we find "fairness" an elusive concept. It is frequently cited as if it were a standard that is capable of a single and precise definition: but there is no such single and precise definition.' As Derek Robinson points out, the concept of fairness adopted by the TSRB is one biased towards the internal needs of the organisations whose pay they are reviewing. This leads to a powerful case for increasing top salaries to avert the crushing of differentials which would otherwise take place and which is viewed internally as 'unfair'.

But Robinson poses the question, 'fair to whom?' What is viewed as fair within the organisation may be looked upon quite differently from outside (for example by those ultimately responsible for footing the bill). In this context it is interesting to note the TSRB's failure to undertake an opinion poll about the prevailing rates of pay for top jobs in the public sector although its first report included the results of some sampling of public opinion taken on the level of salaries paid to MPs and ministers. The results, shown in Table 8.3, make interesting reading.

TABLE 8.3 *Public attitudes to the pay of MPs and cabinet ministers before and after being informed of the actual salary levels*

| | MPs | | Cabinet ministers | |
|---|---|---|---|---|
| | Before % | After % | Before % | After % |
| Overpaid | 36 | 15 | 41 | 42 |
| Adequate | 38 | 50 | 37 | 46 |
| Underpaid | 14 | 33 | 9 | 8 |
| Don't know | 12 | 2 | 13 | 3 |

(*Source*: TSRB, 1971, pp. 11 and 28)

At the time (1971) MPs received a basic salary of £3,250 per year and cabinet ministers £8,500 a year. Only the cabinet minister post would normally qualify for the attentions of the Top Salaries Review Body and, after being informed of the true level of their salaries, 58 per cent of the public considered them adequately paid or overpaid. Moreover, 65 per cent of the public thought MPs adequately or overpaid at the time. Despite this, the TSRB went on to recommend an increase in the salary of MPs to £4,500 per year and a rise to £13,000 for cabinet ministers. There could be no more explicit example of the internal and external dynamics of 'fairness'. It may well be that, in general, the sheer size of a number of public sector salaries is considered a great deal more unfair than the failure in an increasing, but small, number of cases to reward increased responsibility with extra pay.

## Critical comparisons

There have certainly been other hostile reactions to certain aspects of public sector salaries, notably the size of inflation-proofed pensions and what is thought to be the large measure of public sector job security which it is felt should depress pay levels to some extent. The TSRB investigates both questions but its findings cannot be said to be likely to end the debate. On job security 'the broad conclusion is that there is generally greater security of job tenure in some parts of the public sector than in private industry, even though each sector has some areas of substantial stability of employment and some where insecurity is real' (TSRB, 1974a, p. 48). This amounts to a slight understatement of the position. Members of the judiciary are in effect, unsackable. The higher civil service 'have a strong expectation of continuing until the normal retirement age . . . although job security is not automatic' (ibid., p. 48) and senior officers of the armed forces will probably retire early but receive substantial compensation in the form of a large pension. In its evidence to the Royal Commission, ICI, one of the country's leading employers, takes exception to the TSRB's findings on this issue. 'We see real risks to people where career performance has been entirely satisfactory, and the risks arise from the need to ensure the continued viability of the industry as a whole.' To back this up the company produced a diagram illustrating the reasons why senior staff leave ICI. It is reproduced below and clearly indicates the risk to senior management in industry. Clearly a case could be made for the advantages of public over private employment in terms of job security. So, too, could it be made in terms of pensions. The calculations made by the TSRB assess pensions in the public sector as being worth between 14 and 45 per cent of final salary to public sector jobs at the equivalent to permanent secretary level as compared with a value of 22 per cent on average in 80 private sector companies surveyed. For the job equivalent of a deputy secretary the comparable figures are 11 to 33 per cent compared with 19 per cent for the private sector and at under secretary levels to 29 per cent compared with 15 per cent in the private sector. But these valuations exclude inflation proofing. Significantly 'about 70 per cent of members (of private sector pension schemes) are in schemes with some arrangements for post-retirement increases but these arrangements often fall short of full protection against price increases' (TSRB, 1974a, p. 73). In fact 'only about 10 per cent of each of the board members and senior executive posts in private industry are in schemes which provide for post-retirement increases specifically to

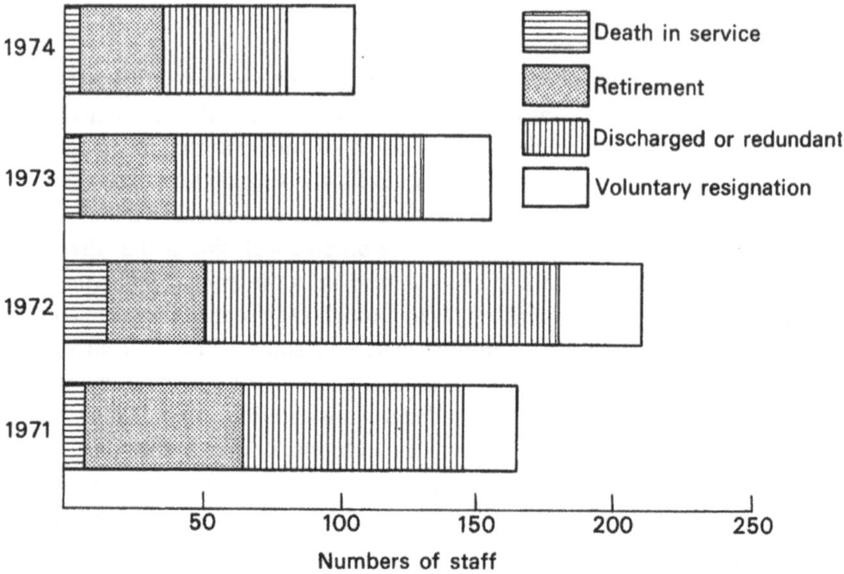


FIGURE 8.1 *Loss of Senior Staff*
(*Source*: ICI Ltd, written evidence to Royal Commission, 1976, pp. 192-3)

match increases in the cost of living' (ibid., p. 167). Whereas all the board members of nationalised industries receive post-retirement increases in pension 85.3 per cent of private sector pensions are similarly protected but 45.2 per cent have to rely on ex gratia projects as compared with 3.6 per cent in the nationalised industries (ibid., p. 180). The figures tend to confirm the impression of superior public sector provision for pensions.

## Conclusion

If the Top Salaries Review Body can be faulted in its examination of the various elements of public sector top pay and its evaluation of them, it has to be said that it faces a thankless task – a fact highlighted by the government's rejection, almost *in toto*, of its seventh, eighth and ninth reports (IDS, 1977b). On the one hand the TSRB is wedded to the concept of comparability but on the other it cannot afford to match the levels of salary which, on its own basis of comparison, it finds paid in the private sector for comparable top jobs. On the one hand it believes explicitly in the need for a rational salary structure and the maintenance of differentials but on the other hand it finds its freedom of action limited by the need to take into account 'fairness' not only in the salary structure concerned but also as it is viewed by the wider public. Before its recommendations are compromised by the government they have already been compromised by the TSRB itself. It is trying to bring some form of objective analysis to an area rich in value judgments and precious little else. It is not altogether surprising, therefore, that its conclusions are open to criticism: the Top Salaries Review Body is merely holding a mirror to inequality, and the reflection of gross inequality in the pay structure, which must by the very logic of the situation then be imitated, is no more pleasing to those who find the degree of inequality in gross income disturbing than the original image. In short, therefore, the real problem lies not with the research and recommendations of the Top Salaries Review Body but in the overall pay structure of the nation. If 88 per cent of the public thought cabinet ministers adequately paid or overpaid at £8,500 per annum in 1971 what would the same public think of the fact that 65,000 people earned in excess of £10,000 from employment in 1974-5 and 300 received more than £50,000? The employment incomes covered by the TSRB's reference accounted for only about 800 of the 65,000 (in 1974). The TSRB is right when it asserts that 'the principle of "fairness" . . . must at the very least require that no category of public servants should suffer permanently because the Government, as employer, may wish to follow a more stringent policy than the private sector.' The onus is on the government to restrain inequalities in all gross incomes if it wishes to see a greater equality of income distribution. The Top Salaries Review Body cannot be expected to do the job for them.

# Appendix

Louie Burghes

The first two chapters referred to various methods of measuring wealth. Here we describe some of those methods in more detail.

One of three methods is now generally used to estimate personal wealth: the balance sheet method, the investment income method and the estate duty method. Of these the estate duty method has been most widely used since it is based on the most readily available, comprehensive and continuous series of data produced by the Inland Revenue. The Inland Revenue data and estimates of personal wealth have certainly contributed to studies of wealth. But there are serious drawbacks and deficiencies to the data which are important, as the Inland Revenue acknowledge, since the data and the series are so widely used as an indication of the extent and distribution of wealth in this country. Before examining the Inland Revenue data we look first at the investment income method of estimating personal wealth.

## Investment income method

We looked in Chapter 1 at the Oxford surveys of wealth and the problems that these surveys face. There are also methodological problems with the investment income approach which estimates personal wealth by capitalising figures for the size and distribution of investment income taken from income tax data. For example, there are problems with assumptions that have to be made about the yields on different assets and the inability to take account of those assets which do not show up in the data. But the approach has yielded some interesting results. Atkinson quotes estimates produced by *The Economist* for 1959-60 which suggest that wealth is much more concentrated than the estate duty figures suggest. All but 9 per cent of total personal wealth was estimated to be owned by the top 10 per cent of wealth holders with the top 1 per cent owning 72 per cent (Atkinson, 1972, p. 15).

More recently Atkinson and Harrison, reviewing the investment income approach, concluded that while its drawbacks make it unsuitable as a replacement for the estate duty method, it can provide a useful check on it (Atkinson and Harrison, 1978, p. 200). Much the same can be said about voluntary surveys of wealth.

## Estate duty method

The estate duty or multiplier method of estimating personal wealth used by, among others, the Inland Revenue, assumes that the wealth of those who die can be taken as a sample of the wealth of the living. These figures produced by the Inland Revenue since 1960 are the official estimates of wealth in the country. Briefly, the method can be defined as follows: the wealth of those who die is taken as a sample of the wealth of the living using data collected through the administration of estate duty and since March 1975 capital transfer tax. A mortality multiplier is then applied to these figures to give estimates of the wealth of the living. If, for example, someone dies and leaves £50,000 and the death rate for that group is one in ten, then the wealth for that group would be estimated at £500,000. But, as Alan Harrison comments in Chapter 2, while the explanation is exact, it makes the choice of mortality multipliers look a much more certain and less important business than it is. We look at the issues involved later; here, at other drawbacks of the data and method.

### *1 Limitations of the sample*

The sample – the estates of those who die – is considerably less than a complete coverage of all estates of those who die within any one year. An estate will only be included if it is known to the Capital Taxes Office (formerly the Estate Duty Office) and this only happens if a grant of representation is needed for the transfer of the estate. Such a grant is not needed where there are special provisions for the transfer of the property or where the transfer is of a 'small amount' which is covered by the Administration of Estates (Small Payments) Act 1965.

Some of the omitted estates will have left no wealth. In 1975–6 there were 690,000 deaths compared with 310,000 estates notified. From this the estate duty method estimated that there were 21m people who owned wealth in 1975, about two fifths of the population. Of the remainder of the population who were estimated to have little or no wealth, about half were under 25 years.

The estimates of wealth are also less reliable for estates below the tax exemption limit (£5,000) because they do not require such thorough examination by the Inland Revenue as those above the limit. There are also problems where the sample numbers for any sub-group are small. This is particularly a problem with very large estates and those of the young. Not only are the number of large estates limited but, as the Inland Revenue point out, they are also very different in size and content. In the younger age groups it is the low death rate that is likely to introduce a margin of error. The Inland Revenue attempt to correct for this by a process known as 'smoothing'. This process and its drawbacks are looked into later in the section.

Atkinson and Harrison have also pointed out that a delay in the reporting of an estate combined with a change, an increase, for example, in asset prices, will result in current estates being larger than the delayed estates appearing in the estate duty figures (see Royal Commission, 1976b, p. 13).

## 2 *Missing wealth*

There is wealth missing from the figures as well as people and their estates. There are two main reasons for wealth to be missing from the estate duty figures. First, because the assets are not subject to estate duty or are specially exempted; second, because the property is part of an estate whose value is not sufficient to be taxed. Examples of the first type of property are gifts *inter vivos* (given more than seven years before death) and discretionary trusts, some settled property is exempt and certain UK government securities. Capital Transfer Tax (introduced in March 1975) has altered this position, but has not as yet affected the Inland Revenue's wealth statistics.

The fact that grants are not required for small amounts (under the Administration of Estates Act) has made a considerable difference to the estimates of those holding wealth:

> Between 1947 and 1965 the limit was £100 when it was raised to £500 and in July 1975, it was raised again to £1,500. The change

> in the limit in 1965 caused most of the apparent decline in the number of identified wealth owners from 1965 to 1968 but the most recent revision has not had a similar effect on the 1975 figures although those for the later years may have been affected (Royal Commission, 1977, p. 231).

In addition to small payments, grants of representation, which establish the right to property, are not required for cash or household goods (the title passes by delivery); for assets where the transfer is to a named person, for example with life assurance; and for jointly owned property where the property passes to the joint owner.

Atkinson and Harrison demonstrated the importance of estimating this missing wealth in their evidence to the Royal Commission by pointing out that figures from the green paper on the wealth tax show that taking settlements into account increases the share of the top 5 per cent of wealth holders by 1 per cent (of total personal wealth) (Royal Commission, 1976b, p. 9). There are other reasons which cause wealth to be 'missing' from the figures – the way that wealth is valued, for example, and tax evasion could both affect the wealth estimates. (For further information on the limitations of the estate duty statistics and the method see Royal Commission, 1976b; Atkinson and Harrison, 1978; Inland Revenue, 1977a.)

### 3 *Mortality multipliers*

Also liable to introduce error into the estimates are the mortality multipliers. Again this problem is recognised by the Inland Revenue. The Inland Revenue uses different death rates for estates of different values to allow for the correlation between wealth and mortality. For estates over £5,000, the death rates are the Registrar General's social classes I and II (from the census of population) while for estates below £5,000 a rate midway between that for the higher estates and that for the whole population is used (again from the census).

Revell and Atkinson have both been critical of the Inland Revenue's use of mortality multipliers. Revell suggested that the swings in the estimates of personal wealth between 1957–8 and 1960–1 were larger than could be accounted for by anything other than sampling errors of important assets. He put the distortion down largely to that introduced by the cases of very large estates, particularly those of the young. Indeed he also considered that the Inland Revenue's mortality multipliers were so inaccurate as to be useless.

There are a number of problems with the data from which multipliers are calculated. First, there may be a discrepancy between the occupation that an individual is classified with for the census and at death. It is the comparison of the one with the other that provides class mortality rates. The discrepancy between the two distorts the rates. Second, the number of people defined as 'unoccupied' will have a similar effect since it includes those people whose occupations are merely insufficiently described for them to be allocated to any particular occupation. Nor do the multipliers allow for the effect that wealth itself may have on life expectancy or the difference in mortality that has been shown to exist by marital status.

As an alternative to the Inland Revenue's census/death certificate constructed mortality multipliers, Revell suggested the use of life office data deriving the mortality multipliers from the continuous mortality investigation of ordinary life and endowment policy holders. There are both advantages and disadvantages with this method. On the positive side the occupations of the population are known so that there is less chance of miscalculation. The holders of such policies are obviously wealth holders. But there are also two drawbacks to the method. First, that it results in an insufficient sample of women, and second, the sample is self-selecting by health – a key variable in this case. Although Revell made adjustments for these deficiencies the Inland Revenue do not consider them ideal. But as the Inland Revenue are unhappy with Revell's adjustments, so other critics are unhappy with the adjustments that the Inland Revenue have made to compensate for the deficiencies in the census/death certificate figures.

The Inland Revenue uses the results from the matching exercise to make adjustments for the errors in the recording of occupational status and allocates the unoccupied population proportionately between the social classes. It is not clear how 'corrective' these adjustments are.

The Inland Revenue also make adjustments for the small numbers of young and of large estates and from errors that may arise from fluctuations in their numbers by what they call smoothing. Smoothing is achieved by using the same mortality multiplier over several age groups or wealth classes. In effect it is combining observations in age or wealth classes and applying a common multiplier.

It is this smoothing, among other issues, that Atkinson has criticised. Ironically, as Alan Harrison recalled earlier, while the choice of mortality multipliers is important, the results are not so sensitive or so distorted by the use of the Inland Revenue multipliers as Revell supposed. However, Atkinson's criticism of the smoothing process points out that in attempting to compensate for small cell numbers the Inland Revenue confuse the importance of age with that of amount of wealth. As he says: 'The reason for concern is not that errors may be introduced through variation in the total number of deaths in a particular age group, since this would be reflected in an exactly offsetting variation in the mortality multiplier' (Atkinson, 1974, p. 283).

Rather, the problem is with the value of the estates and their distribution among the wealth ranges. 'This suggests that any combination of observations before applying the multipliers should not be between age groups (which would introduce errors arising from variation in the overall mortality rate for each group) but between estate classes' (ibid., p. 283).

An additional criticism of the mortality multipliers that Atkinson and Harrison made in their evidence to the Royal Commission was that there was no allowance for changes in mortality rates over time, rather they are assumed to be the same as they were in 1961 (Royal Commission, 1976b, p. 12).

Atkinson's work for 1968 in fact suggests that the estimates of wealth are less sensitive to the mortality multipliers than has been supposed. Atkinson compared the results achieved from three mortality multipliers. First, those used by the Inland Revenue; second, those calculated by Revell from the life office data; and third, because of the criticisms of smoothing, general mortality multipliers.

The results produced using the Inland Revenue's and Revell's multipliers are very similar. For the top 1 per cent of wealth holders there is a difference between the two rates of only 1 per cent in their holding. The differences are less marked between the social class multipliers than those produced using the general multipliers, which produce estimates of the share of the top 1 per cent which are about 3.5 per cent lower than Revell's multipliers suggest (Atkinson, 1974, pp. 287–90). Although these differences are small compared to the difference in the sizes of the multipliers, Atkinson makes the point that they are considerable differences in terms of the share of the top 1 per cent.

## *4 Health and wealth*

One fundamental assumption of the estate duty method is that those who die in any year can be taken, with their wealth, as a sample of the living. It has been pointed out that this may not be true. There is for example a relationship between mortality and social class (for a recent analysis see OPCS, 1978). There may also be a relationship between ill health and wealth holding – or the lack of it. Ill health may affect wealth and the unwell may take steps to change their wealth holding before they die. This is particularly true of steps that may be taken to avoid estate duty. The effect of any actions varies with the type of property being disposed of; in some cases the wealth will be 'lost' from the statistics; in others its value may appear without it being taxed. In the case of gifts *inter vivos* it has been suggested that they may actually be counted twice. On the one hand, if a donor dies within seven years of making a gift then it will appear not only in his estate but in that of the recipient (although perhaps not fully). On the other hand Lampman and Atkinson have suggested that the opposite could apply if those with lower than average life expectancy made gifts *inter vivos* to those with above average life expectancy (Atkinson and Harrison, 1978; Royal Commission, 1976b, p. 11).

## Balance sheet data

Because of the limitations of the estate duty data and the estate duty method for estimating personal wealth – particularly the effect of missing wealth and missing people – an alternative independent estimate has been sought of total personal wealth and its distribution: this is known as the balance sheet method.

The original work on the balance sheet estimates was pioneered by Revell, and Extended by him with Roe, Atkinson and Harrison and the Central Statistical Office (for the Royal Commission) have further refined the method. One difference between the earlier work and that of Atkinson and Harrison and the CSO is that the former only produced estimates of total personal wealth whereas the latter have also made estimates of the distribution.

Revell's interest was in producing a national balance sheet a part of which was for the personal sector. The balance sheet data provides a check on the estate duty totals by using independent estimates of personal sector asset holdings from alternative sources. For example, the amount held in building societies can be obtained from the building societies themselves. In fact the estimates are less than a completely independent check since alternative information is not available for all assets. Where none is available, the estate duty estimates have to be relied on.

The Royal Commission have followed Revell's method in producing balance sheet estimates of total personal wealth and have produced estimates of the distribution of wealth as well. This C Series follows on from the A and B Series produced by the Inland Revenue and allows for wealth holding among the total population. (The A and B Series, because they are based on the estate duty statistics, produce both lower estimates of total wealth and have to assume that almost half the population has no wealth. The difference between the A and the B Series is that the former shows the distribution of wealth among the identified wealth holders only, while the B Series shows the distribution among the total population, i.e. including those people who do not own any wealth.)

Atkinson and Harrison have been critical of the way that the Royal Commission have used the balance sheet method, arguing that, while they themselves have taken Revell's work as their starting point, they have not accepted it uncritically (as the Royal Commission have) and that the balance sheet items for individual assets should not be taken automatically as a better estimate that the estate duty figures. In some cases, for example, Revell's estimates for individual assets are derived as residuals from the other sectors in the national balance sheet. Atkinson and Harrison therefore only adjusted the estate data where there were reasons to believe that the difference between the two estimates could be due to wealth missing from the estate duty figures or because of incorrect valuation.

The Central Statistical Office have produced the most recent estimates for the wealth of the personal sector. Comparing their estimate with that of the Inland Revenue for 1975 (the most recent data) suggests that total personal wealth was some 50 per cent higher, over £280,000m rather than £190,000m. They also provide estimates of the amount of the difference between the two due to different factors, of which there are seven elements. The first two are due to limitations in the estate duty method; £16,000m of the difference is due to problems of timing; estates are included in the statistics for the financial year in which the estates are assessed rather than the year of the death of the owner and in periods of high inflation the difference in asset prices between the two periods may be considerable. Nor are the estimates for identical periods; the balance sheet relates to the end of the year while estates are assessed throughout. A further £5,000m of the difference between the two estimates is thought to result from bias introduced by the mortality multipliers and by smoothing. The sampling of estates below the exemption limit, and the less thorough examination of these estates, is estimated to account for £10,000m.

The largest single item accounting for the difference between the two estimates is that of differences in valuation between the two methods. This amounts to £22,000m. The differences in valuation are fundamental with estates valued at their realisation value at death by the Inland Revenue while balance sheets are based on going concerned valuation. The two items particularly affected are consumer goods and pension rights.

Over 30 per cent of the difference between the two estimates can be explained by missing wealth, i.e. wealth in estates which were below the exemption limit or for which no grant of representation has to be obtained. The total is divided between excluded joint property and small estates – £20,000m – and excluded trusts – £11,000m. Finally, a difference of some £10,000m remains unexplained. There is bound to be some difference between results in such calculations, but it is worth pointing out that the extent of tax evasion is included in this remaining unexplained difference.

## Gini coefficient

The Gini coefficient is a summary measure which is often used to indicate the extent of inequality or equality in the distribution of wealth. The coefficient is calculated by relating the actual distribution of wealth to a hypothetical equal distribution. This relationship can be explained diagrammatically as in Figure A.1. The actual distribution of wealth is presented on a graph by plotting the cumulative wealth shares against cumulative percentages of the population; this is known as the Lorenz curve (line A). An equal distribution of wealth would give a straight line joining the extremes of the two axes (line B). The Gini coefficient, the relationship between the area between the two lines and the whole area (beneath line B), therefore provides a measure of the extent of inequality. The coefficient is either presented as a whole number, in which case it can vary from 0 (complete equality) to 1 (complete inequality) or as a percentage. What the graph makes clear is that the coefficient can be no more than an indication of the extent of inequality. There are a number of differently shaped Lorenz curves that would result in the same (or similar) areas between the two curves and hence in the same (or similar) Gini coefficient.

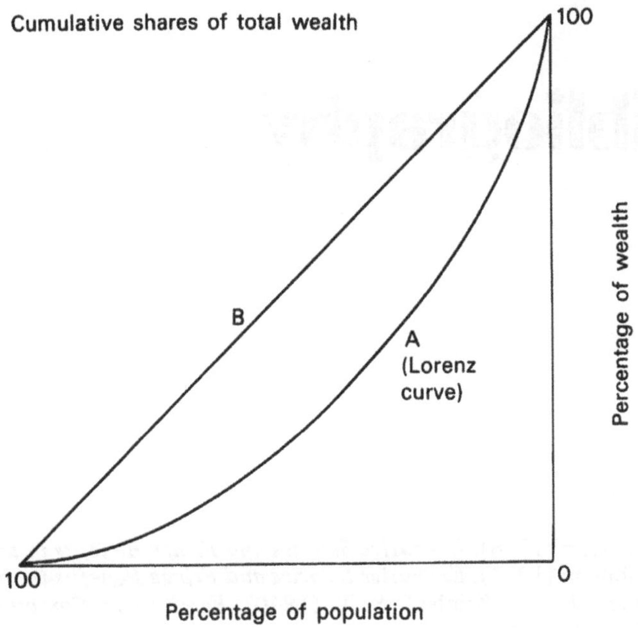


FIGURE A.1 *Cumulative shares of total wealth*

# Bibliography


AIC/Inbucon (1976), *Executive Salaries and Fringe Benefits in the UK.*

AIC/Inbucon (1977), *Executive Salaries and Fringe Benefits in the UK.*

Arensberg, C. and Kimball, S. T. (1940), *Family and Community in Ireland*, Peter Smith.

Atkinson, A. B. (1972), *Unequal Shares*, Penguin Books.

Atkinson, A. B. (1974), 'The distribution of wealth in Britain in the 1960's', in J. D. Smith (ed.), *Personal Distribution of Income and Wealth*, Columbia University Press.

Atkinson, A. B. (1978), 'The wealthy and the wealth tax', *New Society*, 9 February.

Atkinson, A. B. and Harrison, A. J. (1978), *The Distribution of Personal Wealth in Britain*, Cambridge University Press.

Bank Rate Report (1957), *Proceedings of the Tribunal Appointed to Inquire into Allegations that Information about the Raising of the Bank Rate was Improperly Disclosed*, HMSO.

BIM (1974), *Remuneration in the UK*, Review Remuneration Economics.

BIM (1977), *Remuneration in the UK*, Review Remuneration Economics.

Bott, E. (1957), *Family and Social Network*, Tavistock.

Brown, M. B. (1973), 'The controllers of British industry', in J. Urry and J. Wakefield (eds), *Power in Britain*, Heinemann.

Bulmer, M. (ed.) (1975), *Working Class Images of Society*, Routledge & Kegan Paul.

Burgess, G. J. and Webb, A. J. (1974), 'The profits of British industry', *Lloyds Bank Review*, April.

Campion, H. (1939), *Public and Private Property in Great Britain*, Oxford University Press.

Carr-Saunders, A. M. and Caradog Jones, D. (1927), *A Survey of the Social Structure of England and Wales*, Oxford University Press.

Chesterton, G. K. (1908), 'Cockneys and their jokes', in *All Things Considered*, Methuen.
Clay, H. (1924–6), 'Distribution of capital in England and Wales', *Proceedings of the Manchester Statistical Society*.
Coates, B. E., Johnson, R. J. and Knox, P. L. (1977), *Geography and Inequality*, Oxford University Press.
Cowton, R. (1978), 'Managers' lot not so unhappy', *The Times*, 20 February.
Daniel, W. W. (1975), *The PEP Survey on Inflation*, PEP, 1975.
Daniels, G. W. and Campion, H. (1936), *Distribution of national capital*, Manchester University Press.
Day, A. (1974), 'The rich get poorer', *Observer*, 22 September.
DE (1977), 'How individual people's earnings change', *Gazette*, Vol. 85, January.
*Economic Progress Report* (1977a), The Treasury, February.
*Economic Progress Report* (1977b), The Treasury, November.
*Economic Trends* (1971), 'National balance sheet and national accounting – a progress report', HMSO, May.
*Economic Trends* (1978), CSO Evidence to the Royal Commission, 'Personal sector balance sheets', HMSO, January.
*The Economist* (1975), 'Looking after its own', 4 January.
*The Economist* (1976), 'Five years on the dole', 31 January.
Everly, R. (1977), 'The effects of the price code', *National Institute Economic Review*, August.
Field, F., Meacher, M. and Pond, C. (1977), *To Him Who Hath*, Penguin Books.
Flemming, J. S. (1976), 'Trends in company profitability', *Bank of England Quarterly Bulletin*, March.
Glyn, A. and Sutcliffe, B. (1971), 'The collapse of UK profits', *New Left Review*, March–April.
Glyn, A. and Sutcliffe, B. (1972), *British Capitalism, Workers and the Profit Squeeze*, Penguin Books.
Gore, C. (ed.) (1913), *Property: its Duties and Rights*, Macmillan.
Gouldner, A. (ed.) (1959), E. Durkheim, *Socialism and Saint-Simon*, Routledge & Kegan Paul.
Haines, J. (1977), *Politics of Power*, Hodder & Stoughton.
Halsey, A. H. (1978), 'Class-ridden prosperity', *Listener*, 19 January.
*Hansard* (1974a), 26 March, vol. 871.
*Hansard* (1974b), 12 November, vol. 881.
*Hansard* (1974c), 20 December, vol. 883.
*Hansard* (1975a), 14 January, vol. 884.
*Hansard* (1975b), 15 April, vol. 890.
*Hansard* (1976), 6 April, vol. 909.
*Hansard* (1977a), 29 March, vol. 929.
*Hansard* (1977b), 10 May, vol. 931.
*Hansard* (1977c), 27 May, vol. 924.
*Hansard* (1977d), 25 July, vol. 936.
*Hansard* (1977e), 25 November, vol. 939.
*Hansard* (1977f), 15 December, vol. 941.

*Hansard* (1978), 9 February, vol. 943.

Harrop, K. J. and Kirby, A. M. (1975), 'The Byker conference', *Area*, 7.

Harvey, D. (1969), *Explanation in Geography*, Arnold.

Harvey, D. (1975), *Social Justice in the City*, Arnold.

Hill, T. P. (1955), 'Income, savings and net worth – the savings survey of 1952–4', *Bulletin of the Oxford University Institute of Statistics*, vol. 17, May.

Holman, R. (1970), 'Combatting social deprivation', in R. Holman (ed.), *Socially Deprived Families in Britain*, Bedford Square Press.

Hughes, J. (1974), *Profit Trends and Price Controls*, Spokesman pamphlet, 41.

Hughes, J. (1976), *Funds for Investment*, Fabian Society.

IDS (1977a), 'Top salaries in the nationalised industries', Incomes Data Services, *Focus*, April.

IDS (1977b), 'Peers' allowances – more wasted effort', Incomes Data Services, *Report*, May.

Inland Revenue (1970), *Inland Revenue Statistics*, HMSO, 1970.

Inland Revenue (1974), *Inland Revenue Statistics*, HMSO, 1976.

Inland Revenue (1975), *Inland Revenue Statistics*, HMSO, 1976.

Inland Revenue (1976a), *Inland Revenue Statistics*, HMSO, 1977.

Inland Reveue (1976b), *Report of the Commissioners of the Inland Revenue for the year ending 31 March 1976*, Cmnd 6734, HMSO, 1977.

Inland Revenue (1977a), *Inland Revenue Statistics*, HMSO, 1978.

Inland Revenue (1977b), *Report of the Commissioners of the Inland Revenue for the year ending 31 March 1977*, Cmnd 7092, HMSO, 1978.

King, M. (1975), 'The United Kingdom profit crisis: myth or reality?', *Economic Journal*, vol. 85, March.

*Labour Research* (1977a), '£50,000 a year and more', vol. 66, November.

*Labour Research* (1977b), 'Top pay', vol. 67, January.

*Labour Research* (1978), 'Where are the high paid?', vol. 67, February.

Langley, K. M. (1950 and 1951), 'The distribution of capital in private hands in 1936–38 and 1946–47', *Bulletin of the Oxford University Institute of Statistics*, vols 12 and 13.

Lee, R. (1976), 'Surprise and counter production in radical geography', *Area*, 8.

Low Pay Unit (1977), *Supplementary Evidence to the Royal Commission, Lower Income Reference*, forthcoming.

Lundburg, F. (1968), *The Rich and the Super Rich*, Nelson.

Lydall, H. F. and Tipping, D. G. (1961), 'The distribution of personal wealth in Britain', *Bulletin of the Oxford University Institute of Statistics*, vol. 23.

Murlis, H. (1974), 'Employee benefits today', *BIM Management Survey Report*, no. 19.

*National Income and Expenditure* (1977), tables for 1966–76, HMSO.

NBPI (1969), *Top Salaries in the Private Sector and Nationalised Industries*, Cmnd 3970, HMSO.

OPCS (1978), *Occupational Mortality, 1970–1972*, Office of Population, Censuses and Surveys, HMSO.

Pahl, R. E. (1965a), 'Class and community in English commuter villages', *Sociologia Ruralis*, vol. 5, no. 1.

Pahl, R. E. (1965b), 'Urbs in rure: the metropolitan fringe in Hertfordshire', *London School of Economics, Geographical Paper* no. 2.

Paish, F. (1975), 'Inflation, personal incomes and taxation', *Lloyd's Bank Review*, April.

Panić, M. and Close, R. E. (1975), 'Profitability and British manufacturing industry', *Lloyd's Bank Review*, July.

Polanyi, G. and Wood, J. (1974), *How Much Inequality?*, Institute of Economic Affairs.

Pond, C. (1977a), 'Inflation' in F. Williams (ed.), *Why the Poor Pay More*, Macmillan.

Pond, C. (1977b), *For whom the Pips Squaek*, Low Pay Unit, July.

Pond, C. (1977c) *A Jubilee Year for the Low Paid?* Low Pay Unit, October.

Rees, A. D. (1950), *Life in a Welsh Countryside*, University of Wales Press.

Revell, J. (1967), *The Wealth of the Nation*, Cambridge University Press.

Revell, J. and Roe, A. (1971), 'National balance sheet and national accounting – a progress report', *Economic Trends*, no. 211, May.

Roe, A. (1971), *The Financial Interdependence of the Economy 1957–1966*, Chapman & Hall.

Rooker, J. (1978), 'Wealthy win a hidden pay rise', *Labour Weekly*, 17 March.

Royal Commission (1955), *On the Taxation of Profits and Income*, Cmnd 9474, HMSO.

Royal Commission (1975), *Report No. 1, Initial Report on the Standing Reference*, Cmnd 6171, HMSO.

Royal Commission (1976a), *Report No. 4, Second Report on the Standing Reference*, Cmnd 6626, HMSO.

Royal Commission (1976b), *Selected Evidence submitted to the Royal Commission for Report No. 1, Initial Report on the Standing Reference*, HMSO.

Royal Commission (1976c), *Report No. 3, Higher Incomes from Employment*, Cmnd 6383, HMSO.

Royal Commission (1976d), *Selected Evidence submitted to the Royal Commission for Report No. 3: Higher Incomes from Employment*, HMSO.

Royal Commission (1977), *Report No. 5, Third Report on the Standing Reference*, Cmnd 6999, HMSO.

Runciman, W. G. (1966), *Relative Deprivation and Social Justice*, Routledge & Kegan Paul.

Sandford, C. T. (1973), *Hidden costs of taxation*, Institute of Fiscal Studies.

Sandford, C. T., Lewis, A. and Fleming, C. (1978), 'Labour should think again about the wealth tax', *Accountancy*, Sept. 1978.

Sandford, C. T. and Robinson, A. (1975), 'Select committee members who face a daunting task', *Accountants' Weekly*, 21 February.

Sandford, C. T., Willis, J. R. M. and Ironside, D. T. (1973), *An Accessions Tax*, Institute of Fiscal Studies.

Seebohm (1968), *Report of the Committee on Local Authority and Allied Personal Social Services*, Cmnd 3703, HMSO.

Stanworth, P. and Giddens, A. (eds) (1974), *Elites and Power in British Society*, Cambridge University Press.

Stamp, Sir Joshua (1922), *Wealth and taxable capacity*, King.

Tawney, R. H. (1913), Inaugural lecture, 'Poverty as an industrial problem', reproduced in *Memoranda on the Problems of Poverty*, vol. 2, William Morris Press.

Tawney, R. H. (1961), *Religion and the Rise of Capitalism*, Penguin Books.

Tawney, R. H. (1964), *Equality*, Allen & Unwin.

Titmuss, R. M. (1962), *Income Distribution and Social Change*, Allen & Unwin.

*Trade and Industry* (1976), 'Companies' rates of return on capital employed 1960–76', 16 September.

TSRB (1971), *First Report, Ministers of the Crown and Members of Parliament*, Cmnd 4836, HMSO.

TSRB (1972), *Report No. 2, Interim Report on Top Salaries*, Cmnd 5001, HMSO.

TSRB (1973), *Report No. 3, Second Interim Report on Top Salaries*, Cmnd 5372, HMSO.

TSRB (1974a), *Report No. 6*, Cmnd 5846, HMSO.

TSRB (1974b), *Report No. 4, Third Interim Report*, Cmnd 5595, HMSO.

TURU (1974), *Inflation and Company Accounts*, Trade Union Research Unit.

TURU (1976), *The Price Code, Profits and Investment*, Trade Union Research Unit.

TURU (1977), *The 1977 Budget: the Real Picture*, Trade Union Research Unit.

Urry, J. and Wakeford, J. (eds) (1973), *Power in Britain*, Heinemann.

*Wealth Tax* (1975), A green paper, Cmnd 5704, HMSO.

Westergaard, J. and Resler, H. (1976), *Class in a Capitalist Society*, Penguin Books.

Whitley, R. (1973), 'Commonalities and connections among directors of large financial institutions', *Sociological Review*, vol. XXI, November.

Whitley, R. (1974), 'The City and industry; the directors of large companies, their characteristics and connections', in P. Stanworth and A. Giddens (eds), *Elites and Power in British Society*, Cambridge University Press.

Willmott, P. (ed.) (1976), *Poverty Report 1976*, Temple Smith.

Wootton, B. (1962), *The Social Foundations of Wage Policy*, Allen & Unwin.

Wootton, B. (1976), *In Pursuit of Equality*, Fabian Society.

Wootton, B. (1977), 'Free marketeers', *New Society*, 17 February.
Young, M. and Willmott, P. (1957), *Family and Kinship in East London*, Penguin Books.

# Index

For Product Safety Concerns and Information please contact our EU representative GPSR@taylorandfrancis.com Taylor & Francis Verlag GmbH, Kaufingerstraße 24, 80331 München, Germany